WILEY
EXECUTIVE
MBA
Strategies, Skills, Solutions

MASTERING BUSINESS IN ASIA

SUCCEEDING WITH THE

BALANCED SCORECARD

WILEY
EXECUTIVE
MBA
Strategies, Skills, Solutions

MASTERING BUSINESS IN ASIA

SUCCEEDING WITH THE
BALANCED
SCORECARD

James Creelman
Naresh Makhijani

John Wiley & Sons (Asia) Pte Ltd

Other Wiley Editorial Offices
John Wiley & Sons, Inc., 111 River Street, Hoboken, NJ 07030, USA
John Wiley & Sons Ltd, The Atrium, Southern Gate, Chichester PO19 BSQ, England
John Wiley & Sons (Canada) Ltd, 22 Worcester Road, Rexdale, Ontario M9W ILI, Canada
John Wiley & Sons Australia Ltd, 33 Park Road (PO Box 1226), Milton, Queensland 4046, Australia
Wiley-VCH, Pappelallee 3, 69469 Weinheim, Germany

Library of Congress Cataloging-in-Publication Data:

0-470-82141-8 (paperback)

Typeset in 11/15 point, Berkeley by Red Planet
Printed in Singapore by Saik Wah Press Pte Ltd
10 9 8 7 6 5 4 3 2 1

Contents

Dedicated to my Goddaughter Florence Isabella Ada Shilcock,
with all my love
-James Creelman

Dedicated to my parents: G T Makhijani & Geeta Makhijani.
Thanks for all your support!
-Naresh Makhijani

Foreword

It has been well over a decade since Bob Kaplan and I first published the results of our research that led to the Balanced Scorecard. Since that time, the idea has been adopted by organizations in all sectors and in all corners of the world. While every organization has different structures and different cultures, the principles of the Balanced Scorecard have transcended these differences. The Balanced Scorecard has truly become a global management tool.

Since its inception, many books and articles have been written about the approach. Bob Kaplan and I have published three books and numerous articles. James Creelman has authored six reports on the subject. This work by Creelman and Naresh Makhijani is the first to be devoted to the Asian region. They provide an excellent synopsis of the global management principles with the Asian cultural spin. The regional focus is quite powerful and provides an excellent guide to organizations in that region who are considering a Balanced Scorecard program.

While every organization must build its own management system, there is much to be said for the regional sharing of ideas and approaches. One has to look no further than Japan and the tremendous achievements of Japanese manufacturing companies as a result of their early commitment to the principles of Quality Management. My belief is that the Balanced Scorecard and Strategic Management offer a similar opportunity. This book provides a potential first step toward that regionalization, and to the competitive advantages that could follow. The return to the reader will be well worth the investment.

David P. Norton
Boston, MA (USA)
October 2004

Acknowledgments

This book would not have been possible without the help and advice of the following people, all of who are gratefully acknowledged.

The following representatives from companies profiled within the book: Mahdi Syahbuddin, formerly deputy president director and Pak Krisbiyanto, formerly, vice president, human capital, Bank Universal (now merged into Bank Permata); Carol Yong Meng Dai, Senior Manager, Human Resources. Centrepoint Properties; Peter Ryan, Corporate Strategy and Performance Manager, City of Brisbane; Louis Schwendener, formerly Director and Group CEO, The Gold Coin Group; Kwok Yiu Leung, Safety & Quality Manager and Felix Kwok Wah Ng, Standards and Performance Manager, MTR Corporation; Paul Melter, Worldwide Director, CompaSS, Saatchi & Saatchi Worldwide; Titus Kong Ling Chieh, Head of Research and Planning, Shie Yong Lee, Deputy Head Research & Planning, Singapore Prison Service and Matthew Wee Yik Keong, Senior Officer, Research and Planning, Singapore Prison Service; . Chan Wai Yin, Director of Research and Statistics Unit, Subordinate Courts, Singapore; Liliawati Rahardjo, President Commissioner; Lexy A Tumiwa, Director and Herman Nagaria, Assistant Director, Summarecon Agund; KC Girotra, Head, its Business Excellence Services Department, Tata Motors Commercial Vehicles Business unit.

The following Balanced Scorecard advisors: Matthew Tice, Vice-President Asia-Pacific, Balanced Scorecard Collaborative; Andrew Lim, Director, Balanced Scorecard Solutions; JongSup Jung, director, Calebabc; Nigel Penny, managing Director, ClaritasAsia; Ning C S Guzman, De Guzman Associates; Jonathan Chocqueel-Mangan, Director, Tyler Mangan.

We would also like to thank the following: The staff of Balanced Scorecard Solutions, Singapore (notably Ong Hui Beng and Marvin Ang) and OTI, Indonesia (notably Alpin Ginting, Syarif Hidayat Rheno Yusril) and Ajai Singh, OTI India for all their help and support.

Selvamalar Manoharan, Editor, John Wiley and her colleagues for all their work in brining this work to fruition.

And finally we would like to thank Dr. David Norton, President, Balanced Scorecard Collaborative, for contributing a foreword to this work.

1

Introduction

ore than a decade has passed since Harvard Business Review published the article "The Balanced Scorecard – Measures That Drive Performance." [1] Written by Dr David Norton (then CEO of Nolan-Norton and now president of Balanced Scorecard Collaborative -BSCol) and Harvard Business School Professor Dr Robert Kaplan, the article summarized the findings from an in-depth study of 12 manufacturing and service companies that was carried out in 1990 [1].

This research program set out to design a new approach to performance measurement that dealt with a growing managerial problem – that accounting, or financial, measures were increasingly being found wanting in assessing and managing organizational performance. As the business landscape began to take on a knowledge-era rather than industrial-era configuration, Norton and Kaplan premised that what business leaders required was a new mechanism with which to take a holistic view of organizational performance – one that would simultaneously provide views of past, present, and future performance; thus, providing more than the lagging financial metrics on which most organizations based decisions. Consequently, from their research program findings Norton and Kaplan introduced a new performance measurement framework for the knowledge-era: the Balanced Scorecard.

EVOLVING THE SCORECARD

The cited 1992 Norton/Kaplan Harvard Business Review (H BR) article clearly struck a nerve with the readership of that esteemed journal. It became one of the most requested articles for reprint in HBR's history. Indeed, it has passed into corporate folklore – on how organizations first encountered the Balanced Scorecard through a senior executive reading this article and enthusiastically sharing its ideas with management colleagues (Mobil Oil, a famous early scorecard success story being one example).

Such was the success of this article that it was followed by a series of other HBR articles that detailed how the scorecard was being used within organizations and how the experiences of the early adopters was helping to further refine the scorecard methodology. Most notably, the articles traced the scorecard's evolution from a performance measurement framework to a strategy management and implementation framework, of which performance measurement was just one core element.[2] Early usage found that the scorecard was most powerful when it was used at a senior level to steer the execution of strategy and not merely to measure performance.

Kaplan's and Norton's learning from these articles and from their ongoing consultancy assignments shaped their thinking for their three books on the Balanced Scorecard. They began in 1996 with The Balanced Scorecard: Translating Strategy into Action[3], followed up in 2001 with The Strategy-focused Organization: How Balanced Scorecard Companies Thrive in the New Business Environment[4] and culminated in 2004 with Strategy Maps: Converting Intangible Assets into Tangible Outcomes[5]. Thus far the three books have sold over 400,000 copies and have been translated into 23 languages.

SCORECARD UPTAKE

The widespread documentation of Balanced Scorecard successes (mainly from North American and European companies), especially within Norton's and Kaplan's articles and books, but also from others (one of the authors of this book has written six in-depth management reports on North American and European scorecard experiences[6]) has played an important part in galvanizing remarkable scorecard uptake.

An analysis in 2003 from the US-based consultancy Bain & Company, for example, found that no less than 60% of large and medium-sized North American organizations are using the Balanced Scorecard, an increase from 50% in the previous year's survey. Impressively, the survey also found an overall satisfaction rate from scorecard users of about four on a scale of one-to-five (with five being the highest score)[7].

The take-up figures for Europe and Australasia are probably close to this, and we can reasonably expect that take-up figures for Asia will climb to an equally high level over the next few years. Singapore already has a high adoption rate, especially in government departments. Unsurprisingly, therefore, Singapore has a high representation in our case study companies.

> " [Research has] found an overall satisfaction rate from scorecard users of about four on a scale of one-to-five (with five being the highest score). "

DESCRIBING THE BALANCED SCORECARD SYSTEM

We will now provide a broad description of the Balanced Scorecard Management System. The Balanced Scorecard is a strategy management and implementation system that comprises a Strategy Map and an accompanying Balanced Scorecard of strategic measures, targets, and initiatives.

The Strategy Map

The Strategy Map (an example of which is shown in Exhibit 1.1) serves as a strategy implementation roadmap in that it describes the high-level strategic objectives that the organization must deliver if it is to successfully execute its strategy.

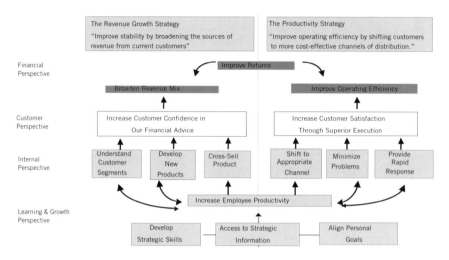

Exhibit 1.1 A template Strategy Map

Central to the premise of the Balanced Scorecard philosophy is that successful strategy implementation is the result of causal relationships within and between typically three non-financial perspectives and one financial perspective. The argument has it that succeeding against objectives from the learning and growth perspective (the foundation of the Strategy Map) has a causal effect on success from the internal process perspective, which in turn creates success from the customer perspective and finally from the financial, or shareholder perspective.

Put another way, from the viewpoint of the knowledge-era where about 85% of an organization value is found in its intangible assets (such as knowledge, information, and skills), a Strategy Map essentially describes how intangible assets are converted into tangible outcomes (such as new products and financial benefits) (see Exhibit 1.2).

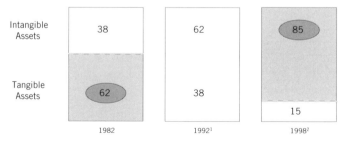

1.Brookings Institute
2.Baruch Lev analysis of S&P500 companies

Exhibit 1.2 The changing values of tangible and intangible assets

Moreover, Strategy Map's often contain strategic themes, such as for revenue growth, new product development, or operational excellence, thus enabling the organization to build competencies and capabilities for the disparate performance thrusts required for success. As an example, Indonesia's Bank Universal (now merged into Bank Pramata) – see Chapter 10 – focused on three themes that would help it emerge from the financial crisis caused by the East Asian economic collapse of 1997/1998: dealing with the legacy of past problems, becoming a good bank, and building confidence in the eyes of shareholders. More conventionally, consider the revenue growth and operating efficiency themes of India's XYZ Cellular, a fictitious name for a real company (see Chapter 6).

> " Although a conventional Strategy Map comprises four perspectives, this is certainly not prescriptive or mandated. Many organizations opt for three, five or even six perspectives, depending on their own cultural or performance requirements. "

Although a conventional Strategy Map comprises four perspectives, this is certainly not prescriptive or mandated. Many organizations opt for three, five or even six perspectives, depending on their own cultural or performance requirements. This divergence from "the norm" is well represented within the case study companies profiled for this book. As examples, the Hong Kong railway network operator MTR Corporation (see Chapter 7) has five perspectives, with "safety" being the addition. Conversely, Subordinate Courts, Singapore (see Chapter 3) has three perspectives, with the financial perspective subsumed into the organizational (or process) perspective.

The Subordinate Courts example highlights two further important factors about Strategy Maps. First, organizations are free to provide labels for the scorecard perspectives that more accurately reflect their culture, structure, or preferred language. Subordinate Courts perspectives are community, organization, and employee. Moreover, the scorecard system itself is called the Justice Scorecard, to better reflect the organization's purpose. The global communications company Saatchi & Saatchi Worldwide (See chapter 11) calls its scorecard CompaSS, partly to describe the navigational qualities of the Balanced Scorecard, but also to capture the organization's focus on branding (it works to enhance the brands of major corporations throughout the world).

> " ...the Strategy Map and accompanying scorecard is a hypothesis. It is management's best guess as to what is required to implement the strategy. "

The second learning from Subordinate Courts is that the typical depiction of a scorecard perspective hierarchy from learning and growth at the base to financial at the top is not sacrosanct. This too can be tailored to the organization's own requirements. Within public-sector, or government, organizations it is not unusual to find the perspective order altered, with financial relegated in the hierarchy. At the Singapore Prison Service, for example, (see Chapter 2), the financial perspective is found at the base of the scorecard.

Accompanying Balanced Scorecard

Continuing with the description of the Balanced Scorecard Management System, a scorecard of measures, targets, and initiatives (see Exhibit 1.3) supports the Strategy Map. This accompanying scorecard shows which measures the organization is using to track the progress it is making toward its strategic objectives. It publishes the performance targets set, lists the strategic initiatives under way to hit the targets, and measures the success against the objectives.

The Balanced Scorecard provides a framework to
translate a strategy into operational terms.

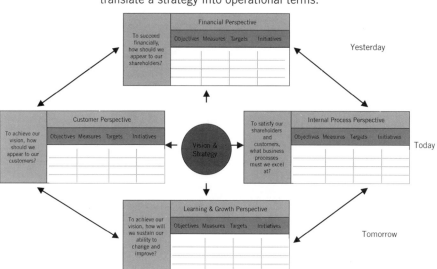

Exhibit 1.3 A template Balanced Scorecard

Crucially, and as shall be explained more fully later in this book, the Strategy Map and accompanying scorecard is a hypothesis. It is management's best guess as to what is required to implement the strategy. In usage, it may be found that there are flaws (major or minor) in the hypothesis, so tweaking, or a more wholesale reappraisal of the scorecard system may be required as learnings are drawn from experience.

The Strategy-Focused Organization

Thus far we have described the constituent parts of the Strategy Map and the accompanying scorecard. But this is not a full explication of the Balanced Scorecard Management System. What we must also describe is the five principles of the Strategy-Focused Organization (SFO). Fully described in Norton's and Kaplan's second book[8], these are principles that the early scorecard adopters generally adhered to in achieving the strategic focus and alignment required for successful strategy implementation (and in many cases, such as Saatchi & Saatchi, an extraordinary financial turnaround). Organizations will rarely adhere to all five principles but exemplary organizations typically incorporate much of the thinking.

Each of the five principles of the SFO is supported by sub-components, as shown in Exhibit 1.4.

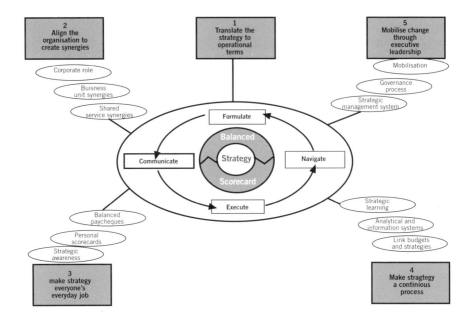

Exhibit 1.4 The five principles of the Strategy-Focused organization

PRINCIPLE 1: TRANSLATE THE STRATEGY TO OPERATIONAL TERMS

Sub-components: Strategy Maps and Balanced Scorecards

As explained above, these are the frameworks for articulating strategic objectives, measures, targets, and initiatives. Strategy Maps and Balanced Scorecards may be created at the enterprise-level and at devolved levels, such as within functions. Indeed, our case study organization Tata Motors Commercial Vehicles Business Unit – CVBU – (see below) has created a total 300 scorecards unit-wide. Crucially, devolved scorecards should be aligned to higher level scorecards. In Chapter 8 we explain how to do this.

PRINCIPLE 2: ALIGN THE ORGANIZATION TO THE STRATEGY

Sub-components: Corporate roles, Business unit synergies, and Shared service synergies

Securing synergistic benefits typically requires the explication of common themes and objectives that are organization, rather than function, specific, such as Saatchi & Saatchi's powerful objective from its "client" perspective: "create permanently infatuated clients," which every unit throughout the world had to focus on and report performance against. Such a "non-negotiable" objective signals what's important to the corporation, but also enables best practice sharing organization-wide.

PRINCIPLE 3: MAKE STRATEGY EVERYONE'S EVERYDAY JOB

Sub-components: Strategic awareness, Personal Scorecards, and Balanced pay checks

This is where we move strategy out of the boardroom and into the backroom, which as Dr Norton has often said is "the holy grail" of most CEOs. Strategic awareness requires concerted, ongoing, educational, and communication efforts. Consider for example the Singapore-based Centrepoint Properties (see Chapter 9), which put all employees through scorecard awareness-raising workshops, and Indonesia's property developer Summarecon Agung (see Chapter 4), which has trained a substantial number of employees in how to build and work with Strategy Maps and Balanced Scorecards.

Singapore's Civil Service College (see Chapter 8) has aligned appraisal and compensations systems to the Balanced Scorecard (unusually for a public-sector organization) as too the private-sector organization Centrepoint Properties. As we explain in Chapter 9, aligning appraisal and compensations systems with the Balanced Scorecard is probably the most complex, challenging, and controversial aspect of scorecard rollout. Compound feed producer Gold Coin is another of our case study companies (see Chapter 5) that tied compensation to scorecard performance.

Scorecards at the individual employee level also provide complex challenges, especially around alignment. Summarecon is one example of an organization that has created personal scorecards for employees.

PRINCIPLE 4: MAKE STRATEGY A CONTINUAL PROCESS

Sub-components: Link budgets and strategies, analytics and information systems, and strategic learning

This is probably the most powerful principle for placing the Balanced Scorecard at the heart of the organization's management system, because it links budgets to strategies and also calls for the inculcation of a robust strategic learning process.

> " Linking budgets and strategies through the scorecard system is crucial if the organization is to become truly Strategy-Focused, as opposed to budget-focused. "

Linking budgets and strategies through the scorecard system is crucial if the organization is to become truly Strategy-Focused, as opposed to budget-focused. Just as the original reason for developing the Balanced Scorecard was the recognized limitations of accounting measures, usage of the scorecard has unearthed equal shortcomings in the budgeting process. Simply put, the annual budgeting cycle can lead to short-term decisions that undermine the chances of strategic success. Saatchi & Saatchi is one of our case study companies that have become Strategy-Focused, as opposed to budget-focused. At Centrepoint Properties the annual Strategy Map formal assessment takes place directly before, and so shapes, the annual budgeting process. We discuss the budgeting process in Chapter 11.

The sub-component "analytics and information systems" takes us directly into the process for scorecard automation. We consider this is depth in Chapter 10. Although there are arguments for and against automation, many of our case study organizations have invested in sophisticated software solutions. MTR Corporation and Bank Universal being two examples.

The final sub-component, strategic learning, is where the scorecard becomes a powerful mechanisms for capturing, and acting on, strategic feedback. It is where performance to the scorecard sets the agenda for monthly management meetings (as at Saatchi & Saatchi) and quarterly strategic reviews (as at Centrepoint Properties). At XYZ Cellular the CEO holds a weekly review of performance to scorecard measures with his direct reports (see also Chapter 11). At Civil Service College Consultants (a business unit of Civil Service College), monthly learning sessions are used to keep a strategic focus and to review how performance from different perspectives fit together. A unit-wide review of performance is held at each six-monthly retreat, where the relevance of objectives and measures is examined.

PRINCIPLE 5: MOBILIZE CHANGE THROUGH EXECUTIVE LEADERSHIP

Sub-components: Mobilization, governance process, and strategic management systems

This final principle speaks not to the process of scorecard creation/implementation, but to the single most important condition for sustainable scorecard success – executive management support. Just about all of our case study companies agree with this, and in several cases, such as Subordinate Courts and Gold Coin it was the CEO (or equivalent) that introduced and championed the scorecard. But the scorecard will stand a much greater chance of success (and surviving a CEO departure) when the whole senior team is galvanized behind the scorecard. The role of senior management is the focus of Chapter 3.

BENEFITS OF SCORECARD USAGE

So far we have provided a thumbnail sketch of the Balanced Scorecard Management System (the rest of the book provides the detail), but what benefits has this framework delivered to organizations? Selected benefits are shown in Exhibit 1.5.

Let's start with financial benefits, which for commercial organizations is what really counts. Saatchi & Saatchi is a good place to start. In the mid-1990s, Saatchi & Saatchi was on the verge of bankruptcy. It brought in a new senior management team who, in 1997, set stretching three-year strategic targets to grow the revenue base better than the market, convert 30% of that incremental revenue to operating profit, and doubled its earnings per share. The senior team chose the scorecard as its framework to implement this strategy globally (after a member of the executive team had come across the scorecard at a Harvard Business School seminar given by professor Kaplan, which incidentally is also how Subordinate Court first encountered the scorecard). As a result, Saatchi & Saatchi reached these targets six months ahead of schedule. Then, in September 2000, the Paris, France, headquartered Publicis Groupe SA (the world's fourth-largest communications group) purchased Saatchi & Saatchi for close on $2.5 billion, equating to about 4.5 times Saatchi & Saatchi's then net worth.

As a further example from our case study companies, MTR Corporation first implemented the scorecard throughout the railway business in 1999. In 2002 it reported the following comparative results. In 1999 value-added per staff stood at just over HK$95, in 2002 it had climbed to just over $110. Moreover, the operating profit generated per staff rose from just under $700,000 to just under $900,000.

In 1999 operating costs per car kilometer was just under $30. In 2002 it had fell to about $23. Also, the railway business reported an operating profit margin (measured by earning before interest, tax, depreciation, and amortization – EBITDA) of 51% on fare revenues of $5,720 million.

Tata Motors CVBU saw revenues grow by 40% in just two years, and it also witnessed dramatic improvements in economic value added (essentially a measure of net operating profit after deducting the cost of capital) and return on capital employed. It also helped Tata Motors Corporation turn a US$108.62 million loss into a US$65.17 million profit in these two years.

In two years of scorecard usage, Gold Coin achieved an average annual increase in EBITDA of 25% and increased profits by 50%. Also, Civil Service College Consultants achieved a 20% increase in revenue during the first fiscal year of scorecard usage (against a targeted 10% increase).

The published literature is littered with impressive financial benefits from scorecard usage. The remarkable financial achievements of early adopts such as Cigna Property & Casualty and Mobil Oil have long since passed into scorecard folklore[9], and others such as Hilton Hotels, Skandia Insurance, and AT&T Canada are equally well reported.

For non-commercial organizations financial success may not be the primary targeted outcome. However, increasing numbers of public-sector organizations are publicly reporting how the scorecard helped them to stretch community-facing objectives. City of Brisbane, Australia, for example, shows that 92% of citizens report that they are satisfied with the way the city interacts with them despite the council having to provide for the needs of a rapidly increasing population in what is the one of the biggest city administrations in Asia-Pacific. Moreover, at the end of 2002, Brisbane reported an accumulated surplus of A$68 million. We shall talk about this exemplary organization further in the book.

Intangible Benefits

But in saying that, scorecard proponents also like to point to the more intangible benefits of scorecard usage – benefits around alignment, focus, accountability, and transparency, as examples. Also, there are the benefits that underpin financial success and set the foundation for sustainable, longer term, success. As a sample of such intangibles, consider these quotes from interviewees from case study companies.

" People now have a far better understanding of how their everyday work links to our vision and mission statements and they can take a more balanced, as opposed to largely internal view of their work. Also as the scorecard is proactive we are better able to identify problems, rectify them and then communicate action and progress to all of our stakeholder groups in a simple format. "

Chan Wai Yin, Director of Research and Statistics Unit, Subordinate Courts.

"The balanced scorecard creates a more team-based, performance oriented culture. The transition the company is experiencing is the move from an operational to strategic mode. That is a major paradigm shift and people across the business are getting better and better at thinking strategically and through the scorecard are sharing a common strategic language."

Carol Yong Meng Dai
Senior Manager, Human Resources, Centrepoint Properties.

"People now have a far better understanding of how their everyday work links to our vision and mission statements and they can take a more balanced, as opposed to largely internal view of their work. Also as the scorecard is proactive we are better able to identify problems, rectify them and then communicate action and progress to all of our stakeholder groups in a simple format."

Chan Wai Yin
Director of Research and Statistics Unit, Subordinate Courts.

Exhibit 1.5 The benefits (pre and post scorecard)

Organization	Pre-scorecard implementation	Post-scorecard implementation
Bank Universal	Blame culture due to lack of understanding of causes of problems.	A culture of performance transparency and accountability.
	Lack of understanding/ communication across functional boundaries.	Better cross-functional teamwork and understanding.
	Difficult to allocate both people and the budget for investments as each group of directors wanted their area to be a priority.	Much stronger clarity around resource allocation.
	Difficulty in explaining to shareholders how they were dealing with the aftermath of economic crisis.	Stronger external communications.
Centrepoint Properties	Overly short-term operational focus.	Strong long-term strategic focus.
	Narrow divisional/functional performance language.	Common organization-wide strategic language.

Civil Service College, Singapore	Goal of growing top-line by 10% annually.	20% growth in year one of scorecard usage.
	Exclusively public sector ethos.	Commercial orientation while keeping benefits of public-sector ethos.
	Potential confusion over how "opposing" strategic thrusts fitted together.	Coherent, and holistic, strategic understanding.
Gold Coin Group	Steady financial improvements.	Average annual increase in EBITDA of 25% and in years 1 and 2 of scorecard usage, and profits increased by 50%.
	Average customer-facing performance.	30% improvement in customer retention, 20% increase in new customer acquisitions. Customer complaints dropped by 40%. Delivery lead times fell by 50%.
	Inconsistent process performance.	15% improvement in manufacturing efficiency, 20% reduction in utility costs.
MTR Corporation	1999 operating profit generated per staff was under HK$700,000.	2002: Increased by 30%
	1999 operating costs per car kilometer was just under $30.	2002: decreased about 23%
	In 1999 the number of serious injuries per 1,000 million passengers was about 0.9.	2002: decreased by 33%
	1999 lost-time injury per 200,000 man-hours worked was 1.2.	2002:decreased by 50%
Saatchi & Saatchi Worldwide	1997, on the verge of bankruptcy.	2000, purchased by Publicis Groupe SA for close on $2.5 billion.
	1997, poor financial performance.	2000, achiever strategic goals of:

	Disconnected business units	Strategically aligned business units.
		• growing the revenue base better than market • converting 30% of that incremental revenue to operating profit • doubling its earnings per share.
Singapore Prison Service	Little understanding organization-wide of performance drivers or outcome measures.	Common performance language and understanding.
	Under-developed performance culture.	Strong performance culture.
Subordinate Courts, Singapore	Internal, operational view of work.	Wider, strategic mindset.
	Under-developed performance communication.	Effective communication of performance.
Summarecon Agung	Poorly developed performance accountabilities.	Well-defined accountabilities.
	Performance management not well linked to strategic goals.	Performance management system hardwired to strategic goals.
Tata Motors Commercial Vehicles Business Unit	2001 baseline	By 2003 revenues grew by 40%
	April–December 2002 total volume sales of commercial vehicles was 72,612 units.	April–December 2003 total volume sales of commercial vehicles increased by 44%
	2001 Tata Motors Corporation reported a US$108.62 million loss.	2003 Tata Motors Corporation reported a $65.17 million profit.
XYZ Cellular	2000, revenue growth of 24%.	2001, revenue growth of 44%.
	2000, reported loss of Rs. 31 million.	2001, profit of Rs. 150 million
	2000, customer acquisitions of 34%	2001, customer acquisitions of 61%.

Caveats and Pitfalls

So we can safely claim that the Balanced Scorecard system can deliver substantial, and wide-reaching, benefits to an organization. However, there are caveats and pitfalls that we should highlight at the outset, and which we will continue to return to as we progress through this book.

First, merely "possessing" a Balanced Scorecard will not in itself deliver benefits. The scorecard is not something that organizations can "plug and play". It is not a neat piece of software that will automatically implement strategy, fix a broken organization, and rectify a dysfunctional culture.

> " ... merely "possessing" a Balanced Scorecard will not in itself deliver benefits. The scorecard is not something that organizations can "plug and play". "

Nor, it should be stressed, will the scorecard make a bad management team a good management team, although it can make a good management team an excellent management team. In just about every successful scorecard implementation that we have encountered throughout scorecard history, the quality of the incumbent leadership was central to subsequent achievements – Saatchi & Saatchi, Subordinate Courts, Singapore, and Centrepoint Properties being three examples. What the scorecard did in each case was to help the senior team better do its job – implement strategy.

Matthew Tice is Vice-President Asia-Pacific for BSCol, and is one of the select group of regional thought-leaders we interviewed for this book. He provides a couple of valuable pointers as to why many organizations fail to secure benefits from the Balanced Scorecard. A typical reason, he says, is simply "fortitude." I've often heard it said that the only place that success comes before work is in the dictionary. You have to keep with

> " I've often heard it said that the only place that success comes before work is in the dictionary. You have to keep with it for a couple of years. A lot of organizations that fail are looking for a quick fix and that causes problems. "

it for a couple of years. A lot of organizations that fail are looking for a quick fix and that causes problems.

A second reason for failure, he says, is not building the capability to sustain the program.

We would certainly endorse Tice's observations, as would the other thought-leaders interviewed for the book. Indeed, observing scorecard implementation over the last decade or so, primarily in North America and Europe, the key reasons for success and failure have become evident. These observations will inform the thinking in this book and will prove valuable to Asian organizations about to take their first steps on the scorecard journey.

The Balanced Scorecard and Asia

This brings us to the reason why we have written this book. Simply put, the Balanced Scorecard is a relatively new concept to most Asian organizations (although organizations such as Subordinate Courts were early adopters for the region, tracing their scorecard usage back to 1998). Consequently, Asian companies can learn much from the experiences collected by their North American and European counterparts.

In saying that, Asian organizations can equally learn a great deal from the scorecard pioneers in this region. The 11 major case studies in this book are primarily Asia-based companies who have evolved the scorecard in a local context. In some cases, such as Saatchi & Saatchi, the organization is headquartered outside of Asia, but with a significant local presence. These organizations are blazing the scorecard trail within Asia and they represent the first dedicated collection of Asia-specific best practice case studies to be published. Indeed, it is reasonable to claim that Asia success stories have been largely

> **... it is reasonable to claim that Asia success stories have been largely overlooked in the scorecard literature to date, much to chagrin of those with best practice stories to tell.**

overlooked in the scorecard literature to date, much to chagrin of those with best practice stories to tell.

What we have also done for this book is interviewed thought-leaders from the region so as to get their expert input into how the scorecard is developing in Asia, and to understand and report on any differences in how the scorecard is implemented within Asia, compared with other geographical regions.

To support this book we commissioned a survey of South-east Asia, where the scorecard is well established. Thus, 121companies responded to a questionnaire on scorecard usage. This questionnaire is shown fully in the Appendix. As shown in Exhibit 1.6 36% were using the Balanced Scorecard, with another 18% planning to do so.

Using the Balanced Scorecard	36%
Planning to use the Balanced Scorecard	18%
Not using the Balanced Scorecard	46%

Exhibit 1.6 Balance Scorecard Usage

Of those companies using the Balanced Scorecards, the most common reason was that implementation was to align the performance of all employees to objectives (47% of respondents rated this "extremely important" – taking the 36% as a 100%), followed by "to better understand the drivers of strategic success," and to "communicate strategy to the employee base" (both of which scored 37%).

Of the 46% of organizations that were not using the scorecard, the main reasons for not implementing it were "we evaluated the Balanced Scorecard, but decided not to implement the framework (22% – taking the 46% as a 100%)," followed by "we have never considered using the scorecard," and "cultural resistance" (both 12%).

Interestingly, with each scoring 10%, other reasons were "management interest faded," "management couldn't reach agreement on the composition of the scorecard," and "it proved too difficult to implement." As we work through this book we will show how to overcome these and other obstacles.

More than anything, we have written this book to meet a compelling need. The East Asian economic crisis of 1997/98 effectively put the normal evolution of management thinking on hold. As regional nations adopted a survival mode, other regions (including Australasia) forged ahead, embracing new approaches such as the Balanced Scorecard. As Asian organizations emerged from the crisis they found themselves facing severe competitive pressures as a result of globalization, increased deregulation, and technological advances.

Today, increasing market share within Asian countries is a strategic priority within a host of non-Asian corporations. Not only are local companies tasked with defending local markets, but the same market forces also provide opportunities for them to make strategic inroads into other regions. But defensive and offensive strategies, however well thought-out at the top of the organization, have to be implemented by the people at the front-line. For this to happen, high-level strategic objectives must be well articulated by the senior team, and must be equally well communicated within the organization via a meaningful and actionable lexicon. Moreover, mechanisms must be in place to monitor, in as near real-time as feasible, the efficaciousness of the strategy implementation efforts and to modify and refocus accordingly.

Throughout the world, increasing numbers of organizations hold that the most powerful framework for articulating, communicating, implementing, monitoring, and modifying strategy is the Balanced Scorecard. This book provides a step-by-step best practice guide in using this remarkable framework based on our observations of global best practice and experienced gained through consulting within over 60 Asia-based scorecard implementations.

CASE STUDY

Tata Motors Commercial Vehicle Business Unit

Summary

Balanced Scorecard Collaborative Hall of Fame inductee Tata Motors Commercial Vehicle Business Unit has achieved breakthrough performance since adopting the Balanced Scorecard. This case study describes the process by which the high-level Strategy Map and Balanced Scorecard was built and subsequently deployed deep inside the organization. Indeed, over 300 Balanced Scorecards exist within the business unit.

Background

Headquartered in Mumbai, India, Tata Motors comprises two divisions, the Passenger Cars Business Unit (it entered this market in the early 1990s) and the Commercial Vehicle Business Unit (CVBU). CVBU is the focus of this case study and Tata Motors has been manufacturing commercial vehicles since its launch in 1945.

Consisting of three plants in India, and supported by a nationwide sales and service network, CBVU manufactures the full range of commercial vehicles, from two-tonne light commercial vehicles to 40-tonne tractor trailers, from 60-seat buses to 6X4 off-road vehicles, and from tippers to defense vehicles. With a workforce of over 26,000, CBVU serves over 60% of the Indian market and is one of the top ten truck manufactures in the world. As we can see on CBVU's Strategy Map (see Exhibit 1.7) it has a top financial objective of being among the world's top five profitable commercial vehicle manufacturers.

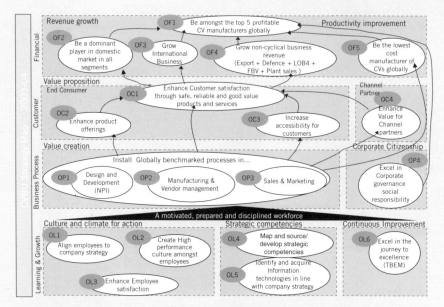

Exhibit 1.7 Tata Motors Commercial Vehicles Business Unit Strategy Map 2003–04

The Balanced Scorecard: The Beginnings

The implementation of the Balanced Scorecard system within Tata Motors CVBU began in 2000. The business unit made notable changes to its leadership team in order to reverse several years of poor financial performance. Mr Ravi Kant was appointed the unit's Executive Director (essentially CEO). With his leadership team, Ravi Kant crafted a strategy that focused first on turnaround and then on sustainable growth and profitability. Being the lowest cost producer would be a central feature of its strategy.

CVBU's leadership team recognized that successfully delivering to its strategy would require the involvement of all of its employees. This would be something of a challenge as the unit had for a number of years taken more of an operational focus with short-term objectives.

Moreover, an external assessment against the organization's Excellence Model (based on the Malcolm Baldrige criteria identified a lack of strategy deployment as a significant weakness within the unit. Mr KC Girotra, who leads CVBU's Balanced Scorecard efforts as head of its Business Excellence Services Department, recalls what happened next: Several of our senior managers attended a one-day workshop on the Balanced Scorecard that was delivered by Dr David Norton. The scorecard seemed to offer a possible solution to our strategy deployment problems, so it was decided to launch a scorecard program.

Scorecard Successes

That the Balanced Scorecard is proving a success within Tata Motors CVBU is without question. One important measure is that the business unit was, during the Balanced Scorecard Collaborative's (BSCol) 2004 Asia-Pacific Summit [10], inducted into BSCol's Hall of Fame (reserved for organizations that achieve breakthrough performance through using the Balanced Scorecard methodology). CBVU, along with City of Brisbane and Korea Telecom, were the first Asia-Pacific specific organization to receive Hall of Fame recognition.

From a company-specific measure of success view, since launching the scorecard system CBVU has seen dramatic improvements in economic value-added (essentially a measure of net operating profit after deducting the cost of capital) and return on capital employed.

Between 2001 and 2003 revenues grew by 40% and are presently at least double the rate of CVBU's nearest competitor. This, coupled with CVBU's aggressive cost reduction program, helped Tata Motors Corporation turn the US$108.62 million loss into a US$65.17 million profit in these two years.

Furthermore, "breakeven point," a critical benchmark for being the lowest cost producer and a key scorecard measure for the unit, has seen equal dramatic reductions. As one further measure, from April to December 2002, total volume sales of commercial vehicles was 72,612 units. In the same time scale in 2003, the figure was 104,626 – an impressive increase of 44%.

Other Scorecard Benefits

KC Girotra states that there has also been a range of other benefits from adopting the Balanced Scorecard. He summarizes these in three words: "Focus, accountability, and ownership."

He elaborates:We now have a greater organization-wide focus on strategic objectives and goals as set by the senior management team. Our workforce is now clearly focused on the customer and on improving critical processes. Furthermore, we have clear ownership for performance and accountability for targets throughout CVBU. And finally we have achieved alignment, and indeed integration, of objectives across the company and from top to bottom.

The latter point has been catalyzed by the fact that there are over 300 Balanced Scorecards in operation within CVBU. We will discuss scorecard deployment later in the case study. First though, we will consider the highest level CVBU Strategy Map and Balanced Scorecard.

Strategy Map

CVBU's Strategy Map is shown in Exhibit 1.7. With 19 strategic objectives, the map comprises the conventional scorecard perspectives of financial, customer, business processes, and learning and growth. The top objective – to "be among the top five profitable CV [commercial vehicle] manufacturers globally" – is fed by revenue growth objectives, such as "grow international business" and productivity objectives such "be the lowest cost manufacturer of CV's globally."

Descending down the map we can see that there are value proposition objectives for end-customers (such as "enhance product offerings') and channel partners ("enhance value for channel partners"), which are in turn fed by value creation objectives from the business processes perspective. These are focused on installing globally benchmarked processes in, for example, design and development.

Note too that from the business processes perspective there is a corporate citizenship objective to "excel at corporate governance and responsibility." In the wake of recent high-profile accounting scandals, corporate governance has become of enhanced importance for all publicly traded organizations (see Chapter 12).

The learning and growth perspective sets out to create a motivated, prepared, and disciplined workforce with emphasis on culture and climate for action, strategic competencies, and continuous improvement.

Balanced Scorecard

The Balanced Scorecard shell for the Business Processes perspective is shown in Exhibit 1.8 (comprising the measures, targets, ownership, and initiatives that support the Strategy Map). Exhibit 1.9 shows CVBU's strategic initiative listing for fiscal 2003/04 detailing functional and individual ownership, and the strategic objectives the initiatives support. According to KC Girotra:

He adds that a template that is used for describing initiatives and their impact forces initiative owners to address financial and human resource requirements, and necessitates that they fully think through and articulate how their proposed initiative would positively impact high-level strategic objectives. As a consequence, KC Girotra points out many initiatives that may have historically been green-lighted no longer receive funding.

Creating the Balanced Scorecard System

The original Strategy Map and Balanced Scorecard were created by putting in place a high-level steering committee (comprising functional heads and some other key officers such as the regional managers in Sales & Marketing), which reported to Ravi Kant.

The committee then appointed a core team of five people (which is part of the Business Excellence Services Department & the Executive Director's Office) to act as the program team that would, working with the Steering Committee, build and deploy the Strategy Map and Balanced Scorecard. However, final validation and ownership would remain with Ravi Kant and the Steering Committee. Status was reported every month. It took one sitting of eight hours with the Executive Director, plus a further month of refinement, to create the Strategy Map.

At this stage, external consultants were not used as part of the scorecard efforts, although the expertise of several consultants was used later for specific purposes. Nigel Penny, the Singapore-based consultant interviewed for this book has, for example, been used several times by the organization.

Sr No	Strategic Objective	Key Performance Measure	Owners	00-01 Actual	00-02 Actual	Status 2002-03	Target 2003-04	2004-05	2005-06	Benchmark	Reporting Resp.	Linkage with Higher level BSC	Supported by Strategic Initiative	Frequency of update
Business Process Perspective														
	management													
OP3	Install globally benchmarked processes in Sales & Marketing													
OP4	Excel in corporate governance and social responsibility													

Exhibit 1.8 The Balanced Scorecard shell for the business processes perspective

Function	Sl. No.	Initiative	Owner	Lead Member	Strategic objective supported
Sales & Marketing + Dealer Dev	1	Trucks Sectoral promotion	SM	RTW	
		Cement	SM	RTW	
		Steel	SM	R TW	
		Petrochemicals	SM	RTW	OF2
		Auto Logistics	SM	RTW	
		Container	SM	RTW	
	2	Fully Built Vehicles	SM/CVS	Vinay Pathak	OF4
International Business	15	Development and deployment of International strategy	RK	PGS	OF4, OF3
	16	Enhance satisfaction of International Customers		PGS	OC1
CRM	17	CRM	KRS	KRS	OC1
Plant	18	Six sigma		MLB/AVA/CVS	
		LPT 1613 TC (Jsr)		MLB	
		LPT 2515 TC (Jsr)		MLB	
		LPT 1613 CMVR (Pune)	APA	AVA	OP2
		LPT 2515 TC (Pune)		AVA	
		407 (Pune)		AVA	
		1613 CMVR (Lko)		CVS	
	19	Cost Reduction	PMT		
		e-Procurement Full source	PMT	VNB/AP	OF5
Business Excellence	23	BSC Deployment	Ravi Kant	KCG / RAB / Probir Mitra	OL1
	24	TBEM ACT 600+	KCG		OL6
HR	25	Career planning for high performers (Talent Pool)	VKV	MM	OL2
	26	Strengthen incentives / disincentives system (PMS)	VKV		OL2
	27	Change organisational structure in line with business needs	VKV		OL1
	28	OHS Action planning	VKV	YM	OL3
	29	Global initiative reporting	VKV		OP4

Exhibit 1.9 CVBU strategic initiative listing

At the outset the core team's knowledge was essentially drawn from the performance management and measurement expertise found within the Business Excellence Services Department (whose head, KC Girotra, was a member of the Steering Committee). As the department had built up considerable knowledge of using performance management frameworks (such as their Excellence Model) it seemed logical that scorecard facilitation and eventual day-to-day ownership would reside here.

The core team's knowledge was enhanced by reading Dr Norton's and Professor Kaplan's first book.

Once the CVBU Strategy Map was drawn and agreed to a concerted program was conducted to provide detailed explanations to all functions and departments of the benefits of the scorecard and its importance to CVBU.

Scorecard Devolution

Despite widespread communication, KC Girotra recalls that in year 1 the key focus was on defining the strategic objectives and their supporting strategic initiatives and essentially this remained a high-level tool. As a consequence, there was limited buy-in to the scorecard below the senior leadership team.

Girotra adds: It was then decided that it should be cascaded to the lowest working level in the organization such as the Area Offices (Sales and Marketing) and Centres of Excellences/Departments (Plant locations).

To start the cascade process senior executives, along with Ravi Kant, attended a workshop delivered by Dr Norton. As a result they better understood the concept of systematic evolution of the scorecard, and the need for a strong review process to support its deployment at all levels.

The cascade process also involved local Business Excellence Service Team members running strategy workshops within plants and functions. Two international experts had trained the team members, Nigel Penny, founder of Clarista Asia, and Henrik Anderson, General Manager of 2GC Australia. Each expert conducted a two-day workshop. Penny explained performance measures and Anderson described the scorecard itself.

Furthermore, Business Excellence Service Team members collaborated with both the CVBU Steering Committee members and managers at lower levels to help evolve the scorecard at these levels, and set in place a review process for monitoring and analyzing performance on their local Balanced Scorecard. Getting lower level buy-in, recalls KC Girotra, was made much easier by the example set by the senior team. He recalls: The use of the Balanced Scorecard by senior leaders such as Mr Kant and other CVBU Steering Committee members to review business performance sent strong messages across the organization about its utility and the value they placed on the system. And the constant visible support and encouragement of the Executive Director and the Steering Committee certainly accelerated the scorecard cascade and buy-in process during year 2.

Importantly, however, he adds: Subsequently, the visible benefits secured from the systematic evolution and review of the scorecard at all levels has led to wholehearted appreciation of the Balanced Scorecard concept.

Evolution and review, for example, led, in year 2, to a sharpening of strategic objectives and initiatives in line with strategic challenges. Moreover, year 2 also saw the introduction of comparative data and benchmarks as a basis for selecting targets.

As cited, more than 300 scorecards have been created within CVBU, covering all functions, departments, manufacturing Centres of Excellence, and Area Offices (deepest work units within the Sales and Marketing organization). How this looks at is shown in Exhibit 1.10.

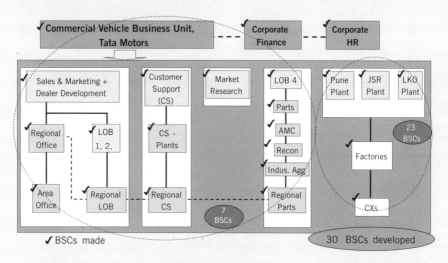

Exhibit 1.10 A schematic of CVBU's 300 scorecards

How this works in practice is that the CVBU level Balanced Scorecard defines the overall goals and timeframes to be achieved by the organization. These goals and targets are then cascaded into Balanced Scorecards for each division/function. Hence, each scorecard is linked to its higher level scorecard through the strategic objectives.

In addition, each division/function also defines its own initiatives to help achieve their own local strategic objectives. For example, the CVBU level strategy of "being a dominant player in domestic market in all segments," was cascaded into all the Lines of Business (LOB) scorecards, where each LOB has targets of achieving a certain market share. The three plants at Pune, Jamshedpur, and Lucknow support this strategy by fulfilling the requirement of products put up by the sales division.

KC Girotra states: Our operational measurement systems of SQDCM (safety, quality, delivery, cost, and morale) deployed in the plants and the

VMCDR (volume, market share, customer satisfaction, dealer satisfaction, and receivables) observed in the Sales & Marketing departments are also aligned to the Balanced Scorecard. Next, the performance plans prepared by individual employees and cross-functional teams align all employees and teams to the company goals.

Devolved Strategy Map

As a devolved example the Strategy Map for the Sales and Marketing organization is shown in Exhibit 1.11. It is clear how this functional map supports the higher level CVBU map. For example, the already cited objective of "be a dominant player in domestic markets in all segments" is directly supported by the Sales & Marketing objective "strengthen presence in domestic CV market by increasing market share."

Day-to-day responsibility

Making the Balanced Scorecard core team responsible for the day-to-day management of the score carding process ensures organization-wide cohesion. Within the plants and locations they are supported by Business Excellence Service Teams, who have local responsibility for evolving the Balance Scorecard, facilitating monthly reviews with senior leaders (divisional and functional steering committees), and escalating important review findings to higher levels.

A key forum for strategic feedback, the Steering Committees looks for gaps in performance that may necessitate the revisiting of action plans launched to achieve strategic initiatives and objectives. According to KC Girotra, "This ensures that the planned strategy gets implemented."

Challenges

Although it has already achieved a great deal through scorecard usage, there are still challenges ahead. Continuous improvements to the Balanced Scorecard process, which are beneficial to all functions and departments, is seen as important to maintaining momentum. KC Girotra adds that maintaining momentum also requires continuous communication to all employees on the scorecard approach and benefits.

Every year the Executive Director initiates this process by sharing the company's vision, mission, future directions, and strategies at a town hall

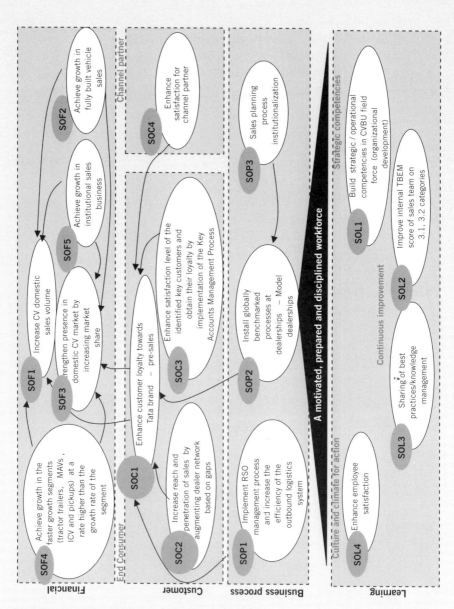

Exhibit 1.11 Sales and Marketing Strategy Map

meeting with all employees. He repeats this communication session personally at all locations of the company, to ensure that all employees have a strong, consistent understanding of the business unit's future.

To ingrain the understanding further, the Balanced Scorecards core team conducts score-carding cascading workshops at each division/function, to communicate the CVBU Strategy Map, Balanced Scorecard, and initiatives. Communication systems include internal publications, intranet websites, presentations made by senior leaders, and so on.

Another challenge is around aligning individual compensation with performance on the Balanced Scorecard (a challenge that is common to most scorecard users). Thus far, the Sales & Marketing organization is the only part of CVBU to explore this alignment.

There is also a project underway to digitize the scorecard at all levels in order to facilitate data uploading, and consequently enable online reviews of the scorecard. This intranet site is expected to be operational in early 2005.

Critical Success Factors
In conclusion KC Girotra says that there are three critical success factors in implementing the Balanced Scorecard:
1. the active and visible support of senior management;
2. a strong review process;
3. a knowledgeable team to drive and support scorecard deployment.

1   Measuring Performance in the Organization of the Future, Nolan Norton institute, 1990.

2   David P. Norton, Robert S. Kaplan: The Balanced Scorecard – Measures That Drive Performance Harvard Business Review, January-February 1992.

3   David P. Norton, Robert S. Kaplan: The Balanced Scorecard: Translating Strategy into Action Harvard Business School Press, 1996

4   David P. Norton, Robert S. Kaplan: The Strategy-Focused Organization: How Balanced Scorecard Companies thrive in the New Economy, Harvard Business School Press, 2001.

5   David P. Norton, Robert S. Kaplan: Strategy Maps: Converting Intangible Assets into Tangible Outcomes: Harvard Business Review, 2004

6   The reports by James Creelman are:
——Building a Strategic Balanced Scorecard: Business Intelligence, 2003
——Understanding The Balanced Scorecard: An HR Perspective HR.Com 2002
——Creating a Balanced Scorecard Lafferty Publications, 2001
——Creating the HR Scorecard (Business Intelligence, 2001
——Building and Developing the Finance Scorecard, Business Intelligence, 2000
——Building and Implementing a Balanced Scorecard Business Intelligence, 1998

7   Bain & Company, 2003.

8   David P. Norton, Robert S. Kaplan: The Strategy-Focused Organization: How Balanced Scorecard Companies thrive in the New Economy, Harvard Business School Press, 2001.

9   See Balanced Scorecard Collaborative Hall of Fame, www.bscol.com

10   The Balanced Scorecard Collaborative's 2003 Asia-Pacific Summit, Brisbane, Australia, November 2003

2

How the Scorecard is Being Used in Practice

A strength of the Balanced Scorecard is its flexibility and adaptability, but this has led to wide interpretations of the term and how it is deployed. A wide variance in interpretation has led to some integrity issues. Typically, the scorecard is perceived, and deployed, as a performance measurement system and not a strategy implementation framework. Therefore, most organizations are failing to reap full benefits. The Strategy Map is the most important component of a scorecard system. Typically, an organization's Strategy Map will comprise four perspectives, but three or five are not uncommon. We will explain what this means for differences in scorecard usage and illustrate how the scorecard is being used in practice through seven scorecard types. We will also describe how the Balanced Scorecard works alongside total quality frameworks such as Malcolm Baldrige and the Singapore Business Excellence Model. A case study on Singapore Prison Service concludes this chapter.

BACKGROUND

Scorecard proponents often argue, and we are no exception, that one of the key strengths of the Balanced Scorecard is its flexibility and adaptability, in that it can be tailored to the structural, cultural, or performance needs of each individual organization.

Simply put, organizations do not have to work within a prescriptive framework, as is the case with most total quality frameworks such as the US-born Malcolm Baldrige framework or the Singapore Business Excellence Model (both of which we describe later in this chapter). Furthermore, organizations are free to build and implement Balanced Scorecards that digress substantially from a classic Norton/Kaplan template.

> **It has become extraordinarily difficult to judge the overall success of the Balanced Scorecard as a management tool because what the term "Balanced Scorecard" means to one practitioner may be diametrically different to what it what it means to another.**

Although this elasticity of description and deployment has contributed to the remarkably high levels of scorecard usage throughout the world, it has led to an array of interpretations and implementations that have often damaged the integrity of the term Balanced Scorecard. It has become extraordinarily difficult to judge the overall success of the Balanced Scorecard as a management tool because what the term "Balanced Scorecard" means to one practitioner may be diametrically different to what it what it means to another.

It is little wonder, therefore, that BSCol, which was founded by the scorecard co-creators, Dr David Norton and Professor Robert Kaplan, was launched with a mission to facilitate the "... worldwide awareness, use, enhancement, and *integrity* (authors itals) of the Balanced Scorecard as a value-added management process."

A "CATCHALL" TERM

Norton and Kaplan recognized that the Balanced Scorecard was fast becoming a catchall term for any management approach that professed a "balanced" composition. And we have certainly seen many Balanced Scorecards that have little in common with Norton/Kaplan's construct. This is not to say such divergent "scorecards" are not without merit. Indeed, many users of such adaptations are happy with their "scorecards" and claim discernable benefits from usage.

A MEASUREMENT SYSTEM

However, in virtually all adaptations we have seen, the Balanced Scorecard is constructed as a measurement system with identified measures and targets (and often articulated initiatives and measure owners), collocated within four, five, or more perspectives. Although this may show, on one piece of paper, performance to articulated measures (and so capturing a key benefit of a scorecard that it provided a "one-page" view of performance), it typically only has a tenuous link to strategy. Therefore such scorecards are typically a performance-measurement system and not a strategy implementation framework. Although it should be stressed that in many instances such frameworks are purposefully construed as performance-measurement systems. And even when organizations set out to adopt a classic Norton/Kaplan scorecard, it is still primarily a measurement system.

> **❝ Probably 30–50% of organizations that pick up the scorecard don't get a great deal of results from it because they create something that is measurement-focused, rather than something that can transform the organization. ❞**

Nigel Penny, managing director of the Singapore-based ClaritasAsia, and previously vice-president Asia-Pacific for BSCol observes:

Despite all the publicity through books and seminars etc, there are very differing degrees of understanding of what the Balanced Scorecard is really about. In Asia in particular, it's only quite recently that organizations have been developing Strategy Maps. Previously, many companies claimed a Balanced Scorecard purely as a result of defining some key performance indicators (KPIs) in each of the four quadrants. There was little link to strategic plans and so the result became yet another numbers report. Unfortunately, this situation has been exacerbated by some consultants, with limited understanding of the rationale behind the Balanced Scorecard, who have lead their clients down totally erroneous routes.

This danger of the "blind leading the blind" is something we come back to in Chapter 5. Matthew Tice, BSCol's present vice-president Asia-Pacific, continues this theme:

The fact is that there are many organizations that as yet don't perceive the scorecard as a strategy implementation framework. And the big challenge is to bring these organizations along as to the power of what the scorecard is. Probably 30–50% of organizations that pick up the scorecard don't get a great deal of results from it because they create something that is measurement-focused, rather than something that can transform the organization. There is still a lot of work to be done in getting people aligned to the strategy execution message.

THE IMPORTANCE OF STRATEGY MAPS

We argue, as would Tice and Penny, that for the scorecard to be a strategy execution framework it has to include a Strategy Map: it is the Strategy Map that describes the high-level roadmap for implementing the strategy. This cannot be described purely through measures. Indeed, in their book *Strategy Maps* Professor Kaplan and Dr Norton write: [1]

We now realize that the strategy map, a visual representation of the cause-and-effect relationships among the components of an organization's strategy, is as big an insight to executives as the Balanced Scorecard itself.

We explain the process for building a Strategy Map in Chapter 6, but what does our research tell us about the usage of Strategy Maps, as this will provide some insights into how organizations view the scorecard system? First, each of our major case study companies has built a Strategy Map. However, our case study Singapore's Civil Service College (see Chapter 8) has not as yet built a Strategy Map, although one has been built within its Civil Service College Consultants business unit.

Moreover, Singapore's Centrepoint Property's first Balanced Scorecard did not contain a Strategy Map. Although that scorecard delivered some benefits, not least in learning to see through "balanced" perspectives, the effort was somewhat constrained by the lack of a Strategy Map to show the causality between objectives.

Now, it may not be that surprising that the best practice case companies in this book have created Strategy Maps, as they were selected by authors who firmly believe that Strategy Maps are the most important element of the Balanced Scorecard System.

NUMBER OF PERSPECTIVES

An important consideration in creating Strategy Maps and Balanced Scorecards is the number of perspectives that are housed within the framework. According to our survey of scorecard adoption in SE Asia (see the Appendix), more that half of the 43 scorecard users opted for the conventional four perspectives, as shown in Exhibit 2.1

Number of perspectives	Organizations
3	3%
4	66%
5	25%
6	6%

Exhibit 2.1 Scorecard use and perspectives

Consider the number of perspectives used by our major case study companies, as shown in Exhibit 2.2

Number of perspectives	Organizations
3	Saatchi & Saatchi (on their most recent Strategy Map, although they used four perspectives for six years). Subordinate Courts.
4	Bank Universal. Centrepoint Properties. Gold Coin Group. Civil Service College. Tata Motors Commercial Vehicles Business Unit. Singapore Prison Service Summarecon. XYZ Enterprises.
5	MTR Corporation.

Exhibit 2.2 The number of perspectives according to case study companies

So as we can see, most of our major case study companies, as with most users, adopt a conventional four-perspective scorecard approach. Where more than four is found it is typically because there is one or more performance dimensions that are particularly mission-critical to that organization. For example, consider the "safety" perspective at MTR Corporation (see Chapter 7). As a further, non-case study company, the administrative support unit of the global consultancy Booz|Allen|Hamilton has a perspective focused on "promoting the brand" in addition to the conventional four perspectives. This highlights the importance of brand management to this organization and that it's promotion is the responsibility of all its employees, including those from support functions.[2]

THREE PERSPECTIVE SCORECARDS

Where we find three perspectives, the typical reason is that the financial perspective is missing (although this is not always the case; for example, the US-headquartered white goods manufacturer Whirlpool Corporation omitted the process perspective, on the grounds that the perspective was well captured in an internal measurement system based on the Malcolm Baldrige Award – see below for more on Baldrige).

> " Where we find three perspectives, the typical reason is that the financial perspective is missing. This is often the case within public-sector organizations... "

The jettisoning of the financial perspective is often the case within public-sector organizations, such as our case study company Subordinate Courts, Singapore (see Chapter 3).

A cursory scan of public-sector organizations in other geographic regions unearths many instances of "three" perspective scorecards. As examples, consider the scorecards at the Royal Canadian Mounted Police and Scottish Enterprise (Scotland's main economic development agency). Both of these organizations have discarded conventional finance perspective and placed "stakeholder" as the top perspective.[3]

SAATCHI & SAATCHI AND THREE PERSPECTIVES

With public-sector bodies this is not that surprising, as the outcomes they typically set out to achieve are not primarily financial and are certainly not shareholder-focused, but couched in stakeholder terms. But why would a commercial organization such as Saatchi & Saatchi

Worldwide (see Chapter 11) not only opt for a three-perspective scorecard in their latest iteration, but also jettison the finance perspective?

On one level this is somewhat surprising, for as explained in the case study, Saatchi & Saatchi can be safely hailed as one of the world's most successful users of a "conventional" four-perspective Strategy Map and Balanced Scorecard, reporting astonishing financial results. Indeed, this book's authors often hold up the Saatchi & Saatchi's four perspective Strategy Map as an example of what a "best practice" Strategy Map should look like (and we explain our reasoning in Chapter 6).

But on another level Saatchi & Saatchi's decision is not surprising for, we now argue, they are indeed taking the scorecard concept to another level.

Saatchi & Saatchi's scorecard houses the three perspectives of sharing the dream (its "top-perspective," which essentially is about identifying and sharing worldwide what it calls "big transformative ideas," or BTIs), a customer perspective (which Saatchi & Saatchi calls "our focus"), and a people and culture perspective (which it calls "our spirit").

Simply put, Saatchi & Saatchi has formulated a Balanced Scorecard that articulates performance goals in a language that resonates fully with the creative people that make up this remarkable organization. Saatchi & Saatchi secures competitive advantage by converting intellectual assets (or intellectual capital) into an intangible product (ideas). Its new scorecard focused squarely on that process.

The lack of a financial perspective does not in any way suggest that judicious financial management, or positive financial outcomes, are no longer important, they are absolutely important, especially as the organization's parent is a major PLC. Rather, the scorecard is saying these are the critical few ideas generating objectives that we must all focus on. Financial objectives may not in themselves inspire ideas sharing in a creative environment. But in saying that, it is only through experiencing extraordinary financial success as a result of transforming intangible assets into financial outcomes that the organization has the confidence, and capabilities, to adapt the scorecard to their own performance requirements. Saatchi's & Saatchi's management team know that a laser-focus on leveraging intellectual capital will deliver financial capital and strategic success. Consequently, they don't feel the need for a financial perspective to prove that this will indeed be the outcome.

However, there are few commercial organizations today with the experience or confidence to dispense with a financial perspective. Moreover, Saatchi & Saatchi is clearly an organization whose value is almost exclusively found in intangible assets (there's nothing more intangible than ideas that transform brands). For those organizations that trade in more "tangible" or capital-intensive industries, dispensing with a financial perspective may be much less appealing, and in most cases not recommended.

SEVEN SCORECARD TYPES

What is certain about Saatchi & Saatchi is that its past and present scorecards are strategy-implementation frameworks. This brings us to a discussion on how organizations are really using the Balanced Scorecard System. Ask most corporations how they are using the scorecard and they will repeat the mantra that they are "turning strategy into action," that the scorecard is being deployed to implement strategies. Typically, however, this is not the case. As we have already said, in most cases the Balanced Scorecard is simply a measurement tool, monitoring progress against targets that are as likely to be operational as strategic.

> **Ask most corporations how they are using the scorecard and they will repeat the mantra that they are "turning strategy into action," that the scorecard is being deployed to implement strategies. Typically, however, this is not the case.**

Art Schneiderman holds a special place in the history of the Balanced Scorecard. Analog Devices was one of the organizations that participated in Norton/Kaplan's 1990 research program that led to their first version of the Balanced Scorecard. At the time Art Schneiderman was Analog's Vice-President, quality improvement and productivity. In a presentation made to Norton/Kaplan and the research group, Schneiderman spoke of Analog's "Corporate Scorecard" that included performance measures relating to customer delivery times, quality and cycle times of manufacturing processes, and effectiveness of new product development, as well as some financial measure. The word "scorecard" took its first step into the lexicon of management speak.

Now an independent consultant, Schneiderman has watched the Scorecard evolve over the past decade and has concluded that the term "Balanced Scorecard" is interpreted differently according to corporate priorities. He has identified seven diverse ways the Scorecard is being applied. These are

1. a project management tool;
2. educating people on the need for "balanced" measures;
3. a communication tool;
4. a control tool;
5. to manage tradeoffs;
6. a deployment tool;
7. a framework for converting strategy into action.

We will now explore each in turn. It should be said that all seven scorecard types are useful and can provide real benefits to organizations. But knowing how you are really using the scorecard can prove powerful in gaining a real assessment of how much work is required before the scorecard truly becomes a strategy implementation framework (a type seven scorecard).

The type one scorecard is essentially a project management tool. This scorecard is used to track the intermediate steps between the beginning of the project and the deliverables.

The type two scorecard is simply based on the recognition that there's a need for a balance of financial and non-financial measures. This scorecard is used to educate people that they can use non-financial measures to manage the business in a proactive way and from a predictive perspective.

The type three scorecard is a communication tool. Strategies often become less and less meaningful, less and less tangible, as you move down through the organization. So this type of Scorecard tries to translate the language of strategy into terms that are meaningful to the people lower in the ranks.

A type four scorecard is used for control purposes. For example, if historically the organization has averaged 95% on time delivery it may conclude that that is good enough, so it is put it on the scorecard and organizations measure it just to make sure it stays at that level.

A type five scorecard exists to introduce balance. It highlights potential tradeoffs (that is, cost and quality) and to stop the pendulum swinging wildly from one focus to the next.

A type six scorecard is as a deployment tool. For example, the CEO asks each subordinate how the company can grow 15%, and what they are going to do to make it happen. They in turn ask each of their subordinates what they are going to do to help achieve the target. As it gets cascaded down through the organization, not only do the goals get deployed, but also means get identified for the achievement of those goals. The process bounces up and down over several months as this very detailed planning process is carried out.

A type seven Scorecard is where the scorecard captures the vital few strategically leveraged improvements that produce a manageable set of objectives that can then be deployed through the organization. It explicitly links the organization's strategy on measures and time-based goals that are deployed throughout the organization to teams and individuals who must make it happen. This deployment will typically take the shape of a series of cascaded scorecards from the enterprise-level through units, functions, teams, and even individuals (which we describe in Chapter 8).

> ...at level seven the management team identify those vital few objectives where performance enhancement will make the difference in delivering to the strategy. And the word "few" means just that.

And note that at level seven the management team identifies those vital few objectives where performance enhancement will make the difference in delivering to the strategy. And the word "few" means just that. There were just 12 objectives on Saatchi & Saatchi's (four perspective) scorecard; for instance, just 14 on the corporate scorecard at Subordinate Courts, Singapore, and there's just 10 on the Strategy Map of MTR Corporation (we talk more about the importance of a "few" objectives in Chapter 7).

Once it is clear which objectives must be leveraged to make a difference, the next step is to ensure that the scarce financial and human resources of the organization are focused on breakthrough improvements against those objectives. Indeed, the "real work" in translating strategy into action is through the initiatives that are launched using those scare resources. This is what distinguishes the scorecard from a measurement system. It enables companies to set criteria for allocating financial, human, and other resources on the basis of their impact on strategy (we discuss this crucial point in more detail within Chapter 7).

A type seven Scorecard is therefore the starting point for translating strategy into action. It is where the whole organization is aligned behind those critical few strategic objectives, measures, ands targets. A type seven scorecard takes us into the relatively uncharted territory of the strategy-focused organization.

TOTAL QUALITY FRAMEWORKS AND THE BALANCED SCORECARD

In the following chapters we will explain the process for using the Balanced Scorecard System to translate strategy into action and further show how exemplary organizations are showing the way towards strategy-focused status. But before we do this, we should note that the Balanced Scorecard is not the only performance management and improvement framework being deployed within organizations.

Indeed, many organizations have achieved breakthrough performance results through the use of total quality management frameworks, such as the Malcolm Baldrige model or the models it inspired – such as the Australian Business Excellence Model and Singapore Business Excellence Model, as just two examples. Most countries (or regions in the case of Europe and the European Foundation for Quality Management's Business Excellence Model[4]) possess "excellence" models that are essentially descendants of Malcolm Baldrige. We will now consider how such frameworks work together.

Malcolm Baldrige

The US-based Malcolm Baldrige framework was launched in 1987 (so predates the scorecard) and assesses performance within seven areas (see also Exhibit 2.3):

1. leadership: with sub-components such as organizational leadership and public responsibility and citizenship;
2. planning: sub-components such as strategy development and deployment;
3. customers: customer knowledge and customer relationships and satisfaction;
4. information: measurement, analysis, knowledge management;
5. people: employee learning and motivation;
6. processes: value creation processes, support processes;
7. results: customer-focused, product and service financial, and market, human resource, organizational effectiveness, governance and social responsibility.

---

1 Leadership (120 pts.)
   1.1 Organizational Leadership (70 pts.)
   1.2 Social Responsibility (50 pts.)
2 Strategic Planning (85 pts.)
   2.1 Strategy Development (40 pts.)
   2.2 Strategy Deployment (45 pts.)
3 Customer and Market Focus (85 pts.)
   3.1 Customer and Market Knowledge (40 pts.)
   3.2 Customer Relationships and Satisfaction (45 pts.)
4 Measurement, Analysis, Knowledge Management (90 pts.)
   4.1 Measurement and Analysis of Organizational Performance (45 pts.)
   4.2 Information and Knowledge Management (45 pts.)
5 Human Resource Focus (85 pts.)
   5.1 Work Systems (35 pts.)
   5.2 Employee Learning and Motivation (25 pts.)
   5.3 Employee Well-Being and Satisfaction (25 pts.)
6 Process Management (85 pts.)
   6.1 Value Creation Processes (50 pts.)
   6.2 Support Processes (35 pts.)
7 Business Results (450 pts.)
   7.1 Customer-Focused Results (75 pts.)
   7.2 Product and Service Results (75 pts.)
   7.3 Financial and Market Results (75 pts.)
   7.4 Human Resource Results (75 pts.)
   7.5 Organizational Effectiveness Results (75 pts.)
   7.6 Governance and Social Responsibility Results (75 pts.)

Exhibit 2.3 Malcom Baldrige Criteria

The Malcolm Baldrige model is the basis for an annual and much-coveted award. Previous winners include AT&T, Ritz-Carlton, and Boeing Aerospace Support.

Australian Business Excellence Framework

Interestingly, Boeing Australia received the "Australian Business Excellence Medal" (ABEM) in 2003. This is the highest ranking honor of its type in Australia and assesses performance against the Australian Excellence Framework, which is very similar to the Baldrige model. Boeing Australia is also fast becoming a recognized best practice scorecard organization.

In an interview with one of the authors for a case study that appeared in the online magazine Scorecard Strategy[5] Michael Whipps, director, quality improvement and innovation, explained how the two frameworks are mutually reinforcing.

> Considered as a cycle, the scorecard shows that which we have decided we must achieve in order to succeed against our vision, such as the customer objective to "improve customer satisfaction and loyalty." The ABEF then provides an assessment to identify any gaps between present state and best practices. Such gaps can then be addressed through strategic initiatives, and these tracked through the Balanced Scorecard.

The successful deployment of quality frameworks alongside the Balanced Scorecard is prevalent within our case study organizations.

XYZ Enterprises (see Chapter 6) gains performance improvement benefits from a total quality management (TQM) program that has been in place since 1998. The program is the basis of an annual Group Quality Award, based on the Malcolm Baldrige National Quality, for which all units are mandated to apply.

According to the former Head, Knowledge Management, the TQM model works well alongside the Balanced Scorecard. The former, he says, provides best practice benchmarks that can feed into the scorecard objectives/measures/targets. As a measure of how well they work together, XYZ Cellular (the unit that we focus on within the case study) was the recipient of the Group Quality Award in the year following its Balanced Scorecard implementation.

As part of it's quality commitment, MTR Corporation also adopted the Malcolm Baldrige framework and finds that it helps the organization identify the vital few things to monitor within the Balanced Scorecard.

Furthermore, Tata Motors Commercial Vehicles Business Unit (see Chapter 1) also uses the scorecard alongside its Excellence Model, which too is based on the Baldrige model.

Singapore Quality Framework

Within Singapore, usage of the Singapore Quality Award (SQA) Framework for Business Excellence, shown in Exhibit 2.4, is widespread, notably within public-sector organizations (also at the vanguard of scorecard usage). One public-sector manager interviewed for this book says:

> **As part of it's quality commitment, MTR Corporation also adopted the Malcolm Baldrige framework and finds that it helps the organization identify the vital few things to monitor within the Balanced Scorecard.**

The SQA model and the scorecard complement each other well. The scorecard is a framework that we use to clarify our strategic focus and to understand the cause and effect relationships across perspectives that deliver strategic success. SQA is more of best practice checklist against all the areas that an organization is required to address if it is to be consistently successful. Furthermore, the scoring system within SQA enables benchmarking against best practice organizations.

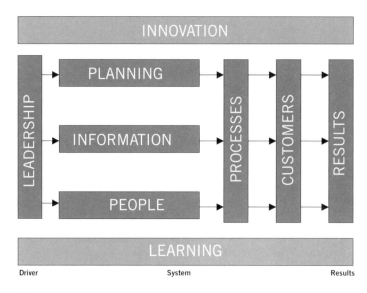

Exhibit 2.4 SQA New Framework

So as we can see, quality frameworks and the Balanced Scorecard are clearly complementary, with quality frameworks enabling comparative assessment against best of class standards, and informing the strategic measures and so on that appear on the scorecard.

Within our survey of scorecard usage in South-east Asia (see the Appendix) we asked the question: Is the Balanced Scorecard used alongside other management tools? Thirty percent of scorecard users were also using quality frameworks (the top answer) and 23% used the scorecard alongside shareholder value frameworks such as economic value-added. But whether the scorecard is used in isolation or in tandem with another performance management framework, enduring scorecard success is dependent on the support and commitment of the senior management team; in particular, the CEO, which we discus in Chapter 3.

CASE STUDY

Singapore Prison Service

Summary

The Singapore Prison Service has created separate Balanced Scorecards for four "strategies for action." Together these scorecards provide an integrated roadmap for how the service dispatches its custodial duties and facilitates the reintegration of offenders back into society.

Introduction

With 2,200 employees managing 14 prisons and 17,000 inmates, the Singapore Prison Service is a government agency within the Ministry of Home Affairs. Its responsibilities encompass the safe custody and rehabilitation of offenders while cooperating in prevention and aftercare with strategic partners.

Strategies for Action

The use of the Balanced Scorecard within the Prison Service traces back to 1999 when the then new director, Mr Chua Chin Kiat, initiated a major exercise to envision, and refocus, how the service could more effectively deliver its responsibilities going forward.

For many years the service had focused more on its security remit than reintegration, and with significant success. Singapore prisons are among the most secure in the world and boast one of the lowest global rates for internal incidents, such as hostage-taking and riots. The challenge for the early years of the twenty-first century was to strengthen its "reintegration of offenders" responsibility without compromising security issues.

A nine-month long "visioning" process, with input from managers, staff, and governmental representatives resulted in new vision and mission statements, both underpinned by a set of core values. It also led to the articulation of four new strategies, which were called "strategies for action," each of which would eventually become the focus for separate Balanced Scorecards.

The vision reads:

We aspire to be captains in the lives of offenders committed to our custody.
We will be instrumental in steering them towards being responsible citizens, with the help of their families and the community.
We will thus build a secure and exemplary prison system.

The supporting mission reads:

As a key partner in Criminal Justice, we protect society through the safe custody and rehabilitation of offenders, co-operating in prevention and aftercare.

The core values are known by the acronym HEART, and serve to inspire prison officers to commit to the vision and mission. The values are:

Honour our vision by placing it above self-interest and inspiring others to our cause.
Excel in our work because we care enough to want to be the best.
Be Agile by being innovative and open to new possibilities, overcoming adversity through continuous learning
Respect our fellow colleagues and the community we come into contact with.

And the four "strategies for action" are:
- enhance inmate management capability;
- maximize inmates' reintegration potential;
- develop staff to make a difference;
- prevent offending and re-offending.

Performance Management
Titus Kong Ling Chieh, Singapore Prison Service's Head of Research and Planning, recalls that the director realized that to successfully implement these new strategies required the inculcation of a performance management and measurement system more robust and informative than was already in place.

Back then we were working with a set of key performance indicators (KPIs) and were creating output plans and performance targets. However, these KPIs, plans and targets were not reflective of our new strategies. The KPIs, for example, were basically lagging indicators and provided little in the way of a forward steer.

Choosing the scorecard

An environmental scan of available performance management frameworks brought the Balanced Scorecard to the attention of the prison service. Although aware that the scorecard was still a somewhat new concept in Asia in 2000, the prison service senior management team was confident enough in its potential to green-light its implementation. This process would be overseen, and championed, by the planning branch.

Consultancy Input

To commence the score-carding process, it was decided to secure consultancy support. The tendering process led to the appointment of Arthur Anderson as expert advisors. Matthew Wee Yik Keong, Staff Officer, Research and Planning, recalls that transferring knowledge from the consultancy to an in-house team (essentially from the planning function) was important.

In workshops with the consultancy we created the structure of the scorecard, picked the objectives, and decided how to measure, what to measure, and what calculations to use. In the process we made sure we grew our own expertise and developed our own staff to own the system.

He also recalls how learning from early scorecard efforts led to an evolution of how the scorecard looked.

The Balanced Scorecard started off as being more representative of our organizational structure than our strategy. Consequently, our first wave of learning about how best to use the scorecard in our context led to the creation of separate scorecards for each strategy.

Shie Yong Lee, Deputy Head Research & Planning, said that as many new projects were rolled out and the Balanced Scorecard was used to track process and performance, there was fear and uncertainty among the line officers.

When the vision was first drafted with an emphasis on rehabilitation and reintegration of offenders, there was some concern that we may divert attention away from security issues. So by offering an integrated solution with the four strategic scorecards, people could see that everything we were doing was geared toward more effectively dispatching out duties and that security is not compromised.

She adds that the performance transparency engendered by the scorecard ensures people can see that security issues are not compromised and is as important as rehabilitation, learning, and growth issues.

Let's consider examples of Singapore Prison Service's Balanced Scorecard.

Maximising Inmates' Reintegration Potential: Scorecard Example

Exhibit 2.5 shows the Balanced Scorecard Strategy Map for the strategy "maximising Inmates" Reintegration Potential. As can be seen this comprises its own vision, "enhancing inmates' potential for reintegration by providing rehabilitative programs and opportunities."

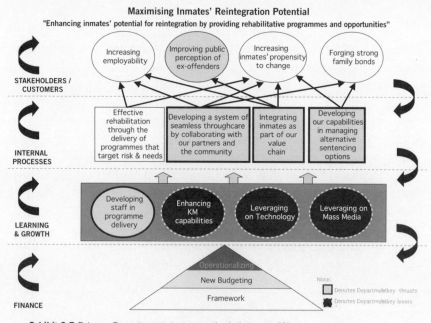

Exhibit 2.5 Prisons Department strategy articulation map (1)

To begin the operations of this vision a Strategy Map was created. It comprised the conventional four perspectives of a Balanced Scorecard. However, the order has been re-jigged, with finance found at the base, rather than the top of the perspective hierarchy (and this is true of each of the four scorecards).

Titus Kong Ling Chieh explains that:

The financial perspective is at the base and not at the top because we use the budget to train our people, to invest in technology and resources. The people in turn deliver the objectives and create value for our stakeholders. The cause and effect is as evident as in a private-sector scorecard, but we are looking for ultimately different outcomes.

Kong Ling Chieh adds, however, that judicious management of financial resources is critical in order to ensure that required investments could be made.

The strategic objectives demonstrate that the prison service recognizes that to "maximize inmates' reintegration potential" requires both an external and internal strategic focus. External examples consider the stakeholder/customer objective: "improving public perception of ex-offenders" and "leveraging on mass media," from the learning and growth perspective. According to Kong Ling Chieh:

We are working to educate the public and government bodies into giving offenders a second chance, which is critical if reintegration is to be successful.

This required orchestrated strategies with other statutory bodies. It has also included a media campaign focused on giving people a "second chance." Also, Singapore Prison Service practises what it preaches. Note, for example, the internal process objective of "integrating inmates as part of our human resources." As a result, ex-offenders may be employed in administrative, non-sensitive areas.

Measuring Re-offending

Given the integrated nature of the Prison Service's scorecards, progress made in this scorecard will directly impact the "prevent offending and re-offending scorecard." Initiatives for the latter include the provision of aftercare services to offenders upon their release, and directing them to community programs and resources that could support them.

About re-offending Kong Ling Chieh states that it is a challenge to identify meaningful performance indicators. He explains:

We could easily set a measure of how many offenders re-offend within a two-year period. However, this may not be all that useful as it's a lagging measure that doesn't help stop re-offending. It may not even be that informative as it may depend on the effectiveness of the police force. So we are working to develop a measurement system that is more forward-looking than lagging. We want to measure on an ongoing basis how released prisoners are successfully being reintegrated into society.

To do this the prison service is looking to assign a potential rating to prisoners on incarceration and on release, and assess that over a period of time. They will look at things like the offenders' relationships with their families, their work profile, and their personal attitude to change. Kong Ling Chieh states:

So we're developing an index for this that is a more dynamic indicator than just measuring things two years after the fact. It will enable corrective interventions when problems are predicted.

Enhancing inmate management capability: Scorecard Example

Exhibit 2.6 shows the Strategy Map for the strategy "enhancing inmate management capability." Its dedicated vision reads: "protecting society by ensuring the safe and secure custody of offenders in a humane environment." As with the other scorecards, the objectives on this Strategy Map are supported by KPIs (such as a measure of "average daily population" to support the objective "coping with increased overcrowding"). KPIs are tracked using a traffic-light system: red (below target) amber (meeting targets) and green (meeting stretch targets). In some cases six or more measures support a strategic objective (for example, there are six for the objective "enhancing security in institutions") and so the metrics are indexed to assess whether or not the objective is being met.

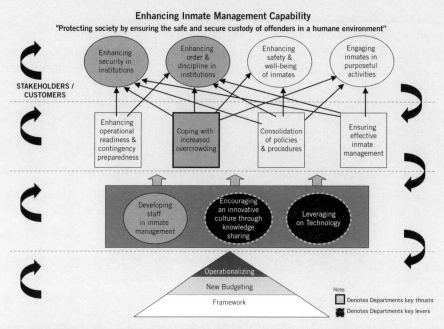

Exhibit 2.6 Prisons Department strategy articulation map (2)

Devolution

Within the Singapore Prison Service each scorecard has been devolved to the three divisions (Operations Division, Staff Development Division, and Corporate Services Division) and the institutions, 14 in total. Each division and institution focuses on the objectives and metrics that are within their sphere of responsibility, and all the scorecards aggregate to the departmental level scorecard, which is owned by the prisons director.

Driven and facilitated by the planning team (which has day-to-day responsibility for the scorecard), devolution required a well thought out communications strategy. Matthew Wee Yik Keong explains:

Awareness-building was crucial. The superintendent on the ground is concerned with day-to-day operations, so the language has to be relevant to them. We have to explain KPI and why they are important in terms that make operational sense to them.

This process involved a series of workshops and both one-to-one and group sessions.

Monthly Meetings

At departmental level, a monthly meeting is held, chaired by the Director, in which KPI performance is discussed. In this session the superintendents report, and are held accountable for the performance of their branches. For Wee Yik Keong:

This monthly exercise ensures that the scorecard remains high on people's agenda. Without this discipline we would probably find that the scorecard would wither.

Benefits

Kong Ling Chieh states that the real benefits being secured through the scorecard also ensures it becomes central to the management agenda.

Two years ago when we talked about KPIs people would say, "What are KPIs?" Two years ago when we talked about lead indicators, people wouldn't know what we were talking about. We didn't have a language around performance drivers or outcome measures. Today, through the Balanced Scorecard, we have a common language that is creating a performance culture internally and a language that makes sense to all our constituent groups.

Shie Yong Lee observes:

Measurement used to be a once-yearly affair, a concern at only the HQ level. Now it's ongoing. We have a better sense of our performance and it is the concern of every institution. At one glance we can see how we have done, and are doing against our strategies and objectives. And from this we can drill down to look at performance against each KPI. Another benefit is that we are fast creating a culture where people can see how their day-to-day performance impacts strategy through the scorecard. The Balanced Scorecard empowers staff as they see the big picture, understand how they contribute, and can make everyday decisions based on that knowledge.

Future Developments

Although well embedded the scorecard journey is far from over within the Singapore Prison Service. Evolution in the future will be required simply because a major rebuilding program will see the present 14 prison system rising to 20 institutions in 5 clusters by 2008. This will substantially impact on the service's structure and ways of working, which will have to be reflected in the scorecards.

At another level the planning team believes there is still some work to be done in refining KPIs and indeed getting better at choosing appropriate ones. Furthermore, the scorecard is presently reported though Excel spreadsheets and a local area network. As the sophistication and usage of the scorecard increases there may be a requirement to automate the scorecard.

Critical Success Factors

Titus Kong Ling Chieh concludes that there are several critical success factors in succeeding with the Balanced Scorecard:

1. It has to be driven by the top – "The senior management team must support the process."
2. There has to be a clear vision and mission statement and strategy – "If these things aren't clear then the scorecard will not help you."
3. It needs a champion, or champions, within the organization – "For us this was from the planning branch. The scorecard must be driven operationally. You need to allocate the resources and the manpower to make it work. We developed our own expertise and made sure our own staff owned the system."
4. Communication is important – "You have to create a communication strategy to allay the fears among prospective scorecard users. First, we targeted the owners and then communicated down to the people on the ground so they could see how it impacts on their daily lives."
5. Don't wait for the perfect scorecard – "The first version is never going to be perfect and we are now in the third iteration of our scorecard. So work with it and improve with experience."

1   David P. Norton, Robert S. Kaplan: *Strategy Maps: Converting Intangible Assets into Tangible Outcomes* : Harvard Business Review, 2001

2   James Creelman, *Building a Strategic Balanced Scorecard*: Business Intelligence, 2003

3   James Creelman, *Building a Strategic Balanced Scorecard*: Business Intelligence, 2003

4   See www.efqm.org

5   Scorecard Strategy, *Business Intelligence*, 2003 (the magazine has since closed)

3

The Role of Senior Management

*T*he single most important condition for success with the Balanced Scorecard is the ownership and active involvement of the executive team. The Balanced Scorecard is a strategy implementation framework, and it is the job of the executive leadership team to execute strategy. Some research finds that although senior management support is crucial over the longer term, it may not always be required at the start of the scorecard program. That the scorecard is seen as primarily a "CEO's tool" is a strength of the scorecard, but maybe also its Achilles heel. We describe the role played by the senior teams within our case study companies and draw key learnings from their involvement. The Balanced Scorecard is most effective when used to drive large-scale change, which has implications for the role of the senior team.

BACKGROUND

If the Balanced Scorecard is to become "the way we manage around here," and if it is to deliver more than marginal benefits to the organization, then it must be the management tool of choice for the senior team, and especially the chief executive officer (CEO). Indeed, in their book The Strategy-Focused Organization, Kaplan and Norton write: "Experience has repeatedly shown that the single most important condition for success is the ownership and active involvement of the executive team"[1]

Of Kaplan's and Norton's five principles of the strategy-focused organization, leadership is most explicitly recognized through principle 5, "mobilize change through executive leadership." But in saying that, the influence of leadership must be felt throughout the organization if strategy-focused status is to be attained.

STRATEGY: THE SENIOR TEAM'S JOB

The importance of leadership is self-evident simply because the Balanced Scorecard is a framework for articulating a strategy implementation roadmap, and for managing and monitoring that implementation. The executive team has collective responsibility for the execution of strategy and the CEO is held ultimately accountable for the success or failure of strategies. In typical Western organizations, if strategies fail, the CEO is typically the first out the door. Culturally this is less true in Asia, where companies are generally more tolerant of poor CEO performance, although we are seeing a trend toward high variable compensation based on performance, especially in Singapore, Hong Kong, and India. This suggests that the tolerance of poor CEO performance is narrowing.

If the top team owns the strategy but not the scorecard, then the scorecard cannot be a strategy management framework. Consequently, ownership of the scorecard cannot be devolved to middle management, and certainly not managed by a consultancy, although as we shall explain in later chapters, both groups can play important roles in scorecard facilitation and rollout.

According to our survey of scorecard usage in South-east Asia (see Appendix 1), the scorecard program was championed by the CEO or equivalent in 51% of cases, other executive board members in 30% of instances, a non-executive board member in 5% and others 7%. This is a heartening finding, as it shows that a majority of organizations recognize the critical importance of CEO buy-in.

SENIOR MANAGEMENT SUPPORT NOT ALWAYS REQUIRED AT THE START

Now there is a caveat to our assertion about senior management ownership, and this was well brought out by a five-month research program involving 29 UK-based organizations undertaken in 2003 by the consultant Jonathan Chocqueel-Mangan (previously an Executive Vice-President with BSCol).2

> " If the top team owns the strategy but not the scorecard, then the scorecard cannot be a strategy management framework. Consequently, ownership of the scorecard cannot be devolved to middle management, and certainly not managed by a consultancy. "

The research, which had both qualitative and quantitative components, unearthed the somewhat surprising finding that although executive support had to be secured eventually, it was not necessary from the start. Much more important in the early stages was that the project team had a clear, long-term vision for their work and the project team leader was able to exploit their experience and influence across the business.

Indeed, during discussions with companies as part of the research it was found that many project managers had not set out to secure top management support from the outset. As a manager from a financial services institution said:

> I didn't need them to buy-in to the long-term vision. I just needed them to want to embark upon the first step. My challenge was to present the Balanced Scorecard in a way that enabled them to address a short-term, critical issues immediately. I knew that once they saw the potential they would want me to deliver the rest of the vision anyway.

A similar observation comes from Peter Ryan, Corporate Strategy and Performance Manager for the City of Brisbane, who comments:

> Launching the Balanced Scorecard into an organization can be problematic if the right preparation has not occurred. In many cases the initial marketing is done by a senior officer rather than at board level. Key board members are selectively targeted and if the organization's conditions are favorable (that is, a burning platform exists) the concept is usually taken up with some enthusiasm by the executive team. It is at this rather precarious point that support networks for the innovator become invaluable. In the state of Queensland, Australia, a cross-departmental team of such transformational officers was formed, resulting in a shared use of resources, contacts, and information across a large number of government agencies.

So, perhaps one of the most striking observations from the above is that top management support is not a prerequisite. Organizations can start on the design of the Balanced Scorecard without support being in place from the outset. Of course, senior management eventually must drive it. Successful rollout and cascade requires top management to communicate and support the objectives of the program. But many organizations have decided to use initial design and development as a way to secure buy-in, rather than wait for an agreement to a long-term vision that may never happen.

> " ... senior managers are continually bombarded with "new" managerial approaches that will solve all their problems, and so may need a more gradual exposure to the potential of the Balanced Scorecard. "

This is a fascinating piece of research and is something that the Balanced Scorecard community should take note of. At its kernel it is saying that yes, eventually the senior team must drive the scorecard, for reasons we've already cited. However, at the outset the scorecard program can legitimately commence without the senior team involvement – as long as it is driven by a middle manager with a strong vision and who is respected organization-wide and by the senior team. After all, senior managers are continually bombarded with "new" managerial approaches that will solve all their problems, and so may need a more gradual exposure to the potential of the Balanced Scorecard.

Indeed, Ning C S De Guzman, a Singapore-based scorecard expert, comments that:

> CEOs can be too preoccupied with other things. He [or she] may have been to too many seminars, seen too many approaches, and so is very confused, so the scorecard may develop slowly.

A scorecard developing slowly and without the support of the senior team from day one may not be a conventional textbook approach to commencing a scorecard program, but in many cases it may be the most practical. Furthermore, and as we will explain in Chapter 4, if the scorecard is to survive over the longer term within organizations, then it has to become much more than the preferred framework of the current "scorecard championing" CEO. This CEO-dependency has for some time been seen as the Achilles heel of the scorecard movement. Indeed, the scorecard annals have many stories of successful, and celebrated, scorecard users who stopped using the framework when the championing (or at least sponsoring) CEO left the organization. One notable example is the celebrated early scorecard adopter Cigna Property & Casualty (P&C). Despite the fact that the scorecard was used to transform the division from a catastrophic financial position in 1992 to being acquired for US$3.45 billion by the ACE Group of Companies in 1998, the scorecard was taken out once P&C president Gerry Isom left the organization following the acquisition.

> " ... if the scorecard is to survive over the longer term within organizations, then it has to become much more that the preferred framework of the current "scorecard championing" CEO. "

THE RESPONSIBILITIES OF LEADERSHIP

Whether they instigate the scorecard introduction or buy-in later in the process, there is no doubt that the CEO (and their senior colleagues) will make the difference between scorecard success and failure. And they have myriad roles and responsibilities: champions, sponsors, and communicators as examples. They have to demonstrate their belief in the scorecard through actions and behaviors. They must show that they pay as much attention to the non-financial drivers of performance as they do to financial outcomes. The most senior management must make it clear to all managerial levels that the scorecard is "the way we manage around here."

> " The most senior management must make it clear to all managerial levels that the scorecard is "the way we manage around here." "

CASE STUDY EXAMPLES

So let's look at the roles played by the CEO and senior teams within our case study companies.

Bank Universal

Mahdi Syahbuddin, who was Bank Universal's Deputy President Director and is now Bank Permata's Managing Director, championed the introduction of the scorecard into Bank Universal (see Chapter 10), ably supported by Pak Krisbiyanto, who was Bank Universal's Vice-President – Human Capital. Syahbuddin, Krisbiyanto, and the rest of the senior management team's belief that the scorecard was a potentially useful strategy implementation tool helped the scorecard survive some early setbacks. If the belief had not been there, the scorecard would have died an early death.

Centrepoint Properties

CEO Jeffrey Heng has been totally committed to the score-carding process within Centrepoint Properties (see Chapter 9). Importantly, he fully understands the critical importance of non-financial components of sustainable success. For example, he values divisions that may not be delivering as well financially, but possess intrinsic value in terms of reputation and branding and are therefore building the foundations for tomorrow's success.

Wider senior management support and involvement has been garnered by the formation of a Balanced Scorecard Deputies Committee comprising senior managers working together to gain clarity and iron out problems. This group has become a driving force for change within Centrepoint.

Civil Service College Singapore

Civil Service College's (see Chapter 8) Dean and Chief Executive Officer Brigadier General (BG) Yam Ah Mee was responsible for introducing the Balanced Scorecard into the organization and was fully supported by his senior management team. BG (NS) Yam was particularly keen on the scorecard as the balanced nature of the framework meant that it was possible to facilitate a mindset shift within the organization to be more outcome-, and indeed financially, driven, while still articulating a commitment to valuing and developing its people.

As well as balance, another catalyst for scorecard adoption was that the framework also served as a transparent mechanism for viewing performance at the organizational, strategic business unit, team, and individual level.

Gold Coin

Gold Coin Group's (see Chapter 5) ex-CEO Louis Schwendener believes that the scorecard is primarily a CEO tool and that the CEO has to own it and drive it. Schwendener states that as CEO it was important that he played a central role in ensuring the smooth progress of the score-carding process. He states:

I had to explain my vision clearly and at times intervene when it was proving difficult to get consensus around a strategic objective. As senior management came from different functions they, quite naturally, had different views and concerns. At times I had to take a decision as to the objective that would be chosen, as I, as CEO, was ultimately responsible for results. I also had to take a holistic, rather than narrow, view of performance.

MTR Corporation

Within MTR Corporation (see Chapter 7) the Operations Director championed the scorecard at executive board level. As he was responsible for the whole railway operations, he was influential enough to raise the likelihood of senior management buy-in and powerful enough to make subsequent rollout possible.

Saatchi & Saatchi Worldwide

Saatchi & Saatchi (see Chapter 11) is one of the most powerful examples of how the most senior team can introduce, champion, own, and drive the scorecard. Moreover, they show through their behavior that the scorecard (or CompaSS as they brand their scorecard) is the way they manage the global corporation and so the way all regional leaders must manage their parts of the business.

Paul Melter, Worldwide Director, CompaSS says:

Without having the unconditional, unequivocal backing of the senior executive group this will fail. All of the 45+ unit-based CEOs have mentors among the senior executive group and if there's a feeling that the CompaSS doesn't have to be done this month, or if they believe there's something more important then it will fade. But our three executive leaders make it clear to all the local unit CEOs that this is a great tool and this is the way we manage the business.

Worldwide CEO Kevin Roberts, for example, uses the CompaSS as the framework for his performance discussions with Saatchi & Saatchi's parent company Publicis.

Singapore Prison Service

The use of the Balanced Scorecard within the Singapore Prison Service (see Chapter 2) traces back to 1999 when the then new Director, Mr Chua Chin Kiat, initiated a major exercise to envision, and refocus, how the service could more effectively deliver its responsibilities going forward. He realized that to successfully implement these new strategies required the inculcation of a performance management and measurement system more robust and informative than was already in place.

Although aware that the scorecard was still a somewhat new concept in Asia in 2000, the Singapore Prison Service senior management team was confident enough in its potential to green-light its implementation.

Subordinate Courts Singapore

The Senior District Judge (equivalent to a CEO) Richard Magnus introduced the scorecard into Subordinate Courts (see below) in 1997. Magus chaired a steering committee that launched a scorecard pilot that included other senior judges and court administrators. He has championed and driven the scorecard ever since.

Summarecon

Summarecon's (see Chapter 4) senior team has played a central role in working to ensure that scorecard capabilities are embedded into the organization for the longer term. Indeed, all of the top 100 people (or one-quarter of the workforce) were taking through scorecard awareness sessions, which were facilitated by the consultancy OTI and supported by top management.

Tata Motors Commercial Vehicles Business Unit (CVBU)

CVBU's (see Chapter 1) Executive Director (the unit's most senior executive) Ravi Kant has from the outset served as an enthusiastic champion of the scorecard. He chaired a senior management steering committee set up to launch the scorecard.

XYZ Enterprises

Although the scorecard was championed by individual CEOs at the business unit level (critical for successful local implementation) at the group level the President of Group Strategic Planning played a crucial championing role. He first introduced the concept to the senior team of XYZ Enterprises (see Chapter 6) as part of the group's knowledge management program. External case studies of companies that had experienced significant business results as a result of their scorecard implementation were shared with the senior teams at corporate level and within business units.

Within XYZ Cellular each of the 21 objectives on the Strategy Map has a designated owner from within the senior team who is held accountable for the performance of that objective. He or she must also champion the initiatives launched to achieve the performance targets. The CEO owns the primary business objective (the top financial objective).

CASE LEARNINGS

So what can we learn about the role of the CEO and senior management team from these case snapshots?

Senior Executive Champion

First, in each case a senior executive championed the introduction of the Balanced Scorecard into the organization. However, this was not always the CEO (or equivalent) as the Bank Universal, MTR, and XYZ examples show. But within each of these three cases the championing leader was powerful and influential enough to drive the score-carding process at the senior level and at deeper levels within the organization. Indeed, and perhaps challenging the research findings alluded to earlier that senior management support is not required from day one, in no cases was the scorecard introduced by somebody outside the executive team.

Senior Management Involvement

Second, concerted efforts have been made to secure the buy-in and active involvement of the wider senior management team. Consider the Deputies Committee at Centrepoint Properties and the neat idea of making senior managers responsible for individual objectives at XYS Cellular.

> " ... the championing leader was powerful and influential enough to drive the score-carding process at the senior level and at deeper levels within the organization. "

A Clear Vision

Third, in each case the championing senior manager (or senior team) has a clear vision of what they wanted to achieve with the scorecard and drove that vision. As examples, at Saatchi & Saatchi the goal was to deliver to stretching strategic and time-based goals and so "survive." At Singapore Prison Service the scorecard was deployed to refocus the service. At Civil Service College creating a mindset-shift to being more commercially oriented while maintaining a public-sector ethos was a key reason for adoption.

> "...the senior teams of our case examples knew why they wanted the scorecard and what they wanted it to deliver. The scorecard, therefore, wasn't just "today's must-have fad." "

Recognizing the Importance of Balance

Fourth, in each case there was recognition by the championing senior executive (which typically extended to the senior team) that non-financial performance dimensions were as important as financial outcomes. The basic scorecard premise that improvement from non-financial perspectives creates, through a cause-and-effect process, improvements from a financial perspective was accepted, internalized, and became intrinsic to how the organization was managed. As examples this was clearly evident at XYZ Enterprises, Centrepoint Properties, and at Gold Coin where CEO Louis Schwendener put a higher performance weighting in the customer perspective than any other. And note too at Saatchi & Saatchi, where CEO Kevin Roberts realized, and communicated, that financial success would only be achieved by creating "permanently infatuated clients."

A visible demonstration from the senior team that non-financial objectives and metrics are as important (if not more so) than financial is a prerequisite for scorecard success. Quite simply nothing can kill a scorecard program quicker than a CEO waxing lyrical about the critical importance of non-financial measures and then demanding that heads roll when quarterly financial results are down, even though performance to non-financial measures have risen (and remember that improvements to non-financial performance objectives may not impact on the financials until subsequent quarters. A key question therefore is whether CEOs and CFOs of publicly traded organizations have the confidence to communicate non-financial performance to shareholders and analysts with the same vigor as they do with financial performance). In recent years we've seen the scorecard being increasingly positioned as a corporate governance tool, which may go some way to getting the message across to the shareholding community of the importance of non-financial performance and, perhaps, of eventually making the scorecard more than just a tool of the present CEO as demands for non-financial reporting grows.

> " ...nothing can kill a scorecard program quicker than a CEO waxing lyrical about the critical importance of non-financial measures and then demanding that heads roll when quarterly financial results are down. "

Large-scale Change

Although the Balanced Scorecard is being deployed within organizations of all shades of performance requirements – in some looking for no more incremental performance advances to those seeking breakthrough performance improvements – it is clear that the most dramatic cases of scorecard success has been found in those organizations with a compelling reason for scorecard introduction and who use the scorecard to drive an all-encompassing change program. For this reason "mobilize change through executive leadership" is a principle of the strategy-focused organization. Nigel Penny, a Singapore-based scorecard expert comments:

> Consider the early success stories of balanced scorecard – Mobil Oil, Cigna, Saatchi & Saatchi etc. Each of these organizations had a compelling need for change and a CEO committed to turning the organization around. The Balanced Scorecard was part of a wider, integrated process of change. It was driven at the highest level. Many organizations seem to lack that imperative for change, or lack the real desire at CEO level, and consequently the results from implementing Balanced Scorecard in these organizations can be disappointing.

He adds:

> For those organizations contemplating a scorecard I would ask "Is the CEO prepared to lead from the top and reengineer the management process within the organization?" The answer to this question is the differentiator between successful scorecard organizations and the rest.

In considering the role of the CEO and the senior team in a scorecard program, Penny's comments are important. The Balanced Scorecard has to be "the way we manage around here." It is not a project happening at the periphery of the enterprise. If the scorecard is to determine everything that happens within the organization (crucial to translate strategy into action), then this must include complex, potentially stressful and politically sensitive areas such as process reengineering and structural reconfigurations (widespread at the start of the scorecard program within Saatchi & Saatchi, for example).

"" For those organizations contemplating a scorecard I would ask "Is the CEO prepared to lead from the top and reengineer the management process within the organization? ""

Clearly, only the most senior executives have the clout to effect large-scale change. Those leaders who truly recognize the power of the Balanced Scorecard system will first and foremost see it as a tool to drive organizational transformation and so achieve breakthrough performance. When this is recognized the scorecard can be used to its full potential, as a full-fledged strategy management framework, and not just as a narrow performance measurement system.

Building Capabilities

Moreover, leaders who fully recognize the true power of the scorecard also ensure that the capabilities to use the scorecard are inculcated deep inside the organization. Indeed, the scorecard becomes a key competence of the corporation. We shall explain how to build these capabilities in the next chapter.

CASE STUDY

Subordinate Courts, Singapore

Summary

Subordinate Courts, Singapore, has created a Balanced Scorecard of three perspectives that has been devolved to each of its divisions. Based on a successful pilot, this scorecard demonstrated the benefits of keeping the scorecard simple and clearly focused on strategic outcomes.

Introduction

The Subordinate Courts deal with more than 95% of Singapore's Judiciary's caseload (the remainder pass through the Court of Appeal and High Court). With about 500 employees, it comprises the District Courts, the Magistrates' Courts, the Coroners' Court, the Family and Juvenile Courts, and the Small Claims Tribunals, collectively handling over 400,000 cases per year.

Harvard Program

The origins of the Balanced Scorecard within Subordinate Courts traces back to 1997 when the Senior District Judge (equivalent to a CEO) Richard Magnus attended a Harvard Business School Advanced Management Program. While there he was exposed to the Balanced Scorecard concept and he returned to Singapore with the belief that this management approach may be of value to Subordinate Courts. He sensed it might enable the inculcation of firmer linkage between vision and actions, and catalyze the evolution of an essentially prescriptive and reactive measurement system, which had been in place since about 1992, into something more predictive and proactive.

A Pilot Program

To assess the effectiveness of the Balanced Scorecard, a pilot project was launched within Small Claims Tribunals. Commencing November 1998, this division was chosen because it was self-contained and, importantly, its management team embraced change.

Overseen by a steering committee comprising Richard Magnus and other senior judges and court administrators, Small Claims Tribunal developed and implemented a conventional scorecard of financial, customer, internal process, and learning and growth perspectives. However, to be more appropriate for a public-sector setting the hierarchical perspective order was modified with customer rather than financial at the apex.

The steering committee reviewed and monitored the scorecard each month and after six months decided it was a useful tool and worth cascading organization-wide. Chan Wai Yin, Director of Research and Statistics Unit recalls:

The pilot program proved that the scorecard provided a clear advance over the existing performance measurement system. As the scorecard is a predictive system we were able to detect early warnings of what was going to happen and so take preventative action. The scorecard made it far easier for us to see what we were doing and how we were doing it.

Wai Yin adds:

We also discovered the scorecard significantly improved communications. Being a two-way system whereby employees could better report and discuss performance we found it actually changed the whole paradigm of performance monitoring, improvement, and measurement.

Communications

With the possibility of full rollout, the Subordinate Courts steering committee made concerted efforts to communicate progress and learnings to the other units during the pilot phase. This was a purposeful strategy in order to build awareness and to pre-emptively tackle cultural difficulties that may emerge, such as around a fear of measurement, for example. The thinking was that when it came to full rollout, the scorecard would be "nothing new." According to Wai Yin, a focused communication campaign would give people enough time to get used to the scorecard idea.

Benchmarking

Full rollout began in late 1999, beginning with the formulation of a corporate-level scorecard, followed by a cascade to the divisions, a process that took about nine months. As well as learning from the pilot, the final scorecard design was also influenced by benchmarking exercises conducted by the scorecard facilitation team led by District Judge Valerie Thean. The team learnt from the implementation of the scorecard by the City of Charlotte, North Carolina, United States, (a celebrated early public-sector adopter of the Balanced Scorecard). Also performance management methods used by various California courts and the National Council of State Courts were assessed and incorporated into the model where relevant.

Moreover, scorecard co-creator Professor Robert Kaplan was also asked to comment on the Subordinate Courts evolving scorecard design. Indeed, the scorecard efforts of Subordinate Courts was highlighted in Robert Kaplan and David Norton's seminal work The Strategy-focused Organization, with the authors stating that this was probably the first application to the judicial sector found anywhere in the world.

The Justice Scorecard

For full rollout the scorecard was branded the Justice Scorecard so that employees could more readily relate to the concept. More fundamentally, the scorecard that was cascaded organization-wide differed from the pilot scorecard in one crucial way. The original four perspectives became three: community, organizational, and employee (see Exhibit 3.1).

PERSPECTIVES/OBJECTIVES	MEASURES	MONITORING METHODOLOGY	TARGETS
COMMUNITY - To Preserve Public Trust & Confidence			
Enhance Access to Justice	Access to Information	**Quarterly** telephone audits to be conducted by requesting information on existing cases (Internal Audit Team)	At least 80% satisfaction rate
	Court Personnel's Courtesy & Responsiveness	**Quarterly** walkabout and telephone audits report (Internal Audit Team)	At least 80% satisfaction rate
		Annual user survey (user refers to AG and lawyers) (RSU)	At least 80% satisfaction rate
	Access to Court Services	**Quarterly** walkabout report (Internal Audit Team)	At least 80% satisfaction rate
		Quarterly report on focus group discussion and feedback (PA & RSU)	At least 80% satisfaction rate
		Annual user survey (user refers to AG and lawyers) (RSU)	At least 80% satisfaction rate
		Annual perception survey (RSU)	At least 90% satisfaction rate
Provide a Fair & Timely Judicial System	Waiting Periods – All Divisions	**Monthly** statistical report (RSU)	At least 80% within timeline
	Age of Pending Cases	**Quarterly** audit of age of pending cases (RSU)	Percentage of files remaining outstanding outside the stipulated time period should not exceed 20% -*Criminal*: Less than 10% of cases remaining outstanding for more than 6 months. -*Civil*: Less than 10% of the cases outstanding for more than 18 months. -*Family*: Less than 20% of the cases outstanding for more than 18 months. -*Juvenile*: Less than 10% of the cases outstanding for more than 3 months. -*Small Claims*: Less than 10% of the cases outstanding for more than 2 months.
	Feedback from Users on Fairness & Timeliness	**Quarterly** user survey (RSU)	At least 80% satisfaction rate
		Annual user survey (user refers to AG and lawyers) (RSU)	At least 80% satisfaction rate
		Annual perception survey (RSU)	At least 90% satisfactory rate
Maintain Quality & Integrity of Justice	% of Cases with Appeals Filed	**Monthly** statistical report (RSU) -[No. of cases appeals filed to No. of cases heard]	Less than 0.2% (including RA & RAS)

PERSPECTIVES/OBJECTIVES	MEASURES	MONITORING METHODOLOGY	TARGETS
COMMUNITY - To Preserve Public Trust & Confidence			
	% of Appeals Allowed	Monthly statistical report (RSU) -No. of appeals allowed by High Court to No. of appeals filed in Subordinate Courts	Less than 20% (including RA & RAS)
	No. of Criminal Revisions by Judicial Officers	Monthly statistical report (RSU)	Zero
Provide Public Education	Community Outreach Programmes		
	No. of Programmes organised and Talks conducted by officers	Quarterly report on number & details of programmes (PA)	At least 6 programmes per quarter
	Feedback from participants	Quarterly report on feedback from participants (PA)	At least 80% satisfaction rate
	Community's Awareness of Courts' Services	Annual perception survey (RSU)	At least 70% of awareness level of Courts' services
Build Community Involvement	Programmes Involving the Participation of the Community		
	No. of Programmes Involving the Community	Quarterly report on number and status of programmes (RSU)	At least 3 programmes per year
	Feedback from participants and focus group discussion	Quarterly report on feedback from participants and focus group discussion (PA & RSU)	At least 80% satisfaction rate
Enhance International Standing	International Benchmarking	Annual surveys of Other Organisation (PA & RSU)	To maintain at least top 10 international ranking.
		Annual perception survey (RSU)	At least 80% perceived that the Singapore Subordinate Courts is better than other jurisdiction
		Quarterly report on focus group discussion & feedback (PA & RSU)	At least 80% of the group feels that the Singapore Subordinate Courts is better that other jurisdiction.

PERSPECTIVES/OBJECTIVES	MEASURES	MONITORING METHODOLOGY	TARGETS
ORGANISATIONAL - To Build a Dynamic Public Institution			
Accountability for Public Funds & Resources	Review of Budgetary Positions	Quarterly report on Budgetary Positions (Finance)	95% utilization of the approved budget Σ
	Monitoring NEV of selected division(s) (Pilot phase of NEV implementation)	Quarterly report on NEV of selected division(s) (Pilot) (Finance)	To monitor the NEV of selected division(s) and ascertain whether the NEV is improving or sustained over the years.
	Feedback on Court's Financial Practices	Annual report on Auditor-General's Office's audit of Subordinate Court's financial practices (FIN)	No adverse report by the Auditor-General

PERSPECTIVES/OBJECTIVES	MEASURES	MONITORING METHODOLOGY	TARGETS
ORGANISATIONAL - To Build a Dynamic Public Institution			
Ensure Adequate Judicial Support	Ratio of Workload to No. of Judicial Officers	**Quarterly** statistical report (PER & RSU)	6,000 workload to 1 JO
	Ratio of Non-JO/JO	**Quarterly** statistical report (PER)	7 Non-JO to 1 JO
	Feedback on Judicial Support	**Quarterly** supervisors' feedback survey (supervisors include JOs and divisional heads) (CS)	At least 80% satisfaction rate
Strategic Use of Technology in the Administration of Justice	Initiatives undertaken for the strategic use of technology in the Courts	**Quarterly** report evaluating the number of initiatives and use of technology in the Courts, including the number of initiatives undertaken (ITD)	At least 1 initiative per quarter
	Feedback on the use of technology in the administration of justice	**Quarterly** report on focus group discussion & feedback (PA & RSU)	At least 80% satisfaction rate
		Annual user survey (user refers to AG and lawyers) (RSU)	At least 80% satisfaction rate
Leading Change	Initiatives for Change Management	**Quarterly** report to be submitted by the Justice Policy Group	At least 3 initiatives per quarter
		Quarterly report to be submitted by all divisions (RSU)	3 initiatives per year per division
		Quarterly report on focus group discussion & feedback (PA & RSU)	At least 80% satisfaction rate Σ
	Number of Staff Suggestions Submitted	**Quarterly** statistical report (DIV & Mr Andrew Chew)	At least 2 staff suggestions per staff per year . Σ
	Number of WITS Project Submitted	**Quarterly** statistical report (DIV & Mr Andrew Chew)	At least 1 WITS project per team per year for 80% of the teams

PERSPECTIVES/OBJECTIVES	MEASURES	MONITORING METHODOLOGY	TARGETS
EMPLOYEE - To Build a Motivated & Knowledge-Driven Team			
Achieve High Employee Satisfaction and Commitment	Staff Turnover Rate (Staff includes JO and non-JO, contract & permanent)	**Quarterly** statistical report (PER)	Less than 6% per year (as per PSD)
	Employment Satisfaction Index (ESI)	**Annual** Employee Climate Survey (PER)	At least 80% satisfaction rate
	Job Commitment Index (JCI)	**Quarterly** supervisor feedback survey (PER)	At least 80% satisfaction rate
Leverage Knowledge Management	Knowledge Management Index (KMI)	**Quarterly** Feedback Survey (KMD)	To be determined Σ
Building A Vibrant Culture	Cultural Index	**Annual** Employee Climate Survey (PER) -Index will include factors such as dynamism, liveliness, honesty, and trustworthiness	At least 80% satisfaction rate Σ
Maximise Individual Potential & Develop Core Competencies	Average Number of Training Hours	**Quarterly** statistical report (HRD)	At least 100 training hours per year
	Effectiveness of Staff Training Index (ESTI)	**Quarterly** supervisor feedback survey (HRD)	At least 95% feedback that all courses are useful

Exhibit 3.1 Justice scorecard 1

Wai Yin states:

Positioned at the apex is the community perspective. It was renamed from customer to community to better reflect the fact that the Subordinate Courts must take into account not only those with whom we deal with on a day-to-day basis in the administration of justice, but also the community whom we protect when justice is administered.

Moreover, the community objectives essentially reflect the five core values of Subordinate Courts, which are:

- accessibility
- expedition and timeliness
- equality, fairness, and accountability
- independence and accountability
- public trust and confidence.

The values and community objectives support the vision of Subordinate Courts, which is "Primus Inter Pares;" that is, the first among equals in world judiciaries, to continue to lead the citizenship of the justice process, and to be a dynamic public institution. Similarly, the community perspective is hardwired to The Subordinate Courts' desired outcome, which is "to uphold the rule of law and public trust and confidence in the administration of justice."

Wai Yin believes that the middle layer, the organizational perspective, represents internal operations – a combination of both the financial and internal process perspectives.

Financial responsibility, though not our bottom line, is still an integral part of the running of an effective and efficient public organization. Thus, the financial component has been subsumed under the organizational perspective. This perspective enables us to determine how the type of service required by the community can be delivered in the most innovative and cost-effective way so as to attain the goal of being a dynamic public institution.

Finally, the "employee" perspective serves as the base, or foundation of the pyramid. According to Wai Yin:

In order to build a motivated and knowledge-driven team of employees, we emphasized on building our people resources to meet the demands of administering justice in a knowledge society. The performance measures developed within this perspective must ensure that every effort is made to equip our staff with the relevant training, motivation, and awareness, as well as to promote a vibrant learning culture within the courts.

To sharpen focus, each perspective has its own goal, or vision. As examples the community perspective's goal is "to preserve trust and confidence," while the organizational goal is "to be a dynamic public institution."

Each goal has supporting strategic objectives. Community objectives include "provide a fair and timely judicial system" and "maintain quality and integrity of justice," while "employee" includes the objectives "achieve high employee satisfaction and commitment" and "building a vibrant culture."

Strategic Measures

Continuing the scorecard design and supporting each objective are strategic measures, targets, and initiatives. For example, the "employee" objective "building a vibrant culture" is measured through a cultural index containing components such as trust and honesty. As a further example, supporting the organizational objective "accountability for public funds and resources" are initiatives, target, and a measure focused on the successful inculcation of the net economic value (NEV) metric, which is mandatory for all Singaporean public-sector organizations.

To explain, NEV is a public-sector version of Stern-Stewart's economic value-added metric (which assesses economic profit by measuring net operating profit minus the cost of capital). NEV assesses the amount of resources exhausted in producing public-sector outputs. Subordinate Courts was one of the first Singaporean bodies to implement NEV.

Wai Yin believes that the NEV metric will prove valuable in demonstrating how each unit adds value to the organization and for identifying opportunities to improve efficiency.

Similarly, efficiency gains will further be achieved through the integration of Six Sigma metrics. To explain this, Six Sigma is a rigorous and disciplined methodology that uses data and statistical analysis to measure and improve a company's operational performance by identifying and eliminating "defects." Six Sigma is commonly defined as 3.4 defects per million opportunities.

Subordinate Courts is looking at processes it can develop to Six Sigma standards. To help achieve this it has an internal Six Sigma black belt. A black belt is fully trained in the Six Sigma methodology and has the ability to lead process improvement teams, as well as to advise management on all aspects of applying the Six Sigma process.

Scorecard Tailoring

Although the top-level Justice Scorecard serves as the focus for Subordinate Courts strategic efforts, the cascade process did see some tailoring in order that local objectives, measures and targets were captured. This required the Scorecard Facilitation team to worked closely with unit managers to create scorecards that were operationally valuable at the local level, while still showing line-of-sight with the high-level corporate scorecard.

Showing line-off-sight, and any misalignment, is aided by the use of an automated software solution provided by the Balanced Scorecard vendor Gentia (now part of Open Ratings). An early Asian adopted of the Balanced Scorecard, Subordinate Courts was equally early in the use of scorecard software.

Scorecard Benefits

Chan Wai Yin is certain that the Balanced Scorecard has delivered real benefits to Subordinate Courts. She says:

People now have a far better understanding of how their everyday work links to our vision and mission statements, and they can take a more balanced, as opposed to largely internal, view of their work. Also, as the scorecard is proactive we are better able to identify problems, rectify them, and then communicate action and progress to all of our stakeholder groups in a simple format.

Critical Success Factors

And for Subordinate Courts "simplicity" is a critical success factor in a scorecard program. Wai Yin states:

We have kept the scorecard simple; for example, we have just 14 strategic objectives on the corporate scorecard, so as to keep ourselves focused on what's critical for driving performance. If the scorecard gets too complex and cluttered you can end up back at square one where you will have a comprehensive set of measures that aren't driving strategy.

According to Wai Yin other critical success factors include:

- top management commitment;
- a clear purpose for the scorecard implementation;
- ownership and accountability at each level.

She concludes: "Quite simply, the scorecard provides a bird's eye view of performance. It shows where problems are and makes it easier to manage a complex organization."

1   Norton, D.P. and Kaplan, R.S. 2001,*The Strategy-focused Organization: How Balanced Scorecard Companies Thrive in the New Business Environment*, Harvard Business Press, Boston, MA.

2   Chocqueel-Mangan, J. 2003, *How to Get Going and Make it Stick, Implementing Performance Management Frameworks for Long Term Success*, Tyler Mangan Ltd, Reigate, UK.

4

Building the Scorecard Team

*T*oo many Balanced Scorecard programs eventually fail because the capabilities to manage with the scorecard over the long-term have not been inculcated. In this chapter we will explicate the process for ingraining internal score-carding capabilities into the organization. Authority and ownership of the Balanced Scorecard reside with the executive management and cannot be devolved to lower level teams, but ongoing management of the scorecard process can be delegated. At the start of a scorecard effort it's advisable to put in place a steering committee comprising senior managers to oversee and review the fledgling program. The scorecard implementation team should be cross-functional, but must avoid any tendency to territorial protection or enhancement. For ongoing success it is important to train a large number of people in working with the scorecard. For large organizations it is typically sensible to employ a fulltime scorecard manager. However, in most companies, scorecard responsibilities dovetail with other performance-improvement requirements. We describe the key skills requirements of a Scorecard Manager. A case study on Summarecon Agung concludes this chapter.

BACKGROUND

If the Balanced Scorecard is to be more than a short-term project it requires the inculcation of permanent Balanced Scorecard "skills" deep inside the organization. Skills include strategy-mapping, building scorecards, working with measures, and knowing how to use the scorecard as a learning mechanism. In the previous chapter we stressed that the Balanced Scorecard has to become "the way we manage around here." Strategy-focused organizations take it to the next step and make it "the way we work around here."

We have seen too many examples of well thought out Balanced Scorecards that worked well as management tools in the shorter term, only to wither and die because the score-carding capabilities were never inculcated. Indeed, we have observed that building the scorecard capabilities for the longer term is often overlooked in the excitement of getting a scorecard up and running. But those organizations that elicit ongoing benefits out of the scorecard system, such as Saatchi & Saatchi (see Chapter 11) invariably ensure that dedicated internal scorecard capabilities are in place at the start of the program, and that they are strengthened, rather than withdrawn, once scorecards are built and deployed.

> " ...building the scorecard capabilities for the longer term is often overlooked in the excitement of getting a scorecard up and running. "

SENIOR MANAGEMENT RESPONSIBILITY

As we begin this chapter we should reiterate a key learning from the previous chapter. The Balanced Scorecard has to be owned and driven by the top team because strategy execution is their primary role – it's what they're paid for. Matthew Tice, BSCol Vice-President, Asia-Pacific makes the unequivocal statement: "The executive team should not devolve the authority for the scorecard program to others – that's absolutely critical."

We agree wholeheartedly, but the executive team should typically devolve responsibility for the ongoing management of the scorecard program to a lower level team. A senior manager who may be just one level below the executive team and who is held in high regard by the executive team typically leads this lower level team.

Dr Norton and Professor Kaplan generally refer to these managers as being "chiefs of staff," and it is notably that some of the most celebrated scorecard success stories are where companies purposefully put in place such "chiefs" – Tom Valerio at Cigna Property and Casualty and Edward Lewis at Mobil Oil being two examples. It would be fair to add Paul Melter of Saatchi & Saatchi to this list, and note that prior to adopting the role of scorecard director he was a Divisional Finance Director with Saatchi & Saatchi and so already carried significant authority within the organization. We will talk more about the personal and professional requirements of such "Chiefs of Staff" or Balanced Scorecard Directors/Managers later in the chapter.

THE BALANCED SCORECARD TEAM

We will now discuss the composition of the Balanced Scorecard team. We will first consider team (or more accurately teams) composition at the start of the scorecard program (that is, those who put the scorecard in place – the implementation team) before considering the makeup of the team responsible for the program's ongoing management. These teams have differing responsibilities but will typically comprise many of the same people.

EXECUTIVE TEAM

In the early stages of a scorecard program it is usually advisable to put in place an executive team to oversee the scorecard efforts, review progress, and to ensure that the team "on the ground" has sufficient authority and resources to get the scorecard moving. For example, this was the case at Subordinate Courts, Singapore (see Chapter 3), where a steering committee comprising the Senior District Judge (essentially the CEO) Richard Magnus and other senior judges and court administrators oversaw a local pilot and reviewed progress on a monthly basis, green-lighting full organization-wide rollout after six months.

> " In the early stages of a scorecard program it is typically advisable to put in place an executive team to oversee the scorecard efforts, review progress, and to ensure that the team ... has sufficient authority and resources to get the scorecard moving. "

Moreover, District Judge Valerie Thean (a high-ranking executive) led Subordinate Courts' scorecard facilitation team. The team benefited from a North American benchmarking trip where they learnt from the implementation of the scorecard by the City of Charlotte, North Carolina, United States (a celebrated early public-sector adopter of the Balanced Scorecard). Also, performance management methods used by various California courts and the National Council of State Courts were assessed and incorporated into the scorecard model. The fact that such a trip was financed speaks volumes for the priority the organizations placed on the scorecard.

At Tata Motors Commercial Vehicles Business Unit (CVBU) (see Chapter 1) a high-level steering committee (comprising the Executive Director, functional heads, and some other key officers such as the regional managers in Sales & Marketing) was set up to oversee the scorecard program. The committee appointed a core team of five people (which is part of the Business Excellence Services Department & the Executive Director's Office) to act as the program team that would, working with the Steering Committee, build and deploy the Strategy Map and Balanced Scorecard. However, final validation and ownership would remain with the Executive Director and the Steering Committee. Status was reported every month.

During the first phase of the scorecard program at Saatchi & Saatchi (see Chapter 11) the scorecard implementation team had to report to the executive management team on a weekly basis. The executive team served as program sponsors and champions, and made sure that the scorecard "got done."

Within Singapore's Centrepoint Properties (see Chapter 9), the establishment of a Balanced Scorecard Deputies Committee comprising senior managers was instrumental for gaining clarity, ironing out problems, and overcoming potential resistance, both at managerial and staff levels.

What we see from the above examples is that the senior teams played a proactive role in the scorecard program. They were not doing the nitty-gritty day-to-day implementation tasks, but they were, through their visibility, making it clear that they have ultimate authority for the Balanced Scorecard and that they were giving top priority to the scorecard program.

Moreover, in order for the scorecard implementation team to be successful, the team will require resources both from human and financial capital perspectives. In today's economic environment, this can be challenging; however, if sufficient resources are not dedicated to scorecard implementation the program will have limited long-term success, or none at all. The senior team, of course, has the power to provide the required human and financial capital.

> " ...if sufficient resources are not dedicated to scorecard implementation the program will have limited long-term success, or none at all. "

CROSS-FUNCTIONAL SKILLS

Once legitimized and empowered by the executive team, what should the composition of the scorecard implementation team be?

All of the regional experts interviewed for this book agree that the scorecard team should be cross-functional in nature, perhaps comprising IT, HR, finance, and commercial people, as examples. Bringing all of this functional expertise into the team is useful for ensuring that all organizational concerns are considered. In saying that, team-members must be made aware that they are not there to protect, or enhance, their functional territories, but to work together for the benefit of the organization.

❝ **S e n i o r e x e c u t i v e s should ask the question, "Would I let this project team member sit in on the monthly executive committee meeting?" If the answer is no, then don't expect this team member to have real insight into the organization's direction. ❞**

Considering our case study examples, Saatchi & Saatchi's implementation team comprised three consultants from Renaissance Worldwide (the then President was Dr David Norton) and three from Saatchi & Saatchi – Paul Melter from finance and colleagues from client services and strategic planning. The role of consultants is something we will explore in detail in Chapter 5.

About the composition of the implementation team, Nigel Penny, a Singapore-based scorecard consultant states:

> Senior executives should ask the question, "Would I let this project team member sit in on the monthly executive committee meeting?" If the answer is no, then don't expect this team member to have real insight into the organization's direction. Consequently, their ability to help design the scorecard will be impaired.

Matthew Tice adds:

> Each of the people involved bring functional skills. But broadly they need to understand change management, communication, measurement, and they need to be credible in the organization. Really, the people you can least afford to have on the program – your 'A' team. That's a challenge for some organizations as the demands on their time for other initiatives is often high.

Interestingly, the skills of the implementation team are the same as those identified for a good Balanced Scorecard Manager (see later in the chapter).

Tice neatly describes the key responsibilities of scorecard team members:

1. There has to be a program manager who has to coordinate all of the stakeholders and resources and consultants.
2. There has as to be an education responsibility, somebody who's out there brining the technology and knowledge to people in the organization.
3. There has to be a strategy responsibility, the people who are doing the front-end work in really developing and translating that strategy into an operational framework.
4. There has to be a measurement and resource responsibility to make sure the measures get created in the right way.

ONGOING MANAGEMENT

Tice states that as the program unfolds governance responsibility comes to the fore. This is really to ensure that management of the framework is ongoing. He says:

> There's responsibility in finance to make sure the budgets line up and from HR to make sure that training and education is embedded, and ultimately that remuneration is aligned. There's a responsibility in technology to make sure that reporting systems get rationalized and that the technology is able to support a broad-based reporting requirement around the scorecard."

As we can see once the scorecard is in place, responsibility for the scorecard program lies within many organizational places. The original implementation team may disband, although typically many, especially the program manager, will continue as part of the ongoing management team. And this is something we would encourage, as it brings consistency, and a sense of permanence to the program.

And this brings us to an exploration of the importance of inculcating scorecard capabilities deep inside the organization so that the scorecard system can be effectively managed as an organization-wide framework.

Looking at our case study companies we find powerful examples of where scorecard skills inculcation has been a central focus of the executive team. At Summarecon, for example (see below), a team of

55 employees (about one-eighth of the entire workforce) has been trained by in-building and working with Balanced Scorecards. The team regularly hold roundtable meetings with senior managers to review (and if required amend) the Strategy Map and supporting Key Performance Indicators at corporate or divisional levels.

Moreover, as part of the early communication efforts, all of the top 100 people (or one-quarter of the workforce) were taking through scorecard awareness sessions.

So with corporate and business unit management teams building strategy maps and balanced scorecards, and with a 55-employee-strong balanced scorecard team, and the top 100 people going through scorecard awareness programs, Summarecon quite quickly reached the point where scorecard awareness and expertise was widespread.

According to Assistant Director Herman Nagaria:

> We have a small team from business development and information technology that maintains the scorecard on an ongoing basis, but strategy implementation cannot be the responsibility of a small group. It has to be everybody's job. This is why we have put so much effort into internalizing the scorecard competency.

Nagaria is right – strategy implementation has to be everybody's job.

Often the Balanced Scorecard internal expertise comprises both full-time and part-time members. At Saatchi & Saatchi, for example, a full-time scorecard team of three is supported by over 40 part-time scorecard champions in the business units who are responsible for collecting and collating their own CompaSS (or scorecard) and forwarding these to the center.

Booz|Allen|Hamilton Case Example

As a powerful example from outside of our case examples, consider The GO-Team (essentially an organization comprising support units) within the US-headquartered Booz|Allen|Hamilton. It has a full-time Balanced Scorecard Manager, John Monkzewski, who is supported by three other full-time employees.[1]

One scorecard team member is from an IT background and is charged with looking for better ways to collect and automate data.

The other two team-members are tasked with continually working with unit teams, sub-teams, and individuals to help them better understand the scorecard process and to share best practices.

In addition to the central fulltime Balanced Scorecard team, a further scorecard team exists within Booz Allen's Go-Team, the existence of which, Monczewski says, is a success prerequisite. This is the core team. Monczewski goes on to say:

> The Core Team comprises one person from each of the nine main teams within the organization. It is part-time and team members had shown an interest in the Balanced Scorecard and a willingness to oversee scorecard implementation and usage within their own areas. This team was quickly brought up to speed with the scorecard through the workshop process and also through web-casts, their own reading, and attending monthly meetings with the central scorecard team.

Scorecard Manager

As we can see, Monkzewski is a full-time Balanced Scorecard Manager, as is Paul Melter at Saatchi & Saatchi, who has the title "Worldwide Director, CompaSS."

Of our case study companies, Saatchi and Saatchi is the only one with a full-time scorecard manager. About the need to be full-time, Paul Melter pulls no punches:

> I find it difficult to imagine how any large organization can manage the scorecard as a part-time effort. When we set up the steering committee it was essentially a part-time responsibility, but once CompaSS was being rolled out it had to be full-time. To do the CompaSS on a quarterly basis there's a great deal of education, training, and logistics that go into the process.

But he stresses that the job isn't over when the CompaSS is up and running.

Then you get into managing the scorecard as an ongoing program. We are using the scorecard with the aim of building a strategy-focused organization. The scorecard therefore impacts planning, communication, people and culture, budgeting, and feedback as examples. It focuses the discussions of every management meeting. In short, the scorecard is an essential tool in the way the way we manage our global organization. It's the means for setting priorities and allocating resources.

He asks:

Where the scorecard is managed part-time I'd be interested to know how effective the scorecard is, whether the company is truly setting out to become a strategy-focused organization and how deeply ingrained it is in their cultures.

> **" If the scorecard has to be the focus for all strategic and operational activities, then does it make sense to manage the scorecard process on a part-time basis, especially for large organizations? Probably not. "**

To a large extent Melter's comments are difficult to argue against. Scorecard proponents maintain that the scorecard must become "the way we manage around here" and "the way we work around here." If the scorecard has to be the focus for all strategic and operational activities, then does it make sense to manage the scorecard process on a part-time basis, especially for large organizations? Probably not.

In saying that, some of our case study companies have managers whose scorecard responsibilities dovetails naturally with other duties. For example, at Tata Motors CVBU KC Girotra leads CVBU's Balanced Scorecard efforts as head of its Business Excellence Services Department, which also has responsibility for the unit's Excellence Model.

At MTR Corporation (see Chapter 7) Felix Kwok Wah Ng, the Standards and Performance Manager, is responsible for overseeing the whole Balanced Scorecard process within the organization. This includes report compilation and presentation for the monthly operations performance meeting, formulating measures, negotiating targets with departmental heads, and providing advice to the departments on the deployment of measures and other aspects of working with the scorecard.

He says that scorecard work accounts for about 30% of his time, with the remainder of his time focused on performance benchmarking, which is an important improvement process within MTR, engineering standards management, and statutory compliance management. Importantly, Ng works within the safety and quality team, which was given responsibility for the scorecard as it understood organization-wide processes and systems.

As another case example within Bank Universal (see Chapter 10), Pak Krisbiyanto, Vice-President, Human Capital was project manager for the scorecard and assumed responsibility for the scorecard on an ongoing basis. He speaks from experience:

Placing responsibility in the human capital group made sense because this was essentially about change management, leadership, and communications. And as part of their work in the bank, human capital has primary responsibility for ensuring those performance aspects are well managed as a process.

Within Bank Universal each of the three strategic themes on the Balanced Scorecard had a designated program manager from within the group. Each theme "manager" was charged with securing data from an identified scorecard contact in finance and for putting that data into reporting formats.

Although we would suggest (especially for larger organizations) that a scorecard manager should be in situ full-time (the Chief of Staff or Transformation Officer that works closely with the scorecard-owning CEO), practically speaking this may not happen that often. However, whether full-time or part-time, our observations and research have identified key personal and professional skills that are required for a scorecard manager to efficaciously dispatch their duties.

FUNCTIONAL BACKGROUND

Before we consider this, we will first look at which function the scorecard manager should come from. We have already seen from

Bank Universal that the manager came from HR, which was also the case at Centrepoint Properties. If scorecard rollout is largely about "people" issues then a HR background may be sensible.

However, it is probably more common for the scorecard manager to be plucked from finance, as was the case with Saatchi & Saatchi's Paul Melter. Finance people typically have good analytical skills, understand data collection and data integrity, and may be particularly rigorous in proving the causal links between non-financial performance drivers and financial outcomes.

REQUIREMENTS OF A SCORECARD MANAGER

> " ...in the final analysis, where the manager comes from is perhaps of lesser import than the breadth of the skills-set they posses. "

> " A scorecard manager has to take the back off the clock and figure out how it all fits together. They move away from the slice-of-pie view to a systems way of thinking. "

In the final analysis, where the manager comes from is perhaps of lesser import than the breadth of the skills-set he or she possesses.

Understanding the business

A first important requirement is that managers have a deep understanding of the business they are in. As Melter says: "I have to know about the communications business [in which Saatchi & Saatchi competes] and what we are trying to achieve from a business perspective."

Whether scorecard managers come from finance, HR, quality, or elsewhere, it is critical that they quickly jettison their view of the world and build a multifunctional perspective. Peter Ryan who, as Corporate Strategy and Performance Planner for City of Brisbane, is essentially the scorecard manager. He puts it nicely: "A scorecard manager has to take the back off the clock and figure out how it all fits together. They move away from the slice-of-pie view to a systems way of thinking."

Continuous Improvement

This takes us into the next job criteria, which is about building on the understanding of the business to ensure that the scorecard drives continuous, or breakthrough, performance. A scorecard manager from a Singapore-based organization interviewed for this book said:

> Specifically, the scorecard manager has to be able to quickly detect when critical indicators are not performing to plan and convey the urgency of corrective action to the head of the organization and to then facilitate the dialogue for launching required performance improvement initiatives. For this the organization's leadership expected the scorecard manager to be able to see both the big picture (the organization's vision) and the small picture (the performance indicators) and how they relate to each other, and so to understand strategy and tactics.

Credibility

A further requirement is that managers have credibility with senior management and the ability to be respected by other managers and by staff deeper inside the organization. They must bridge the strategy world and the operations world and feel at ease in each.

Change Management

If the skills listed thus far are not enough, an overriding requirement is the ability to drive a large-scale change program deep inside the organization. Recall that some of the famed early scorecard managers (or transformation officers) such as Tom Valerio at Cigna Property and Casualty were essentially charged with deploying the scorecard as part of a major corporate change program. Indeed, from our observations the ideal scorecard manager has a driving commitment to change.

So the scorecard manager has to understand the business, be a strategist and a tactician, and also a change master. No wonder Peter

> " ...the scorecard manager has to understand the business, be a strategist and a tactician, and also a change master ... There's no better apprenticeship for going into a leadership role than managing a scorecard rollout. "

Ryan says: "There's no better apprenticeship for going into a leadership role than managing a scorecard rollout."

This is a view echoed by just about every scorecard manager we have interviewed.

Passion

There are a number of other skills that scorecard managers require: listening skills, political skills, communication skills, and so on. Paul Melter highlights one other requirement that is certainly a prerequisite: "I quickly became passionate about the scorecard and was convinced that this was the way to manage our business. Such passion and conviction are key requisites for this job."

Simply put, the scorecard manager has to have an unshakeable belief in the efficacy of the Balanced Scorecard and be able to pass on this belief to others.

To complete the section on the requirements of a scorecard manager, we asked several of our scorecard managers to describe the critical success factors for success. Here are their answers:

Felix Kwok Wah Ng, MTR Corporation

It's important to possess good interpersonal and diplomatic skills. And it's critical to have the ability to present information and data in a logical fashion.

Paul Melter, Saatchi & Saatchi

Apart from common sense, patience, and listening, the CSFs are helping units be successful, helping them figure out action plans and initiatives that enable them to achieve their objectives. And in the final analysis, it's about helping the corporation become financially successful by being a strategy-focused organization.

Peter Ryan, City of Brisbane

The good scorecard managers move quickly and easily from the big picture to operational detail and back again. That is not as common as people think. They are also compelling communicators and have the courage to challenge the status quo. The best scorecard managers are good at both building support and taking criticism. And they are good at making complex things easy to understand, rather than they other way around. They re-invent the scorecard every few years with the future in mind. What's around the corner and how can the scorecard help? How do I need to adjust? In short, they think over the horizon, and have strategies for getting there. The best scorecard managers practice what they preach.

Scorecard manager, Singapore-based organization

They have to fully understand the dynamics by which the organization operates. For this they have to have the opportunity to be involved in strategic planning, vision and mission-building, and the development of action plans. Unless the individual has a strong grasp of the company's business objectives and strategic approach, they will have difficulty in appreciating the real contribution that can be made by implementing the Balanced Scorecard. If the individual does not develop these skills then the job of Balanced Scorecard manager may not be satisfying and it would be unlikely that the Balanced Scorecard would deliver any benefits to the organization.

Another key skill often required of scorecard managers is to work with consultants, especially early in the scorecard program. We look in detail at the role of consultants in a scorecard program in Chapter 5.

CASE STUDY

Summarecon Agung

Summary
When looking for a performance management solution, Summarecon came across the Balanced Scorecard. Through scorecard design and implementation, the organization has been able to better link performance management to corporate strategy. As this case study explains, Summarecon's senior team has, from the outset, recognized the importance of making scorecard usage a core organizational capability.

Background
Based in Jakarta, Indonesia, Summarecon Agung is concerned mainly with property development, but has a growing property investment interest. Established in 1975 by Soetjipton Nagaria, Summarecon now has about 400 employees and has been listed on the Jakarta Stock Exchange since 1990. Examples of its property developments include the Kelapa Garding. In the mid-1990s it launched Gading Serpong, now a town of more than 5,000 houses, shops, and a popular 18-hole Graham Marsh-designed golf course: Gading Raya Golf & Klub (Graham Marsh being an Australian golfer who was a world-famous player in the 1970s). A more recent residential development is the exclusive launched Gading Nirwana in Jakarta in 1999. Investment properties include Mal Kelapa Gading and its Gading Food City and Plaza Summarecon, both also in Jakarta.

Introducing the Scorecard
A longstanding commitment to a strategy of coordinated, incremental growth and development that allows time for evaluation and redirection has served the company well in Indonesia's often volatile property sector, where economic overheating and copycat development can lead to severe cyclical swings in the market.

Summarecon introduced the Balanced Scorecard in 2002 as a mechanism to help it maintain a market leadership position. Liliawati Rahardjo, President Commissioner explains:

Despite our history of success we are acutely aware of growing competition and know that to continue to prosper we cannot stand still. As an organization we must be able to continually reinvent ourselves and stay ahead of the curve if we are to survive in a much tougher, and more global, competitive environment.

Continuous Improvement

The introduction of the Balanced Scorecard as Summarecon's strategic management framework was somewhat eased by the fact that since the Asian Currency Crisis of 1998, which led to several tough years for the organization, in common with most companies in the region, Summarecon has paid close attention to inculcating a culture and mindset of continuous improvement. This required ongoing training in new performance-enhancing tools and techniques. Consequently, the organization, at each level, was generally accepting of a framework that sets out to enhance that continuously improvement ethos.

Given the training/continuous improvement infrastructure, it should be stressed that Summarecon first encountered the scorecard while seeking a better way to improve the performance management of its people. By the turn of the decade it had recognized that strengthening human resource management was fast becoming a success perquisite. While interviewing prospective consultants, they were shown by other consultants from Indonesia-based Balanced Scorecard specialists OTI how by focusing first on the business and its strategies, and linking performance management to that via the Balanced Scorecard, would both dramatically improve human resource management and also ensure that people management would be better positioned to help the organization to contend with growing competition.

According to Liliawati Rahardjo, "So what began as a performance management agenda became a business agenda".

Creating the Scorecard

Facilitated by OTI consultants, Summarecon began the process of building Strategy Maps and accompanying Balanced Scorecards in late 2002, which it would do at a corporate level and for its four business units of Real Estate, Mall, Club, and Apartment and Food City. It became a textbook scorecard cascade as director Lexy A. Tumiwa explains: "Based on the corporate vision, we built the corporate Strategy Map first and then created aligned unit Strategy Maps."

Summarecon's vision is to be "a well-known property company in Indonesia that provides high-quality, high-value products. ... by doing continuous improvement on our management skills, innovation and services, which in the end benefit our stakeholders." Its stakeholders are employees, customers, and shareholders.

The corporate Strategy Map and scorecard were created through dedicated workshops, in which the senior team and scorecard team were fully briefed on the Balanced Scorecard concept, taken through an implementation case study and, with the facilitation of consultants from OTI, created Strategy Maps at the corporate level and for the four divisions.

The corporate Strategy Map comprises the conventional perspectives of learning and growth, internal process, customer, and financial, with the map's theme developed according to revenue growth, cost efficiency, and capital expenditure strands.

Learning and growth objectives include objectives such as employee productivity, satisfaction, and competencies/skills; internal process objectives include optimum traffic productivity, service excellence, and project management. From the customer perspective we find objectives such as tenant satisfaction, retention, and acquisition. While financial objectives include increase revenue, improve cost efficiency and capital expenditure, all financial objectives (and in a causal effect all perspective objectives) focus on a top financial goal to grow normal profits.

Tumiwa stresses that the workshop process proved a powerful learning experience for the senior team: "At the end of the sessions we gained a stronger consensus around what will drive strategic success and how strategic programs could be devolved and communicated to the front-line."

A Balanced Scorecard Team

Particularly noteworthy about Summarecon's scorecard experience is that from the outset the management team was cognizant that to ingrain the Balanced Scorecard into the organization required that the scorecard became a core organizational capability. Consequently, a Balanced Scorecard team of 55 employees (about one-eighth of the entire workforce) have been trained by OTI in building and working with Balanced Scorecards. The team regularly hold roundtable meetings with senior managers to review (and if required amend) the Strategy Map and supporting KPIs at corporate or divisional levels. Employees show their commitment to the scorecard by turning up for these meetings with focused questions, comments, and suggestions for improvement.

Assistant director Herman Nagaria states:

We have a small team from business development and information technology that maintains the scorecard on an ongoing basis, but strategy implementation cannot be the responsibility of a small group, and have to be everybody's job. This is why we have put so much effort into internalizing the scorecard competency.

Communication

Summarecon's executive management team also understood that scorecard rollout was a major change management and communication effort. Training the 55 members of the Balanced Scorecard team also ensured that the scorecard would become a working tool in the short-term, as well as becoming a long-term competence.

As part of the early communication efforts, all of the top 100 people (or one-quarter of the workforce) were taking through scorecard awareness sessions, which were facilitated by OTI and supported by top management.

So with corporate and business unit management teams building Strategy Maps and Balanced Scorecards and with a 55-employee strong Balanced Scorecard team, and the top 100 people going through scorecard awareness programs, Summarecon quite quickly reached the point where scorecard awareness and expertise was widespread. As Herman Nagaria comments: "The scorecard is an extremely effective management tool, but it should be a topic of conversation for everybody."

Automation

The scorecard dialogues are sharpened further through the organization's decision to automate the Balanced Scorecard through the Pbviews' software solution. With the scorecard now on desktops throughout Summarecon, managers and staff have direct access to the latest performance information. Although of value, automation has highlighted some problems as Nagaria states:

The benefit of Pbviews is that the reports are clear and the software is easy to use. However, as yet we don't have all the data we need for all of our key performance indicators, making sure that all the numbers are correct is something of a challenge.

Challenges

This isn't the only challenge of scorecard implementation. As with most organizations that adopt the Balanced Scorecard, Summarecon found it a challenge to define, clarify, and gain consensus on the strategy, but, also in common with other organizations, the "doing" proved a significant benefit.

Another commonly experienced challenge that Summarecon encountered was concerns around measurement, as Lexy A Tumiwa explains:

People can be afraid of the performance transparency that the measurement component of the Balanced Scorecard brings. Managers, for instance, may be afraid of their poor performance being visible to other managers.

He adds that overcoming this is work-in-progress.

We are working hard to get the message across to managers that prior to the scorecard they didn't always know how they were performing against strategically critical performance indicators. With the scorecard they have this information and where they find poor performance they are presented with an excellent opportunity to focus attention on improving that performance. And that improvement will be visible to all the other managers in the organization.

In short, the scorecard is being purposefully positioned as a continuous improvement tool, and thus keeping with the corporation's history of improvement.

Individual Scorecards

In saying that, the scorecard is instilling more defined accountabilities into the organization. And this is being achieved by hardwiring the performance management system to the Balanced Scorecard. Recall that Summarecon came to the scorecard while seeking a performance management solution.

The performance management/scorecard link is through individual scorecards, which has been rolled-out down to departmental managers. On these individual scorecards, managers have accountability statements and have objectives and measures set against the perspectives they most impact, thus enabling line-of-sight from individual performance up to unit and corporate scorecard performance.

Over the next couple of years, bonuses will also introduced to support individual scorecard performance and more widely to reward employees for success against the scorecard. Although an important element of moving toward becoming a "performance-based" organization, there is some caution around paying for performance, largely for local, cultural reasons. Liliawati Rahardjo explains:

When it comes to performance, in Indonesia we do not have the same approach to reward and punishment as the United States and some other countries. It's not a question of a big bonus if you do well and you're fired if you don't. Culturally, we still have more of an emotional connection with employees and so tend to put as much emphasis on personal relationships as we do on individual performance. However, competition is becoming increasingly global so individual performance is becoming more of an issue.

►► Conclusion

In conclusion, Summarecon is certainly finding the scorecard to be a powerful decision-making tool. Liliawati Rahardjo adds:

Through the scorecard we are able to identify problems quicker and we can dig deeper to see why these are occurring. And sometimes we find that problems are out of the control of line managers and require a more organization-wide change. So, [by] being aware of what has to be done, senior managers can order, and resource, the interventions that will solve the problem, so performance is improved throughout the company. ... And this is a strength of the scorecard. We all have the same focus and we all speak the same language. It creates a sense of oneness."

1 Creelman, J. 2003, *Building a Strategic Balanced Scorecard*, Business Intelligence, London.

5

A Template for Choosing Consultants

M anagement consultants can play a vital role in a Balanced Scorecard program, but there are definable responsibilities they can hold and those they cannot. Consultants cannot own the scorecard program, and certainly must not build the scorecard. Both are the responsibility of the executive team. Beware of consultants that see the scorecard as a measurement exercise. This can cause significant problems to the scorecard program. There is a wide variation in the quality of consultants, from poor to excellent. Indeed, one practitioner says that some of the worst are effectively "reading the book under the table" during consultant engagements. Time and resource restraints can make engaging a consultancy a compelling solution. It can take a long time to build the requisite internal skills and knowledge. Scorecard consultants should have outstanding facilitation skills, most importantly around facilitating dialogues among the executive team. It is also important that consultants know how to relate with people at all levels of the organization, and sensitively capture and deal with their concerns. We explain that it's important to ensure that knowledge transfer takes place from the consultancy to the host organization. Companies have to be able to manage the scorecard program once the consultancy leaves. It's also important to clearly define the timetable of the consultancy project and the deliverables expected. A case study on Gold Coin Group concludes this chapter.

BACKGROUND

This chapter considers the role of consultants in a Balanced Scorecard program. That consultants can play an important role in ensuring the scorecard gets off to a proper start is without question, as we shall show. There are clear delineable boundaries around the responsibilities that consultants can, and should, hold, and those they must not.

THE DANGERS OF CONSULTANTS BUILDING THE SCORECARD

> " Engaging a consultancy to build the scorecard and simply getting the senior team to "sign it off" will deliver no benefits whatsoever, short term or long term. "

First, reiterating a key message of this book that we have made in earlier chapters, the Balanced Scorecard must be owned and driven by the executive team and it is they who must debate and agree on strategic objectives and so on. Engaging a consultancy to build the scorecard and simply getting the senior team to "sign it off" will deliver no benefits whatsoever, short term or long term.

Indeed, we have been amazed, and appalled, to hear of consultancies offering to build an organization's scorecard with virtually no input from the senior team, and equally of senior teams who purposefully seek out consultants to do this. As a US-based consultant said to one of the book author's in a previous work:[1]

I, or most other consultants, could quite easily interview a few business leaders, sit in an office and whip up a scorecard in half a day. But that's not going to drive the business. … Leaders know their business and it is they who must identify the key objectives, measures etc. You can't have somebody come in and create your scorecard for you. The leadership team has to do this. At the end of the day it is their scorecard and they have to manage with it.

We would agree wholeheartedly with this view. Both of the authors of this book could create a "nice-looking" Strategy Map and Balanced Scorecard for any organization in any sector in a few hours. But it will have no value to the organization as it will have no ownership of it and, lacking consensual buy-in at the highest level, it will quickly disappear once its validity and appropriateness is questioned. We have both been approached on many occasions by organizations that ask us whether we have a scorecard template for their industry.

So to our readers we say this: if any consultancy comes to you and offers to build your Strategy Map and Balanced Scorecard for you, don't show them your strategy, show them the door. But equally, don't ask them to do it for you.

> " ... if any consultancy comes to you and offers to build your Strategy Map and Balanced Scorecard, or you don't show them your strategy, show them the door. But equally, don't ask them to do it for you. "

METRICS-FOCUSES CONSULTANTS

Another set of consultants who should be shown the exit door are those who treat the scorecard as a measurement exercise. We made it clear at the start of the book that the Balanced Scorecard is not a measurement system, that metrics are essentially a way to monitor progress toward strategic objectives, as articulated on the Strategy Map. Unfortunately, just as there are organizations that cling to the myth that the scorecard is essentially about metrics, there are also consultants who still peddle that belief. One of the authors of this book has profiled companies for previous works that suffered serious setbacks to their scorecard efforts due to engaging "measure-focused" consultants. For example, John Monczewski, the Balanced Scorecard Manager within the GO-Team (essentially the collective support functions) of the US-headquartered Booz|Allen|Hamilton explained in Building a Strategic Balanced Scorecard how a metrics-focused effort derailed its first scorecard effort.[2]

The consultancy held workshops for the senior team and then at the manager level within the GO-Team. They organized the scorecard into perspectives, but then made a mistake. They focused on selecting measures for each perspective that could be used by the top team and then at team and sub-team level.

As a consequence, teams at each level had exactly the same measures, such as employee turnover, productivity index, professional association involvement etc on their scorecards.

So it became a measurement exercise that had nothing to do with strategy and had nothing to do with creating a culture of learning.

A second attempt at the scorecard, this time with consultancy input from Hyperion Solutions, was successful. Monczewski sums up the crucial difference that Hyperion brought to the scorecard effort.

They focused on strategy first, measures second. In the workshop sessions for each level, the focus was on what could the team or sub-team do to help deliver to the GO-Team's strategic objectives, rather on what could be measured from an operational standpoint on a day-to-day basis.

We also know of an example where a first scorecard attempt failed because the consultants "delivered" a list of 600 possible strategic key performance indicators (KPIs). How the organization was supposed to manage with 600 strategic KPIs is anyone's guess. Not surprisingly, the fledgling scorecard effort soon withered.

WIDE VARIATION IN QUALITY

> " [The] quality of consultants varies widely from excellent to poor ... "

It should be stressed that not all consultants are of equal ability and knowledge. Peter Ryan, Corporate Strategy and Performance Planner at the City of Brisbane, says that in Australasia client feedback indicates that quality of consultants varies widely from excellent to poor and that it in many cases consultants are essentially "reading the book under the table" during the consultancy engagement. And this wide variation in consultancy quality is also true in other geographic regions, and will certainly be true as the scorecard gathers momentum throughout Asia. This chapter will give some pointers in what to look for from a consultant.

CASE STUDY COMPANIES AND CONSULTANTS

It's worth stating that most of our case study organizations benefited from consultancy support during their scorecard program. Many used the services of Balanced Scorecard Solutions, Singapore, or OTI, Indonesia (the book authors are involved in both of these organizations), but certainly not all. Saatchi & Saatchi (see Chapter 11) contracted the services of Renaissance Worldwide (the President of which was Dr David Norton and the consulting nucleus of which became the Balanced Scorecard Collaborative – BSCol) and Singapore Prison Services (see Chapter 3) worked with Arthur Andersen.

Within our survey in South-east Asia (see the Appendix) 44% of Scorecard adopters had used the services of a consultant, of which just over two-thirds had used a specialized Balanced Scorecard consultancy.

WHY USE A CONSULTANT?

So let's consider why organizations commencing a scorecard journey should use consultancy services; after all, there are many examples of companies that have built scorecards without any, or significant, consultancy support. This was true at Subordinate Courts, Singapore (see Chapter 3), which is generally regarded as one of the most impressive scorecard stories in Asia (and was indeed mentioned as such in Kaplan/Norton's second book The Strategy-Focused Organization)[3]. However, Professor Kaplan did review Subordinate Court's evolving scorecard. Also, although some of the units within XYZ Enterprises (see Chapter 6) used consultancy support, most did not.

Furthermore, Tata Motors Commercial Vehicles Business Unit (see Chapter 1) did not use external consultants when starting their scorecard efforts, although the expertise of several consultants was used later for specific purposes. Nigel Penny, the Singapore-based consultant interviewed for this book has, for example, been brought in several times by the organization.

What these organizations did was build an internal scorecard team that worked diligently to enhance their own scorecard knowledge and to understand fully the intricacies of the design and implementation process. We explored the process for building in-house capabilities in the previous chapter.

This is a good question to pose to a consultancy: Why should we use your services when we can do it ourselves?

TIME AND RESOURCE CONSTRAINTS

> ❝ ... **many organizations doing it all themselves from day one is not a realistic option, given the time and resource restraints, which in itself may be a compelling reason to secure consultancy support.** ❞

In saying that, for many organizations doing it all themselves from day one is not a realistic option, given the time and resource restraints, which in itself may be a compelling reason to secure consultancy support.

It can be a lengthy process to build internal knowledge and expertise. At Subordinate Courts, for example, a pilot was launched in November 1998 and it was a year later before learnings from the pilot and learnings from, for example, a North American benchmarking tour, led to full scorecard rollout. Most organizations will be looking to get the scorecard up and running quicker, especially if there's a compelling business need for a scorecard, such as a burning platform, which was certainly the case at Saatchi & Saatchi where, with Renaissance Worldwide assistance, the corporate scorecard was build in a three-month period (and essentially became the scorecard they used for the next five years).

A consultancy can play a catalytic role in getting the scorecard up and running quickly, as long as they have the requisite knowledge and skills and are not "reading the book under the table."

However, our survey of scorecard usage within South-east Asia found that over 50% of respondents believed their consultant to be effective or totally effective. Indeed, no respondents said they believed their consultant to be ineffective, as shown in Exhibit 5.1.

Totally effective	21%
Effective	32%
Moderately effective	42%
Ineffective	0%
Totally ineffective	0%
Too early to say	5%

Exhibit 5.1 How effective was the consultancy in supporting your scorecard effort?

FACILITATION SKILLS

Something you certainly want from the consultancy is a proven ability to expertly facilitate the process by which the Executive Team reaches agreement on the makeup of the corporate-level Strategy Map and Balanced Scorecard. As Pak Krisbiyanto, Vice-President, Human Capital of what was Bank Universal (see Chapter 10), says: "We are experts in financial services, not in building Balanced Scorecards, so it seemed sensible to bring in consultancy support."

It should be said that where such facilitation skills exist they are quite impressive. After all, being able to facilitate dialogues, and challenge the assumptions, of very senior

> " ...being able to facilitate dialogues, and challenge the presumptions, of very senior and successful executives is not an easy task. There can be a lot of very powerful and dominant egos in the room. "

and successful executives is not an easy task. There can be a lot of very powerful and dominant egos in the room. Moreover, these functional heads may typically see the world through their own functional lenses and it can be a skill to, for example, get a manufacturing vice-president to see the world through the eyes of the HR vice-president and vice-versa. A skilled facilitator has to be diplomatic and apolitical.

The facilitator has to be able to ask probing questions, such as are you choosing an objective or measure because they are easy to achieve, or because are they the right strategic measures? Also, a facilitator may sometimes have to ask questions such as, "I don't get this. You say that these objectives are very important in delivering to the strategy, but I can't see why they're so critical. Please explain it to me?" This is a useful technique for getting leaders to really challenge their ingrained presumptions.

Skilled facilitators should bring with them a wealth of experience of successfully running senior management scorecard workshops, and organizations commencing a scorecard journey should make this a key criterion for consultancy selection. Just as organizations would want to know that the consultancy has a proven record in successfully facilitating scorecard rollouts.

The latter is an important point, because most scorecard efforts fail at the implementation phase, and not the design stage, largely due to cultural, structural, or logistical reasons (which we cover in depth in chapters 8 and 9). Therefore it is important that consultants know how to relate to people at all levels of the organization, and sensitively capture and deal with their concerns.

KNOWLEDGE TRANSFER

Ensuring that the scorecard succeeds over the longer term requires, as we explained in the previous chapter, the inculcation of scorecard capabilities into the organization. This implantation process should begin during the consultancy's tenure. The host organization should make sure that the consultant transfers essential knowledge in the form of capabilities, know-how, and best practices to the in-house scorecard team. An experienced consultancy would have seen how scorecards are successfully deployed in a range of industries and sectors, and seen how cultural or logistical barriers have been circumnavigated. All this is invaluable knowledge that can make all the difference to the likelihood of long-term scorecard success.

Simply put, one of the primary responsibilities of consultants is to pass on their knowledge so that the organization is capable of successfully managing the scorecard on their own. To readers we say that this is what you pay consultants for, so make it clear that you expect this to be delivered.

> " ... one of the primary responsibilities of consultants is to pass on their knowledge so that the organization is capable of successfully managing the scorecard on their own. "

We would agree with Jonathan Chocqueel-Mangan, a UK-based consultant and once Executive Vice-President, BSCol, who says: "Companies should bleed the consultants dry in terms of sucking out their knowledge and experience. This is crucial, but doesn't happen too often."

This knowledge transfer was certainly evident in some of our case study companies. Pak Krisbiyanto says that knowledge transfer from the consultancy OTI Indonesia was an important outcome of the engagement. Saatchi & Saatchi's Paul Melter says that the great value of working with Renaissance Worldwide was knowledge transfer. "They really worked hard to ensure that took place. They constantly kept us focused and on track throughout the project."

Matthew Wee Yik Keong, Staff Officer, Research and Planning at Singapore Prison Service, recalls the importance of transferring knowledge from the consultancy to an in-house team (essentially from the planning function).

In workshops with the consultancy we created the structure of the scorecard; picked the objectives; and decided how to measure, what to measure, and what calculations to use. In the process we made sure we grew our own expertise and developed our own staff to own the system.

Simply put, a measure of the success of the consultancy project is if at the end of the assignment the consultant leaves the organization and isn't missed, which was certainly true at Bank Universal, Saatchi & Saatchi, and Singapore Prison Service.

CLEARLY DEFINE THE TIMETABLE AND DELIVERABLES EXPECTED

This brings us to the next important consideration when engaging a consultant – to clearly define the timetable and deliverables expected from a consultancy assignment. In short, be very clear about what you want and by when, and hold the consultancy accountable for that. For example, OTI's involvement with Bank Universal came to an end, as agreed in August 2001, eight months after the program began. In this period, the pilot was completed and the pilot scorecard automated, a corporate scorecard created, and importantly, knowledge transfer took place between OTI and bank employees.

> **... be very clear about what you want and by when, and hold the consultancy accountable for that.**

A benefit of being clear as to timetables and deliverables is that it helps overcome a potential problem of a consultancy, once through the door, looking for ways to extend the project or sell other services. Make it clear that you are buying their scorecard knowledge, and nothing else, and that you want to "own it" by a specified date. These requirements should be set out in hard, tangible outcomes and, importantly, within the contract.

▶▶ CONCLUSION

To conclude this chapter we would certainly state that consultants can bring substantial value to a Balanced Scorecard program, most tellingly in the early stages. But to get the most from a consultancy engagement organizations should keep in mind the following pointers:

1. Choose a consultant with a depth of experience in scorecard design and implementations, and who has done so successfully. If possible, find out the results achieved by the organizations as a result of the consultancy project.

2. Beware of consultants who treat the scorecard as no more than a measurement exercise. If the consultant speaks about metrics rather than strategy, then they cannot be considered as scorecard consultants.

3. Make sure that the consultant transfers essential knowledge in the form of capabilities, know-how and best practices to the in-house scorecard team. This is absolutely essential for ensuring the longer tem viability of the scorecard.

4. Define the timetable and deliverables expected from a consultancy assignment.

5. Be clear that ownership of the scorecard program must always remain with the senior team, not the consultant. It has to be the executive team's scorecard. It cannot belong to anybody else.

As explained, with the roles and responsibilities of the consultants defined, they can play a very important role in facilitating the process of building the high-level Strategy Map and Balanced Scorecard. We describe the process for building a Strategy Map in the next chapter, and for building a high-level Balanced Scorecard in Chapter 7.

CASE STUDY

Gold Coin Group

Summary

At Gold Coin Group, the CEO's leadership, involvement, and support was pivotal to the scorecard design and implementation process. Moreover, as this case study explains, Gold Coin's customer perspective has a higher weighting than any of the other three quadrants.

Background

Gold Coin Group is a Swiss-owned business with operations in Singapore, China, Hong Kong, Malaysia, Thailand, Indonesia, Sri Lanka, Vietnam, and Laos. With a turnover measured in the hundreds of millions of US dollars, and with more than 2,000 employees, Gold Coin Group is Asia's leading producer and distributor of compound feed for livestock and aquatic animals, and for the production and distribution of wheat flour. It boasts 21 feedmills, 8 flourmills, 2 fishmeal factories, and several trading subsidiaries.

Since its inception as a feedmiller in 1953 the Gold Coin brand has been synonymous with products of the highest quality. Since the early 1990s the Group has paid equal attention to delivering top-quality service. This has combined to form the Group's competitive differentiator of "better quality and better service at the same price." This in turn supports the corporate vision of "leadership in our core business: Feed and Flour Milling."

The Scorecard Explained

Exhibit 5.2 provides a high-level overview of Gold Coin's corporate Balanced Scorecard, detailing vision, business idea, areas of focus, strategic goals, critical success factors, and strategic measures.

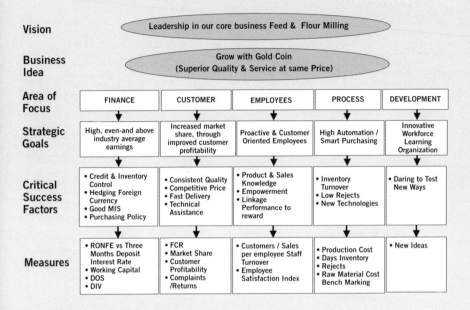

Exhibit 5.2 Overview of Gold Coin's Balanced Scorecard

The Group's corporate Balanced Scorecard is shown in Exhibit 5.3. Although it consists of the classic financial, customer, internal, and learning and growth perspectives, note how the weightings signal a shift in the importance typically ascribed to scorecard perspectives. Within the Gold Coin scorecard the customer perspective is awarded a 45% weighting, with 20% assigned to both the financial and internal perspectives and 15% to learning and growth. Note too that the strategic objectives within each perspective are also weighted.

The reason for a higher customer weighting is quite simple, explains Louis Schwendener, formerly Director and Group CEO, and now an independent consultant:

In the industries in which Gold Coin competes products are essentially viewed as commodities. The real differentiator is quality and service, so it is by focusing clearly on customer-perceived quality and service that superior financial performance will be attained. Placing a higher performance weighting on the customer perspective sends an unambiguous message to managers and the general employee-base as to what really matters to the senior management team.

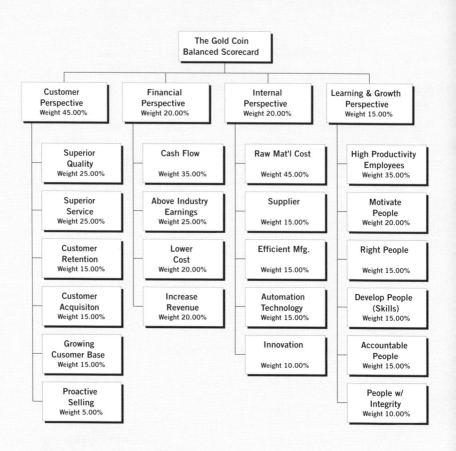

Exhibit 5.3 Corporate Balance Scorecard

Exhibits 5.4, 5.5, 5.6, and.5 7, show the measures that support the objectives for each of the four perspectives. Note too how these measures are also weighted according to their importance. For example, the objective "superior quality" (which itself has a 25% weighting for the customer perspective) is supported by the measures "internal rejects" (35%), "returned stock" (25%), and "number of quality complaints" (30%). So the measure of "customer complaints" accounts for 13.5% of the total scorecard performance score

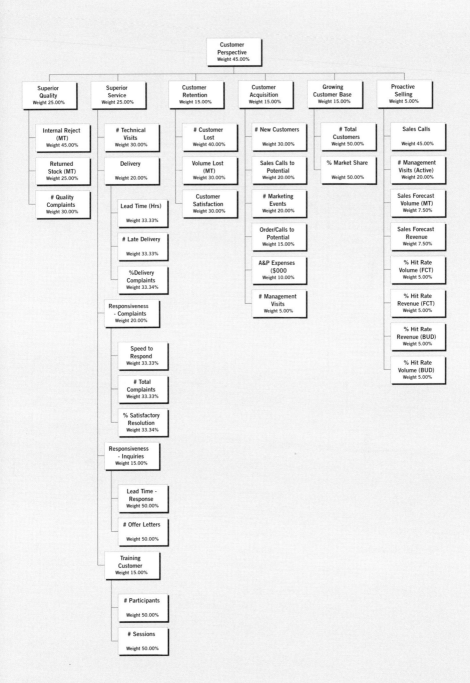

Exhibit 5.4 Corporate Balance Scorecard

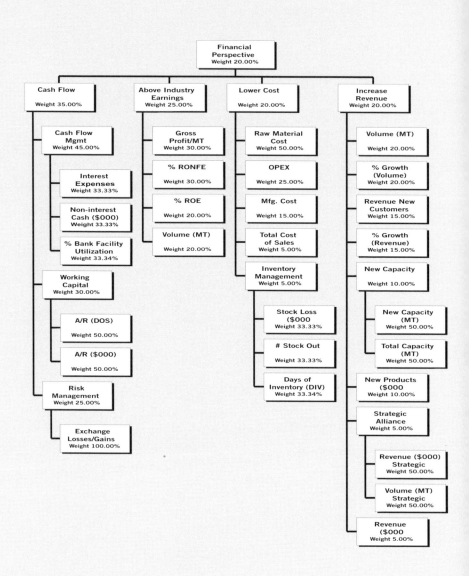

Exhibit 5.5 Corporate Balance Scorecard

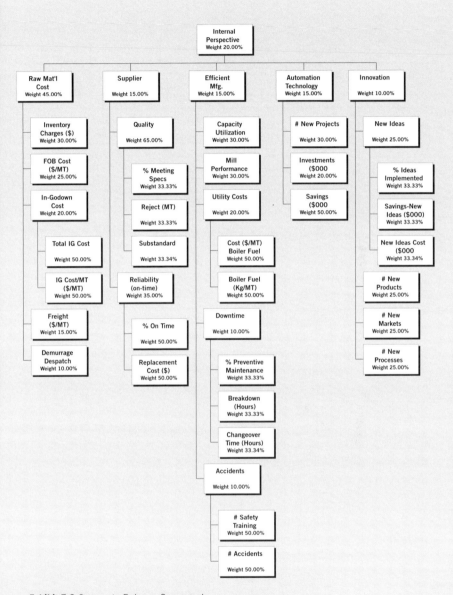

Exhibit 5.6 Corporate Balance Scorecard

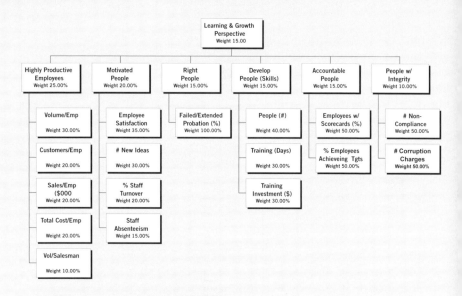

Exhibit 5.6 Corporate Balance Scorecard

As a further example, the objective "motivated people" (which has a 20% weighting in the learning and growth perspective) is supported by measures of "employee satisfaction" (35%), "number of new ideas" (30%), "% staff turnover" (20%), and "staff absenteeism" (15%). So the measure of "employee satisfaction" accounts for 8.5% of the total scorecard performance score.

It should be stated that although Gold Coin only possesses one scorecard, this being at the corporate level, there are some slight differences in the measures used with flourmills and feedmills. Moreover, the weightings of individual measures might be different according to the local needs of each country or operation.

Results

It is evident that the Group has achieved excellent results since adopting the scorecard. Consider these results from the first two years of full scorecard usage (2001 and 2002). From a customer perspective the Group enjoyed a 30% improvement in customer retention and a 20% increase in new customer acquisitions. Customer complaints dropped by 40% and delivery lead times fell by 50%. From an internal perspective the Group achieved a 15% improvement in manufacturing efficiency, a 20% reduction in utility costs, and a substantial improvement in automation. And from a financial perspective the group achieved an average annual increase in EBITDA (earnings before interest, tax, depreciation, and amortization) of 25% and over the period the Group increased profits by 50%. According to Schwendener the financial results justify the Group's decisions to pay greater attention to the customer perspective than any other.

A more intangible benefit is around strategic understanding, as Schwendener explains:

With the scorecard so visibly delineated and weighted, the Group quickly found that employees gained, largely for the first time, a clear sense, and an understanding, of their role in implementing the Group's vision and strategic goals, which led to their identifying potential strategic initiatives.

Consider the following as just one example of an initiative that came from the employee base (and recall from Exhibit 5.2 that developing "proactive and customer-oriented employees" is a strategic goal). A group of storekeepers initiated the idea of creating waiting rooms for lorry drivers at each of our locations. These rooms are air-conditioned, have televisions, and free food is available. As a result, more than 5,000 lorry drivers in Asia prefer visiting Gold Coin locations than they do its competitors. Taking care of drivers leads to improvements in delivery performance and the drivers typically become Gold Coin ambassadors to potential customers.

Building the Scorecard

Having described what the Group scorecard looks like and how it has delivered superior financial and customer-facing performance, let's step back to 2000 and consider how the scorecard was originally built. Facilitated by one of this book's authors, Naresh Makhijani, the scorecard was created through a series of one or half-day s workshops from January to March 2000, attended by senior and some middle-level managers. The initial workshop focused on familiarizing the senior team with the scorecard concept, on helping secure their buy-in, and assuaging any fears. According to Schwendener, "It was important to get the message up front that the Balanced Scorecard is about strategy implementation and performance improvement and not about cost-cutting, restructuring, or firing."

The subsequent workshops focused on the classic score-carding process of identifying objectives, measures, targets, and initiatives. This itself was a powerful learning experience, as most managers had typically only previously been used to working with financial, sales, and some quality measures. They were basically inexperienced in customer satisfaction process or learning and growth measures as examples. At the time of commencing the scorecard journey, recalls Schwendener, only about 30% of what was really driving corporate performance was being systematically measured.

The CEO's Role

Raising the senior team's understanding, and acceptance, of "balanced" performance objectives and measures required Schwendener to focus on coaching his senior team in the use of the scorecard. Indeed, based on his experience, Schwendener believes the role of the CEO is central to succeeding with the Balanced Scorecard:

As CEO it was important that I played a central role in ensuring the smooth progress of the score-carding process. I had to explain my vision clearly and at times intervene when it was proving difficult to get consensus around a strategic objective. As senior management came from different functions they, quite naturally, had different views and concerns. At times I had to take a decision as to the objective that would be chosen, as I, as CEO, was ultimately responsible for results. I also had to take a holistic, rather than narrow, view of performance.

Schwendener went on to stress, "The Balanced Scorecard is primarily a CEO tool and he has to own it and drive it." In saying that, a clear benefit that came out of the workshops was the fact that senior management gained a deeper appreciation of how their work impacted on that of the other members of the senior team. From sourcing to shipping and from production to selling, the management team collectively moved to a more holistic view of Gold Coin's operations.

Lower Management Buy-In

The next step was to get middle and junior managers to the same level of enthusiasm and buy-in as the senior team. The Balanced Scorecard was devolved down to the lowest of the Group's managerial levels. Managers at this level are in turn responsible for ensuring that all staff in touch with customers (such as telephone operators, storekeepers, and so on) are focused on the Group's strategic goals.

To achieve this devolution Naresh Makhijani conducted face-to-face meetings with general managers to explain the concept and answer questions.

Furthermore, an in-house-trained project manager made scorecard presentations within each country and plant, and Schwendener too would made it a priority to get the message across in all of his meetings with country/plant leaders and staff.

Incentive Compensation

Also, key to ensuring management buy-in to the Balanced Scorecard was tying incentive compensation to scorecard results. Throughout the Group the split between fixed and variable pay is standard according to management level. So group directors received 50% fixed pay and 50% variable, and sales managers received 60% fixed and 40% variable. However, the variable percentage will alter depending on local needs. As an example, in one country customer retention may be a pressing priority, while in another it may be customer acquisitions. Therefore, the variable compensation may be configured according to local needs, as will the measures weighting on the local scorecard.

Performance Reporting

Within Gold Coin, performance to the Balanced Scorecard is monitored throughout the group within regular management meetings. At the most senior level the scorecard is monitored on a monthly basis. Schwendener states:

What has been incredibly powerful is that instead of receiving a 50-page report from all 30 plants, the senior team now only receives an update of the few key performance indicators. This means the senior team is able to manage performance rather than people and reports. And from a CEO's viewpoint it certainly enables a more holistic view of performance, while providing the capability to drill down for more detailed analyses.

The reporting and analysis process has been aided by the use of the scorecard software solution Pbviews. Gold Coin chose this software because of simplicity, easy handling, and ultimately the senior team felt it offered a good price–value ratio.

According to Schwendener Gold Coin also found it easy to align the budgeting process with the Balanced Scorecard, as they already had experience of budgeting bottom-up. Setting new targets for all the measures goes hand in hand with the annual budgeting process.

Challenge

Although scorecard implementation was successful within Gold Coin, there were clear challenges, as Schwendener recalls:

In hindsight I would admit that we were probably a little over ambitious in trying to cover each and every angle of our business. If we were to start over again, we would probably choose fewer measures, and ensure a greater focus on the most important ones. Having probably chosen too many measures it required us to be highly disciplined in their proper management.

However, from his experience, Schwendener firmly contends that the Balanced Scorecard is simply the best tool available for translating vision and strategies into a language that is understood by virtually everybody in the organization. "… it is also a sophisticated tool in helping to guide and control the progress of targets set and for substantially improving transparency within the corporation."

▶▶ Conclusion

Schwendener provides six critical factors for succeeding with the Balanced Scorecard:

1. Senior management commitment: "Don't think of starting with the Balanced Scorecard if top management is not convinced by it, aware of its benefits, and fully behind the idea."
2. Education: "Allow ample time to ensure that middle and lower management is trained very well, and that they understand the personal benefits to them."
3. Choose the right software: "Choose software suitable to your needs, but ensure that it is simple enough to be managed and understood deeper inside the organization."
4. Pick the right consultants: "If you hire a consultant, choose one who takes the time to understand your business, who will train and educate your employees, and who will understand the process of implementation."

[1]   Creelman, J. 2001, *Creating a Balanced Scorecard*, Lafferty Publications, London.

[2]   Creelman, J. 2003, *Building a Strategic Balanced Scorecard*, Business Intelligence, London.

[3]   Norton, D.P. and Kaplan, R.S. 2001,*The Strategy-focused Organization: How Balanced Scorecard Companies Thrive in the New Business Environment*, Harvard Business Press, Boston, MA.

CHAPTER

6

Creating the Enterprise-level Strategy Map

*T*he Strategy Map is the most important component of the Balanced Scorecard Management System. The Strategy Map is a visual representation of the cause-and-effect relationships among the components of an organization's strategy. Organizations globally, and more recently in Asia, are becoming aware of the requirement to build robust strategies. In building a Strategy Map ensure that the executive team has a common understanding of the term "strategy." A compelling vision statement can play an important role in shaping the Strategy Map. However, the vision should be inspirational and should differentiate the organization in the marketplace. Reaching consensus among the executive team as to the objectives that appear on the Strategy Map can be a challenge, but it is a critical outcome. Strategy Maps are typically organized according to strategic themes. Organizations should work toward creating Strategy Maps with a limited number of objectives – these should be the critical few processes that truly make a difference in delivering the strategy. A case study on a major Indian telecommunications company concludes this chapter.

BACKGROUND

The most important component of the Balanced Scorecard Management System is the Strategy Map – everything else that takes place within the system is geared to delivering to the strategic objectives and themes articulated on the map. At the enterprise-level the Strategy Map describes the critical few high-level objectives that, if delivered, will mean the successful execution of strategy (we will return to the importance of "the critical few" later in the chapter).

A sample Strategy Map is shown in Exhibit 1.1, which shows that it is the cause and effect relationships between, and within, the non-financial and financial perspectives that propels successful strategy execution. Put another way, it shows how desired financial and customer outcomes are created by excellence in the dispatching of strategically critical internal processes, which in turn are delivered by ensuring that the requisite people and IT capabilities (as described from the learning and growth perspective) are aligned with the internal process requirements.

THE IMPORTANCE OF THE STRATEGY MAP

The importance of the Strategy Map is unequivocally illustrated through the fact that the originators of the Balanced Scorecard system, Dr David Norton and Professor Robert Kaplan, called the third of their trilogy of Balanced Scorecard books "Strategy Maps" with the sub-title "converting intangible assets into tangible outcomes"[1]. They wrote:

> ... the strategy map, a visual representation of the cause-and-effect relationships among the components of an organization's strategy, is as big an insight to executives as the Balanced Scorecard itself.

This is an observation with which we would certainly agree. Although many organization gained significant benefits from the process of articulating objectives, measures, targets, and initiatives within the early Balanced Scorecard framework (see Exhibit 1.3), it was really when executives began to visualize how objectives interrelated by laying the objectives out separately on a linkage model (that later became known as the Strategy Map) that the full power of the scorecard system truly emerged. And this was something that our case study company, Centrepoint Properties (see Chapter 9), realized. Stage one of using the Balanced Scorecard, which occurred within one of its four divisions, did deliver some benefits, not least in learning to see through "balanced" perspectives, but the effort was somewhat constrained by the lack of a Strategy Map to show the causality between objectives. This was rectified in stage two when maps were developed for all of the divisions, with the help of their consultants, Balanced Scorecard Solutions, Singapore.

> " … it was really when executives began to visualize how objectives interrelated by laying the objectives out separately on a linkage model (that became the Strategy Map) that the full power of the scorecard system truly emerged. "

In this chapter we will not provide an in-depth explication of the process of strategy mapping, which is done in remarkable detail in over 400 pages in Norton/Kaplan's book Strategy Maps[2]. In that book they provide a thorough step-by-step guide on how to map strategies, be they focused on customer-intimacy, product leadership, operational excellence, or lock-in. They explain how to identify objectives, perspective by perspective for each strategic approach. We will not repeat this work here.

What we will do is, based on our observations of exemplary corporate practices, including the learnings from our case study organizations, provide a best practice template for creating an enterprise-level Strategy Map. We will detail the tangible benefits (such as the executive team agreeing upon, and articulating, the delineable components of the strategy) and the intangible benefits (such as the formation of a much more team-based and much less fractured senior team).

A NEED FOR STRATEGY

A first important point to note is that creating a Strategy Map is in itself an explicit recognition that in today's business world there is a clear requirement for a well-defined strategy. Such is the speed of change and the pressures brought to bear by global competitors descending avariciously on local markets that Asian organizations, as has happened in other geographic regions, are having to become more adept at planning for, and describing, how they will secure short-term and long-term competitive advantage – which is the essence of strategy. Moreover, to secure such advantage, formulated strategies should describe how the organization will differentiate itself in what, for most commercial corporations are typically crowded marketplaces.

Importantly, of course, strategies must be implemented, and on an ongoing basis monitored and tweaked, or more wholly revamped, when economic conditions or customer demands dictate (the power of the Balanced Scorecard system as a strategic feedback system is something we cover in detail in Chapter 11).

DEFINING STRATEGY

If the need for a more robust strategic planning process is something that's new to a proportion of Asian companies then organizations should also be careful that they don't assume that all senior managers will have the same definition of the word "strategy." People view strategy differently. Norton and Kaplan write in Strategy Maps how they realized this wide variation in understanding in their consulting practice[3]: "Some described strategy by their financial plans for revenue and growth, others by their products or services, others by targeted customers, others from a quality and process orientation, and others still from a human resource perspective."

They continued to say that this narrowness of interpretation was compounded by the fact that the members of the executive teams applied their own functional, and so narrow, take on strategy – finance, sales, IT, manufacturing, and HR leaders saw strategy through their particular lenses.

A Singapore-based scorecard manager interviewed for this book recalls that when his organization began the process of strategy mapping it was found there wasn't consensus as to what the word strategy meant. In hindsight, he says, it would have been useful to get an agreed definition up front at the outset.

We would argue that strategy is essentially about how an organization intends to attain its vision for creating value for its key stakeholders. This, we also maintain, is typically achieved by describing value creation from financial, customer, internal process, and learning and growth perspectives. However, the perspectives may alter, depending on industry or sector nuance, or more obviously due to differing public- and private-sector requirements.

VISION STATEMENTS

In considering strategy we have purposefully highlighted the importance of an organizational vision. To some extent corporate vision statements have fallen into disrepute in recent years, largely because organizations rushed to articulate a vision (and indeed mission statements and sets of values) that was then pinned on a wall and instantly forgotten. To be honest, most vision statements were hardly inspirational. They failed to differentiate the organization from its competitors. For example, "to be the number one supplier to our chosen customers" was, and is, a common vision, but does not differentiate the organization in the marketplace and is hardly likely to prove a stirring motivational rallying call to front-line troops.

> " ... to be the number one supplier to our chosen customers was, and is, a common vision, but does not differentiate the organization in the marketplace and is hardly likely to prove a stirring motivational rallying call to front-line troops. "

Consider the vision of Saatchi & Saatchi (see Chapter 11) as a marked contrast" "To be revered as the hothouse for world-changing creative ideas that transform our clients' businesses, brands and reputations."

This is certainly more inspirational than the standard vision "to be the no 1..." Furthermore, it provides a clarity that fits perfectly with the scorecard concept. Two words that are always used to describe key benefits of the scorecard are "alignment" and "focus." It is clear how the Saatchi & Saatchi vision can be used to align the key activities of this global organization and it certainly provides an overarching focus for the corporation. Finally, it is also clear how this vision can be decomposed into financial, customer, process, and learning and growth perspectives – therefore it is the perfect strategic vision.

The ultimate goal of the Saatchi & Saatchi vision was financial success, or success in the eyes of shareholders (which was achieved); however, for public-sector organizations a vision serves wide stakeholder needs. At Singapore Prison Service (see Chapter 2), for example, a nine-month visioning process to reposition the service for the twenty-first century, and with input from managers, staff, and government representatives, led to the following visions:

We aspire to be captains in the lives of offenders committed to our custody.

We will be instrumental in steering them towards being responsible citizens, with the help of their families and the community.

We will thus build a secure and exemplary prison system.

This was supported by a mission statement which reads:

As a key partner in Criminal Justice, we protect society through the safe custody and rehabilitation of offenders, co-operating in prevention and aftercare."

A set of values was also articulated.

The Singapore Prison Service vision/mission therefore has broad goals comprising the rehabilitating prisoners with the protection of society. Indeed, to deliver to the four strategic components that would deliver the vision/mission the service created four Strategy Maps and Balanced Scorecards (see below). And, with a robust and focused vision the next step was to create the enterprise level Strategy Map itself.

Carol Yong Meng Dai, Senior Manager, Human Resources at Centrepoint Properties (see Chapter 9) observes the following about senior managers: "If they are clear about vision and direction, then the map is not difficult to create. If they lack this clarity, they will not be sure whether the critical success factors are right."

An important consideration is how long to spend on building the Strategy Map and the accompanying Balanced Scorecard. Within our survey of scorecard usage within South-east Asia (see the Appendix) we asked our scorecard users how long it took to build the Enterprise Balanced Scorecard System. The replies are shown in Exhibit 6.1.

Less than 1 month	0%
1–3 months	13%
3–6 months	22%
6–9 months	22%
9–12 months	5%
Over 1 years	36%

Exhibit 6.1 Building the Enterprise Balanced Scorecard System

Our own view on this is that the process should take between three and six months (which was the case in 22% of scorecard users). If it takes any longer, and certainly if it takes more than a year (which was true in 36% of cases), then the scorecard runs the real risk of being significantly out of date. Simply put, the strategy may have changed (and perhaps failed) before the scorecard is ready.

Our survey found that only 6% of scorecard users have found their corporate level Balanced Scorecard system to be ineffective or totally ineffective, as shown in Exhibit 6.2. This shows that generally the scorecard is proving a success within South-east Asian companies at least.

Extremely effective	29%
Effective	33%
Moderately effective	32%
Ineffective	3%
Totally ineffective	3%

Exhibit 6.2 How effective is the corporate-level Balanced Scorecard proven to be in improving performance at the corporate level

STRATEGY MAPPING

A typical strategy mapping exercise follows the following process.
1. facilitated interviews with individual members of the executive team to tease out what each leader believes to be the drivers of strategic success;
2. creation of a draft Strategy Map by the program team (which may typically involve consultants);
3. a one-day workshop where the draft map is presented to the team, debated, refined, and agreed.

Reaching final agreement, of course, is easier said than done as leaders, as already stated, typically come to the strategy mapping exercise with their own takes on the world. Sometimes this means final agreement proves elusive, as was found at Gold Coin (see Chapter 5). Ex Group CEO Louis Schwendener explains:

As CEO it was important that I played a central role in ensuring the smooth progress of the score-carding process. I had to explain my vision clearly and at times intervene when it was proving difficult to get consensus around a strategic objective. As senior management came from different functions they, quite naturally, had different views and concerns. At times I had to take a decision as to the objective that would be chosen, as I, as CEO, was ultimately responsible for results. I also had to take a holistic, rather than narrow, view of performance.

Most of our case study companies did gain consensus from the senior team, an outcome they typically found in itself of great value.

Summarecon's (see Chapter 4) Director, Lexy A Tumiwa, stresses that the workshop process proved a powerful learning experience for the senior team. "At the end of the sessions we gained a stronger consensus around what will drive strategic success and how strategic programs could be devolved and communicated to the front-line."

Consensus was certainly achieved within Civil Service College Consultants business unit (see Chapter 8). Director Gavin Tan took his own management team and some five staff members through a two-day workshop in early 2002 that was facilitated by the local consultancy Balanced Scorecard Solutions. Staff members were included in the training to generate buy-in and to act as a sounding board to the eventual Strategy Map that management came up with.

Out of the workshop came a first draft of the Strategy Map. This was refined, and simplified, during subsequent in-house discussions with the group that had been through the workshop training.

STRATEGIC THEMING

Reaching consensus concerning the Strategy Map focused on the strategic objectives, but also typically the strategic themes within the map. As Norton and Kaplan write:[4] "The critical few strategic processes are often organized as strategic themes. Strategic themes are the building blocks around which the execution of strategy occurs."

Strategic theme creation was certainly evident in our case study organizations. For example, Bank Universal (see Chapter 10) identified three strategic themes required to be the best Indonesian bank. The first theme was around handling past problems caused by the non-performing loans from the previous years. The goal here was to minimize loss for the shareholders. The second theme was focused on becoming "a good bank." This was about were setting out to build a new business model and launch a new market strategy post-crisis. So here the goal was to create future value for shareholders. The third theme was around communication and building confidence in the eyes of the stakeholders – government, shareholders and customers. Hence, setting the organization on its way, one that would be profitable and ensure trustworthiness.

Summarecon has themes around revenue growth, cost efficiency, and capital expenditure. Revenue growth and cost efficiency also shape the Strategy Map of MTR Corporation's Railway Business and are the two most common themes to find on a map.

SEPARATE "THEMED" STRATEGY MAPS

As a different approach to theming at Singapore Prison Service, four "strategies for action" were identified to deliver to their vision (see above).

- enhance inmate management capability;
- maximize inmates' reintegration potential;
- develop staff to make a difference;
- prevent offending and re-offending.

Rather than show these on one map the service created four separate maps and scorecards, each dedicated specifically to one of the themes. Each map, however, comprised the same four perspectives of stakeholder/customer (at the top), internal process, learning and growth, and financial (at the bottom).

Given the clear difficulty of combing markedly differing themes such as "prevent offending and re-offending" and "enhance inmate management capability" on one map in a simple, uncluttered and easily communicable format, separate maps certainly make sense in this instance.

THE NUMBER OF OBJECTIVES

With themes identified, the next consideration of the Strategy Map process is how many strategic objectives to identify? There is no textbook answer to this question. Some organizations, such as Summarecon, design enterprise-level maps with up to 50 objectives. More common is a map comprising between 20 and 30 objectives. The map of XYZ Cellular, for example, has 21 strategic objectives, and at just under 20 we find Tata Motors Commercial Vehicles Business Unit (see Chapter 1) with 19.

> " Although it is for each organization to decide the number of objectives they wish to work with and feel comfortable working with, generally we would urge organizations to focus efforts onto identifying the critical few strategic objectives. "

Other organizations opt for a smaller number of objectives. As examples, divisional maps within Centrepoint Properties typically house only about 15 objectives, Subordinate Courts has 14, and Saatchi & Saatchi just 12. According to our survey of scorecard adoption in South-east Asia, there was a wide variation in the number of objectives reported from less than 10 to more than 50.

Although it is for each organization to decide the number of objectives they wish to work with and feel comfortable working with, generally we would urge organizations to focus efforts onto identifying the critical few strategic objectives. In many instances, organizations may wish to start with a larger number of objectives. This may be in order to begin the process of inculcating a strategic mindset into the organization and also perhaps for dealing with tricky political concerns around making sure that everybody is represented on the map (which may be important for buy-in purposes). However, over the longer term the goal should be to reduce the number of objectives to the critical few. .

Chan Wai Yin, Director of Research and Statistics Unit at Subordinate Courts explains why they opted for just a few objectives.

We have kept the scorecard simple ... so to keep ourselves focused on what's critical for driving performance. If the scorecard gets too complex and cluttered you can end up back at square one where you will have a comprehensive set of measures that aren't driving strategy.

Paul Melter, Worldwide Director, CompaSS (how they brand their Balanced Scorecard) adds:

A Strategy Map should show the critical few objectives that will make the difference in delivering to the strategy. And these should be strategic objectives, not operational. Too many Balanced Scorecards and Strategy Maps include both."

This is an important observation. What we are talking about in this chapter is the creation of a Strategy Map, not an operations map, or even a hybrid, however tempting a hybrid may be. And it certainly isn't an organization map. Early efforts at Singapore Prison Service led to a scorecard that was more representative of the organizational structure than its strategy.

> " ... a Strategy Map [is] not an operations map, or even a hybrid ... And it certainly isn't an organization map. "

And we should stress that creating the Strategy Map provides the executive team with an excellent opportunity to really think through the critical few objectives that will differentiate the organization in the marketplace, For example, "create permanently infatuated clients," which is the only strategic objective from Saatchi & Saatchi's customer perspective.

OWNERSHIP

A final consideration of creating the Strategy Map is assigning ownership for objectives (although overall responsibility for themes may also be assigned). However, when assigning ownership some care should be taken. First, a Strategy Map is the collective responsibility of the executive team. An overriding purpose of creating the map is to cement a group responsibility where the team is collectively responsible for strategy rather than each being just concerned with a narrow function. In saying that, the practicalities of running a complex organization means that responsibility typically has to be placed somewhere.

Within XYZ Cellular each of the 21 objectives on the Strategy Map has a designated owner from within the senior team who is held accountable for the performance of that objective. He or she must also champion the initiatives launched to achieve the performance targets. The primary business objective of "achieve sustained profitability (profit before tax) from March 2001 and retain market leadership," which was the top objective on the Strategy Map, was owned by the CEO.

With the CEO owning and championing the primary objective it was found that he took a keen interest in ensuring clarity in thinking as to which supporting objective should appear on the map.

Within Saatchi & Saatchi ownership was assigned during the process of building the Strategy Map. When reporting to CEO Kevin Roberts, owners were identified for each perspective. For Finance it was Bill Cochrane, from North America, the Group CFO. For Client it was a Senior Executive/Regional Director from Asia. For Product and Process it was another Senior Executive/Regional Director from Australia, and for People and Growth it was another Senior Executive/Regional Director, from China. These perspective owners then worked with the steering committee to choose objectives that would eventually be essential links in the Strategy Map.

From here, senior executives, typically CEOs from agencies around the global network, were assigned responsibility for detailing how specific objectives would be achieved, such as identifying the key measures. And identifying key measures, as well as the targets and initiatives that appear on the enterprise-level Balanced Scorecard, is the focus of the next chapter.

C A S E   S T U D Y

XYZ Enterprises

Summary

XYZ Enterprises has implemented the Balanced Scorecard throughout its diversified business units. This case study highlights the critical importance of assigning ownership for strategic objectives to individual senior managers, for replacing performance appraisal frameworks with individual scorecards, and for ensuring that green-lighted initiatives are clearly aligned with strategic objectives. Best practice is illustrated through a successful scorecard implementation within the XYZ Cellular business unit.

Background

XYZ Enterprises (the name has been changed for this case study) is one of India's largest diversified conglomerates, reporting turnover in excess of US$1.5 billion and with assets of about $1.8 billion.

Scorecard beginnings

The group-wide Balanced Scorecard implementation effort began in March 2000, as a mechanism by which to inculcate within the employee-base a clear focus on business objectives and to ensure that all performance improvement initiatives were hard-wired to the achievement of those objectives. According to a former senior member of the Balanced Scorecard rollout team, XYZ was at the time experiencing a problem common to most organizations:

Prior to implementing the Balanced Scorecard we had a tendency to launch large-scale initiatives that were tactical in nature, isolated from other improvement efforts, and not clearly linked to strategic objectives. We saw the Balanced Scorecard as a potentially powerful framework for rectifying these problems.

Performance benefits

The manager states that the balanced scorecard has certainly delivered to its potential.

The Balanced Scorecard helped us to align the efforts of every single employee to the achievement of our primary business objectives and to ensure that employees not just focused on what was important but understood why it was important.

It's safe to say that the balanced scorecard has helped to totally eliminate the dissipating of time or resources onto work that did not contribute to the achievement of our business objectives.

But what about the impact on financial results? After all, positively impacting the bottom line is the ultimate goal of any private-sector scorecard implementation. As a sample from just one business unit, XYZ Cellular, revenue grew by 44% in the financial year 2000–01 (the first full year after scorecard implementation), compared to 18% (1997–98), 27% (1998–1999), and 24% (1990–2000). And profit before tax was Rs. 150 million against a budgeted loss of Rs. 72 million and an actual loss of Rs. 31 million in 1999–2000.

Although factors such as investment in technology and capacity expansion played an important role in impacting these results, the part played by the Balanced Scorecard (which is after all a unifying management framework) should not be underestimated.

Importantly, the senior management team of XYZ Enterprises fully agreed with the central balanced scorecard premise that it is success against non-financial performance objectives and metrics that, through causal relationships, leads to eventual financial success.

And considering "non-financial" results from XYZ Cellular, there was a 61% growth in the gross additions to the customer-base in 2000–01, compared to 14%, 26%, and 34% during the previous three years. Moreover, there was a 54% growth in the closing customer base (net customer base at the end of they year) in 2000–01, contrasted with 40%, 29%, and 10% in the preceding three years. Exhibit 6.3 shows how XYZ Cellular performed against customer-base additions in 2000–01 against that year's budget and Balanced Scorecard target.

	Budget 2000–01	Balanced Scorecard target	Actuals 2000–01
Gross new additions to customer-base during the year	55,000	55,000	71,600
Closing customer-base as on March 31, 2001	53,886	64,400	69,200
Profit before tax (Rs. cores)	(7.21) loss	3.9 profit	15 profit

Exhibit 6.3 XYZ Cellular performance – budget to scorecard target

From an internal process perspective, the unit achieved demonstrable improvements in the quality of customer service, the billing and collection process, and successfully implemented a corporate account management process. And from a learning and growth perspective the unit experienced a greater focus to their training and a significant enhancement to the unit's customer knowledge base.

Strategy Map and Balanced Scorecard

The Strategy Map for XYZ Cellular is shown in Exhibit 6.4. Note that a total of 21 strategic objectives were chosen. These in turn are supported by a total of 50 strategic measures, each of which has a specified performance target. Targets for each measure are achieved through time-bound initiatives, thus ensuring the original goal that green-lighted objectives are demonstrably strategic. Indeed, no initiative is launched or funded unless it clearly maps one of the strategic measures/objectives.

Linkage Model

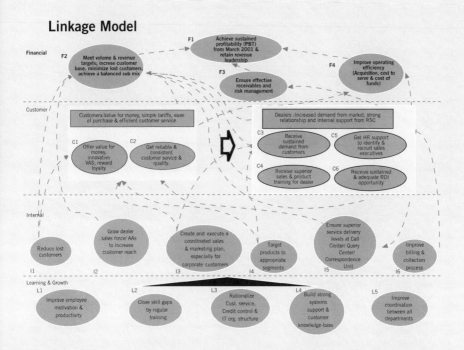

Exhibit 6.4 Strategy Map

As one example of how initiatives track through to objectives, a XYZ Cellular strategic objective from the "customer" perspective was articulated as "offer value for money, innovative, value added services, reward loyalty." One of several measures for this objective was "growth in revenue per user from value-added services." This measure had a supporting target of a 10% monthly growth. A time-bound initiative to achieve the target was launched. It comprised a project leader from sales and a dedicated support team, working to set milestones and utilizing proven project management templates (a sample template is shown in Exhibit 6.5).

Initiative / ID: 3. To open 4 more city Outlets Purpose: To provide better access to customers Dedicated Financial Resources:t The initial investment works out very high for dealers. Advances/ rent are very high as compared with our calculations. Support expected from Group. Dedicated People Resources (# involved and expected man hours):	Sponsor: VP-Mktg Owner: Manager - Distribution Priority: A

Supports the Strategic Objective of the Balanced Scorecard:
Benefits: • Opportunity for the dealer to execute the services of as Franchise. • Loyalty of the dealer • Easy reach for customers
Schedule / Milestones: Start Date: 01-APR-200X Key Milestone: Identification of location - Completed Key Milestone: Shortlist existing dealers and Identifying new franchise - Partly complete. Key Milestone: Approval for revised costing - 25-MAY-200X - Complete Completion Date: 30-JUL-200X
Dependencies: • Finance & IT for integration of the systems for activation, Marketing - Signages H R - Manpower.

Exhibit 6.5 Sample monitoring template

Senior management ownership

Creating the Balanced Scorecard itself involved a combination of familiarization workshops within each unit to introduce the concept to each unit's CEO and his or her senior management team. This was followed by a focused interview with the CEO to identify the primary business objective for that unit, which was subsequently ratified by the senior team.

For XYZ Cellular the primary business objective was identified as "achieve sustained profitability (profit before tax) from March 2001 and retain market leadership," which is the top objective on the Strategy Map. The former senior member of the Balanced Scorecard rollout team explains why it was crucial that the CEO identified the primary objective: "Each of the 21 objectives on the Strategy Map has a designated owner from within the senior team, who is held accountable for the performance of that objective. He or she must also champion the initiatives launched to achieve the performance targets."

According to this manager:

Therefore, with the CEO owning and championing the primary objective it ensures he [or she] takes a keen interest in ensuring clarity in thinking as to which supporting objective should appear on the map and, crucially, goes a long way to ensuring the scorecard gets implemented. After all, he [or she] can green-light the required initiatives.

Objectives to support the primary objectives were created in joint workshops between the CEO and his senior team and the result was the Strategy Map depicted in Exhibit 6.4.

Facilitation

Although the scorecard was championed by individual CEOs at the business unit level (critical for successful local implementation), at the group level the President of Group Strategic Planning played a crucial championing role. He first introduced the concept to the senior team of XYZ Enterprises as part of the group's knowledge management program. External case studies of companies that had experienced significant business results as a result of their scorecard implementation were shared with the senior teams at corporate level and within business units.

Unsurprisingly therefore, members from the Strategic Planning Unit were primarily responsible for facilitating the scorecard design and implementation efforts, although some units did use external consultants. The facilitator's role (whether internal or external) was to guide the discussions for the identification of business objectives that would feed into the primary objective, categorize these under the correct scorecard perspective and define robust linkages between the objectives.

Of course, the Balanced Scorecard has to become "the way we manage the business" and not a one-off project. Therefore, a manager from the Strategic Planning Unit has been assigned group responsibility for facilitating the scorecard as an ongoing process. Her main duties include ensuring that each function and department maintains their scorecards (which feed into the higher-level unit scorecard), making sure that the standard templates to monitor initiatives for achievement of targets on performance measures are updated and reviewed regularly, and for highlighting any issues or delays in the achievement of targets. In addition, most business units have identified a single responsibility point for Balanced Scorecard facilitation.

Individual scorecards

As indicated, therefore, within XYZ Cellular, as one example, the Balanced Scorecard has been devolved to function and department levels. Impressively, scorecards have been created at individual employee levels, thus ensuring clear line-of-sight between performance and objectives at the individual level and that of the function and business unit. An individual scorecard typically includes achievement of targets on specific measures and completion of initiatives as per timelines. The individual scorecards serve as the organization's performance-appraisal process. No other performance frameworks exist apart from the individual scorecards.

The senior member of the rollout team stresses that the alignment of the performance measurement system with the Balanced Scorecard and the simultaneous scrapping of the earlier performance appraisal system also sent a very powerful message as to the seriousness with which the senior management team took the scorecard concept.

Moreover, he states that such a tangible demonstration of senior commitment as scrapping conventional appraisals was largely responsible for the fact that very little resistance to the scorecard as a concept or management tool was experienced, despite being devolved so deeply into the organization.

Once the CEO and respective functional heads showed through their commitment and, more importantly, behavior, that this was a serious initiative and not just another "fad," the enthusiasm and participation of staff was forthcoming. ... It is important for senior management to "walk the talk" and to demonstrate total seriousness and focus in implementing the Balanced Scorecard.

Performance review process

Another powerful demonstration of senior management commitment within XYZ Cellular is that each week the CEO conducts a review of performance to scorecard measures with his direct reports. Each functional head conducts regular reviews, with respective initiative-owners, of the initiatives that they personally champion. Reviews are enabled through the functional scorecards being maintained in Excel worksheets and updated on a weekly basis by respective owners.

Furthermore, there's a periodical (typically quarterly) review by the senior team of the objectives, measures, weights, and targets on the scorecard to ensure that it remains aligned with changes in the business environment or strategy. This h elps ensure that the balanced scorecard continues to remain relevant. All in all, the Balanced Scorecard is central to all performance reviews, be that individual performance appraisal or strategic initiatives.

Total Quality Management

Although the Balanced Scorecard is the only strategic management framework used within XYZ Enterprises, the organization gains performance improvement benefits from a total quality management (TQM) program that has been in place since 1998. The program is the basis of an annual Group Quality Award, for which all units are mandated to apply. The award is based on the US-based Malcolm Baldrige National Quality Award, which assesses performance against criteria such as customer and market focus, human resources focus, and process management.

According to the former Head, Knowledge Management, the TQM model works well alongside the balanced scorecard. The former, he says, provides best practice benchmarks that can feed into the scorecard objectives/measures/targets. As a measure of how well they work together, XYZ Cellular was the recipient of the Group Quality Award in the year following its Balanced Scorecard implementation.

Critical Success Factors

To conclude, the former Head, Knowledge Management, provides the following five critical factors for succeeding with a Balanced Scorecard implementation.

1. There has to be total commitment, involvement, and seriousness of the CEO and their senior management team. Without this the scorecard will not work.
2. Alignment of employee performance measurement with the company's overall performance measurement system is critical. This ensures direct line-of-sign from employee-level performance and business unit performance.
3. There has to be regular scorecard reviews by the CEO and the senior management team. It has to be a working tool and must remain relevant.
4. Make sure that the scorecard and its purpose is clearly communication to all employees. This is vital if their buy-in is to be secured.

And finally, he stresses the absolute importance of ensuring that initiatives support strategic goals.

5. For a Balanced Scorecard implementation to succeed and deliver breakthrough results, the company must guard against "noise" or "distractions" by ensuring that the balanced scorecard is the central initiative to achieving strategic business objectives. Also, an initiative must not be undertaken unless it clearly contributes to achieving a target for a measure that supports a strategic objective.

[1] Norton, D.P. and Kaplan, R.S. 2004, *Strategy Maps: Converting Intangible Assets into Tangible Outcomes*, Harvard Business Press, Boston, MA.

[2] See end note 1.

[3] See end note 1.

[4] See end note 1.

CHAPTER

7

Creating the Enterprise-level Balanced Scorecard

*M*easurement is a vitally important component of the Balanced Scorecard system, but the Balanced Scorecard is not a measurement system. A Balanced Scorecard comprises the strategic measures, targets, and initiatives that support a Strategy Map. We describe the process for selecting strategic measures. Organizations should select a critical few measures. Choosing too many turns the scorecard into a measurement exercise. A balance of leading and lagging metrics should be chosen. It is important to articulate robust and standard definitions of measures. Measure owners should be identified. We explain the process for selecting strategic targets. These targets should be stretching but achievable. They should also be time-bound. We explain the process for selecting strategic initiatives. Also, that it is through initiatives that the real work of the Balanced Scorecard takes place. Initiatives must be prioritized according to strategic needs. We provide examples of prioritization processes. A case study on the MTR Corporation concludes this chapter.

BACKGROUND

"What gets measured, gets done," a maxim originally attributed to the celebrated management guru Peter Drucker has become a mantra for most Balanced Scorecard-adopting organizations. When we ask executives why they were originally attracted to the scorecard this adage is a typical reply, along with similar sayings such as "if you can't measure it, you can't manage it."

The idea of measurement, or more accurately "'balanced" measurement, has more than anything else been responsible for catapulting the scorecard concept to the front of the minds of senior management, and is a massively important component of the Balanced Scorecard Management System, as we shall show in this chapter. However, the predilection by leaders to focus so much attention to measurement has somewhat stymied attempts to gain global consistency in how we understand the term Balanced Scorecard.

> ... so much attention to measurement has somewhat stymied attempts to gain global consistency in how we understand the term Balanced Scorecard.

At the outset of this chapter we will repeat a central message of this book that we made in Chapter 1. The Balanced Scorecard system is not a measurement system. It is a strategic management system of which strategic measurement is but one component and which, crucially, plays a supporting role to strategic objectives. So measures exist purely to monitor progress toward the implementation of strategy, as described through a Strategy Map (see Chapter 6).

Within this chapter we will place the contextual role of measurement within a Balanced Scorecard Management System, and indeed within a Balanced Scorecard itself – by which we mean the accompanying Balanced Scorecard of strategic measures, targets, and initiatives that support the Strategy Map.

However, typically, the accompanying Balanced Scorecard will also list the strategic objectives the scorecard components support. Exhibit 1.8 shows the shell Balanced Scorecard for the customer perspective of our case study company Tata Motors Commercial Vehicle

Business Unit (see Chapter 1). As we can see this Balanced Scorecard also includes other key performance information, such as on measure owners, actual versus target performance, and frequency of updates, again not uncommon on a scorecard.

To be honest, we do find that the multifarious use of the term Balanced Scorecard does cause confusion. Does a Balanced Scorecard denote the complete management system, or just a set of measures, targets and initiatives? Is it a visual collocation of objectives with measures and so on, but without the Strategy Map? Further clarification of terminology will, we think, be useful as scorecard proponents further evolve the Balanced Scorecard concept and language.

In this chapter we will focus on the Balanced Scorecard measures, targets, and initiatives that accompany a Strategy Map. We will not overtly discuss objectives as we did this in the previous chapter.

When these strategic objectives are articulated, the next step is to identify measures, and the targets for the measures, and finally the initiatives that are required to drive performance toward the targets.

At the enterprise-level, and this chapter is about creating an enterprise-level Balanced Scorecard, this scorecard creation process typically takes place during the same workshop series that begins with the selection of objectives. As examples from our case study organizations, this was true for the Gold Coin Group (see Chapter 5) and Summarecon Agung (see Chapter 4). But even when a different process was used, each of our case studies began by identifying strategic objectives.

SELECTING STRATEGIC MEASURES

We will now describe the process for selecting strategic measures. A first key consideration is the number of measures to choose. Of course, this is largely dependent on the number of strategic objectives that have previously been identified. In Chapter 6 we asserted that ideally the number of objectives should be limited to the critical few, those that are critical for delivering the strategy. This holds true for strategic metrics, these too should be the critical few for assessing progress toward the objective. About two measures for each objective will typically suffice, although there will always be variations depending on individual corporate requirements, but note the advice of Louis

Schwendener, formerly Director and Group CEO of the Gold Coin Group: "If we were to start over again, we would probably choose fewer measures, and ensure a greater focus on the most important ones."

> **" If a scorecard has too many measures, managers can become obsessed with measurement. "**

Andrew Lim, Director of the Singapore-based consultancy Balanced Scorecard Solutions puts it nicely: "If a scorecard has too many measures, managers can become obsessed with measurement." According to our survey of scorecard adoption in South-east Asia (see the Appendix) the reported number of key performance indicators ranged from less that 10 to 80.

Case study examples

Let's consider metric numbers from some of our other case study examples. At XYZ Cellular (see Chapter 6), 21 strategic objectives are supported by 50 strategic measures. At Saatchi & Saatchi Worldwide (see Chapter 11), 12 strategic objectives are supported by 26 strategic measures: four financial measures for four objectives; four client measures for one objective; 12 product and process measures for six objectives; and six people and culture measures for one objective.

Note that Saatchi & Saatchi has more measures, and more objectives, in the process perspective than any other. This is typical as the process perspective is where the real work is done to convert the knowledge and skills developed within the learning and growth perspective to deliver value to the customer.

Lead and lag

As well as the number of measures, organizations should be careful to ensure a balance of lagging and leading metrics, as this is central to creating a "balanced" scorecard and to driving causality into the scorecard system.

To explain, a lagging measure tells you what has already happened. As a simple example profit is a measure of past performance, it does not provide information on what will happen in the future. A leading measure provides information on what is happening today that will impact on performance tomorrow. For example, for an organization competing on product leadership the new product pipeline provides a powerful indication of future sales potential.

> *... organizations should be careful to ensure a balance of lagging and leading metrics, as this is central to creating a "balanced" scorecard and to driving causality into the scorecard system.*

To fully understand leading and lagging measures in the scorecard model, there are times when a metric is both leading and lagging. For instance, customer satisfaction is a lagging measure as it tells an organization how satisfied a customer was with services/products already received. However, it is also a leading measure as it provides an early warning signal regarding likely future levels of customer loyalty and profitability.

Singapore Prison Service Case Example

Singapore Prison Service (see Chapter 2) recognizes the importance of leading performance indicators. Its decision to opt for a scorecard approach was partly driven by its potential for shaping a leading/lagging balance, as Titus Kong Ling Chieh, the Service's Head of Research and Planning explains:

> ... we were working with a set of key performance indicators (KPIs) and were creating output plans and performance targets. However, these KPIs, plans, and targets were not reflective of our new strategies. The KPIs, for example, were basically lagging indicators and provided little in the way of a forward steer.

Using its strategy "prevent offending and re-offending," which has its own dedicated scorecard as an example, Kong Ling Chieh says:

We could easily set a measure of how many offenders re-offend withi a two-year period. However, this may not be all that useful as it's a lagging measure and doesn't help stop re-offending ... So we are working to develop a measurement system that is more forward-looking than lagging. We want to measure on an ongoing basis how released prisoners are successfully being reintegrated into society.

To do this the Prison Service is looking to assign a potential rating to prisoners on incarceration and on release, and to assess that over a period of time. They will look at things like the offenders' relationships with their families, their work profile, and their personal attitude to change. Kong Ling Chieh states:

So we're developing an index for this that is a more dynamic indicator than just measuring things two years after the fact. It will enable corrective interventions when problems are predicted. ... Two years ago when we talked about KPIs people would say what are KPIs? Two years ago, when we talked about lead indicators, people wouldn't know what we were talking about. We didn't have a language around performance drivers or outcome measures. Today, through the Balanced Scorecard, we have a common language which is creating a performance culture internally and a language that makes sense to all our constituent groups.

As a slightly varied take on the leading/lagging balance, at Saatchi & Saatchi where there are subjective measures, they try and include at least one substantive measure to support it (for example, Client Satisfaction rating, supported by a Brand Sales Growth measure).

MEASUREMENT MEANING

Yet another measurement requirement, and something of a challenge, is that of gaining consensus on what a measure means. This is not typically the case with financial metrics as we have 500 years' experience of working with these measures and reaching accepted agreement around meaning (although how we arrive at a metric score has many variations, as the recent accounting scandals showed).

Regarding non-financial measures there can be variances in meaning within individual organizations, as well as across organizations and industries. For example, a large trucking organization may have many definitions of what it means by on-time delivery. As a consequence, reported performance from one part of the organization cannot accurately be compared with another. One unit may claim 95% on-time delivery according to their definition, while another part scores 85%, according to their interpretation. But from the customer's perspective the latter may be more "on-time" than the former.

Therefore, organizations need specific, documented, and published definitions for measures so that people in the organization can calculate data in the same way. This will mean that accurate comparisons can be made and Balanced Scorecard reports can be truly meaningful and useful.

> " ... organizations need specific, documented, and published definitions for measures so that people in the organization can calculate data in the same way. "

As a case study example, MTR Corporation (see below) has a strategic measure of a "training hours ratio." This is defined as "technical training hours/working hours of OD direct staff X 100%." In short, given that specificity of objectives and measures is critical to succeeding with the Balanced Scorecard, organizations should afford the same rigor to metric formulas.

ACCESSING DATA

A further consideration with metrics is that it may prove difficult at the beginning of a scorecard effort to access the data for preferred non-financial measures – the data may simply not exist or be stored in various information systems.

Centrepoint Properties (see Chapter 9) is, for example, still grappling with the challenge of how best to capture the most meaningful non-financial metrics, as they find that the best metrics are often difficult to measure while easy-to-find metrics are not necessarily good measures. Furthermore, a senior executive of a larger financial services organization comments:

An excellent performance measure may be identified, but it may cost millions of dollars and take years to create and implement. Therefore, the challenge here becomes how to take that "perfect" measure and from it create a measure that is both useful to the business and cost-effective to implement.

Nigel Penny, of the consultancy ClaritasAsia, makes the following observations:

The availability of data needed to populate the scorecard is also a problem. It's incredible to me that after the billions of dollars of investment in IT over the years, that many companies still don't have simple information on, for example, profitability by customer. This isn't a defect in the Balanced Scorecard – more an issue on our data systems. The Balanced Scorecard can often make these issues very visible and I'm surprised that organizations don't make more use of the Balanced Scorecard to highlight information deficiencies and put plans in place to correct the situation.

Proxy measures

Sometimes proxy, or substitute, measures may be required. As a simple example, absenteeism is sometimes used as a proxy in the absence of a staff satisfaction metric. We should also state that absenteeism could also be a leading indicator of staff satisfaction. Scorecard experts often remark that at the beginning of a score-carding effort only about 50% of preferred metrics are available. Schwendener recalls that at the time of commencing the scorecard journey within Gold Coin that only about 30% of what was really driving corporate performance was being systematically measured.

> " ... bear in mind that people at all levels, including the most senior, can be afraid of measurement. "

There are problems with proxies, as Penny observes:

There are many "soft" areas that are difficult and maybe impossible to measure. Learning and growth is often a real problem here. ... This often results in somewhat fatuous measures being developed just to satisfy the need for a measure in each area. Its fine to say that if you "can't measure it, you can't manage it," but if the reality is that we look at "training hours" as a proxy for becoming a "knowledge-based organization," then the tenuous nature of the link all but nullifies the value of the measure.

I have seen many very "unbalanced scorecards" where some measures are clearly critical components of long-term business success, while others are almost meaningless."

MEASURE OWNERS

It is also important to identify measure-owners, just as it is to identify owners of objectives. This is a typical part of how the score-carding process drives performance accountability deep inside the organization. On the Tata Motors Balanced Scorecard, for example (see Exhibit 7.1), the name of the measure-owner appears alongside the performance metrics.

Although such assigned accountability is important, bear in mind that people at all levels, including the most senior, can be afraid of measurement. Professor Andy Neely, a noted performance measurement expert at the UK's prestigious Cranfield School of Management, said to one of the authors for a previous work:[1]

> **Scorecard experts often remark that at the beginning of a score-carding effort only about 50% of preferred metrics are available.**

Measurement is incredibly political in most organizations. Furthermore, people have a natural fear of measurement, as they are afraid it will expose their weaknesses and shortcomings. People in positions of influence in organizations have succeeded against a certain set of measures and the measures effectively define the rules of the game in the organization.

> People in positions of power understand the rules of the game well, so if you come along and say "we're going to change the rules of the game," they may resist if they fear they can't succeed under the new set.

As a consequence, he says, there can be a tendency for managers to push for metrics with which they feel comfortable and are sure they can work with.

STRATEGIC TARGETS

If managers can't get the metrics they want, they may still push for targets that are easier to achieve. This brings us to an examination of choosing strategic targets, which is the next step in the scorecard design process.

Simply put, a performance target is where you want to get to in the implementation of strategic objectives. Interestingly, Kwok Yiu Leung, Safety & Quality Manager at MTR Corporation, says that although there was some resistance around a willingness to change and to agree on required leading and lagging indicators, the biggest challenge is around setting stretch targets. He states that key to getting stretch targets is to get people to understand that the scorecard is about continuous performance improvement, and not a system for punishing people for poor performance. This, we would contend, is equally true of the whole measurement process.

> **... the scorecard itself is a powerful medium for putting meaning around performance targets.**

Before discussing targets as a specific component of the Balanced Scorecard system it is worth stating that the scorecard itself is a powerful medium for putting meaning around performance targets. To explain, all organizations set targets – most commonly, of course, financial targets. The scorecard explains how these targets will be met, what has to be done where, and by whom.

Moreover when targets are not met, the scorecard can show what went wrong and why. Pak Krisbiyanto, formerly Vice-President, Human Capital at our case study organization, Bank Universal (see Chapter 10), comments: "Previously, we would blame each other, but through the scorecard we could see the actual causes of problems that led to targets being missed, and so knew where to direct our efforts."

Stretch targets

We would maintain that targets within a Balanced Scorecard should be stretching. The target should take the organization to a performance level that is markedly better than present level. So baseline, present, and target performance should be evident in the scorecard-tracking process.

Now, setting stretch targets should take into account the performance of competitors and increasingly relevant best practice standards from outside the organizations' own industry or sector. Tata Motors, for example, has introduced comparative data and benchmarks as a basis for selecting targets.

> ... just as there's a danger that those who resist measurement may push for easy targets there are other who may, in a rush of -blood for the scorecard, set targets that are too stretching in the allotted time-scale.

Targets should be time-bound. For example, rather than articulate a target of "90% customer satisfaction," say "90% customer satisfaction by end of quarter 3."

As a caveat to the above, targets should also be achievable. There is little to gain from setting targets that are way out of reach and which may take many years to build the requisite strategic capabilities to meet. Centrepoint Properties Carol Yong Meng Dai says that the CEO will challenge managers if he thinks that targets are too low, or alternatively if he thinks the targets represent too much of a stretch.

Simply put, just as there's a danger that those who resist measurement may push for easy targets there are others who may, in

> " ... it is within the strategic initiatives component where the real work of the Balanced Scorecard takes place. "

a rush of -blood for the scorecard, set targets that are too stretching in the allotted time-scale.

Although we would counsel organizations to set stretching targets for all metrics, we would suggest that the level of stretch varies, depending on where strategic performance is the weakest or where there is a present need to substantially drive up performance. This is because moving from the present performance level to a substantial higher performance level typically requires the launch of strategic initiatives and the allocation of additional financial and human resources.

In their book Strategy Maps, Professor Kaplan and Dr Norton write:

> The strategy map describes the logic of the strategy, showing clearly the set of critical processes that create value as well as the intangible assets required to support them. The Balanced Scorecard identifies measures and targets for each objective in the strategy map. But objectives and targets are not achieved simply because they have been identified. For each measure, managers must identify the strategic initiatives needed to achieve the target. And they must supply the resources – people, funding, and capacity – required to successfully complete each initiative. ... The initiatives create the results; they are the basis for successful strategy execution.[2]"

The final line is important, for it is within the strategic initiatives component where the real work of the Balanced Scorecard takes place. And this takes us into an exploration of selecting strategic initiatives, the next step in creating a Balanced Scorecard.

STRATEGIC INITIATIVES

Successful initiatives enable targets to be hit and for objectives to be implemented. At XYZ Cellular, for example, targets for each measure are achieved through time-bound initiatives. No initiative is launched or funded unless it clearly maps to one of the strategic measures/objectives.

As an example of how initiatives track through to objectives, an XYZ Cellular strategic objective from the "customer" perspective was articulated as "offer value for money, innovative, value-added services, reward loyalty." One of several measures for this objective was "growth in revenue per user from value-added services." This measure had a supporting target of a 10% monthly growth. A time-bound initiative to achieve the target was launched, comprising a project leader from sales and a dedicated support team, working to set milestones and utilizing proven project management templates (a sample template is shown in Exhibit 1.9).

According to Tata Motors' KC Girotra says:

> ... initiatives are chosen to close the gaps between the actual and the intended levels of performance required to accomplish our strategic objectives. These are also prioritized based on a matrix of business impact versus time to results. Initiatives are reviewed during our monthly steering committee meetings at all levels.

He adds that a template which is used for describing initiatives and their impact forces initiative owners to address financial and human resource requirements and necessitates that they fully think through and articulate how their proposed initiative would positively impact high-level strategic objectives. As a consequence, Girotra points out that many initiatives that may have historically been green-lighted no longer receive funding.

The Tatar Motors approach also forces initiative prioritization. And a robust approach to prioritization is critical, given resource allocation consideration. A valuable approach from a non-Asian organization comes from the Department of Revenue, State of Washington, United States. This approach was detailed in the report "The Balanced Scorecard: A HR Perspective," written by one of this books authors.[3]

The Department has a three-tiered hierarchical system for initiative prioritization, and therefore for resource allocation to initiatives. These three tiers are:

- Tier 1: Essential – initiatives with the Department's highest level of commitment, which are certain of funding.
- Tier 2: Important – those that are very important, but must be considered against others if funds are limited.
- Tier 3: Beneficial – initiatives that are only pursued if they do not infringe upon higher level priorities.

Initiative identification begins with brainstorming in each division after which an executive coordinating team, comprised of divisional heads, selects initiative candidates. Team members individually sort these candidates into the three-tier order with the final priorities being agreed to by consensus within the group, rather than by any numerical ranking.

As a result, the Department has created a common understanding with upper management on resource priorities. If budgets need to be scaled back during the year for any reason, it is clear which initiatives will be affected. As a further example, consider this approach at the Royal Canadian Mounted Police, which has developed an approach called initiative-funneling.[4]

First, criteria were set for a "qualified" strategic initiative – as a result, non-strategic initiatives were immediately "binned." Next, all "qualified" initiatives were mapped against strategic objectives and ranked in priority. Those with the lowest priority would have no real chance of securing scarce human and financial resources.

Higher ranking initiatives, but with a need for a stronger business case, were deferred, while the highest ranking initiatives were prioritized and rationalized. The output was a robust process for ensuring that strategically aligned initiatives would have first call on resources.

In their book Strategy Maps, Norton and Kaplan write:[5]

Integrating the strategy map's measures, targets and initiatives provides a complete description of how value is created – that is, a complete description of the organization's strategy and its successful execution."

In this and the previous chapter we have explored how to create an enterprise-level Strategy Map and accompanying Balanced Scorecard of measures, targets, and initiatives. In the next two chapters we will explain how to devolve the map and scorecard deep inside the organizations – the logistical and cultural challenges of organization-wide implementation.

MTR Corporation

Summary

MTR Corporation has created a Balanced Scorecard that integrates into a wider management system. With five perspectives rather than the conventional four, the Balanced Scorecard has helped MTR Corporation to achieve impressive financial and non-financial results.

Background

MTR Corporation was established in 1975 as a Hong Kong government-owned corporation with the principal business of operating a mass transit railway system. When privatized in 2000 its shares were traded on the Hong Kong Stock Exchange. With almost 7,000 employees, MTR currently operates a railway network of 87.7 kilometers with 49 stations. With a daily patronage of over 2.3 million passengers, the railway system is one of the most intensively utilized in the world.

Besides railway operations, the corporation is also actively involved in the development of key residential and commercial projects above existing stations and along new line extensions, as well as many other commercial activities associated with the railway. These include the rental of retail and poster advertising spaces, ATM banking facilities, and personal telecommunication services. MTR also provides consultancy services to organizations worldwide.

Vision and Mission Statements

The MTR Corporation's vision is to be "a fast-track to Hong Kong people," which is essentially about creating a service that makes the lives of Hong Kong residents faster and easier. This vision is supported by a key mission, which is: "To develop and manage a world-class railway, together with property and other related businesses, and to enhance the quality of life in Hong Kong." This, in turn, is supported by a dedicated mission for the Railway Business (its core business and where the scorecard has been deployed), which is:

To plan and deliver a safe, reliable, efficient and profitable Railway Business to Hong Kong community and derive maximum value from all railway assets, through values and policies that provide highly competent and motivated staff.

This railway business mission clearly speaks to performance that is typically captured within a Balanced Scorecard – Hong Kong community (customers), value from assets (shareholders), and competent and motivated staff (employees).

Scorecard Results

First successfully piloted within the Engineering Department from 1997, the Balanced Scorecard was implemented within the corporation's railway business in 1999. So far the results have impressive. A snapshot of examples include:

- In 1999, value-added per staff stood at just over HK$95. In 2002 it had climbed to just over $110. The operating profit generated per staff rose from just under $700,000 to just under $900,000.
- In the same 1999–2002 timeframe, safety improvements (a key scorecard focus) were also evident. As just two examples the number of serious injuries per 1,000 million passengers fell from about 0.9 to 0.6, and lost-time injury per 200,000 man-hours worked fell from 1.2 to just under 0.6.
- In 1999, operating costs per car kilometer was just under $30. In 2002 it had fell to about $23. Note, too, that in 2002 the railway business reported an operating profit margin (measured by earning before interest, tax, depreciation, and amortization) of 51% on fare revenues of $5,720 million.

These results clearly show that safety enhancements and financial success are not mutually exclusive.

Success and the Scorecard

Kwok Yiu Leung, MTR Corporation's Safety & Quality Manager, is certain that these achievements are in no small part the result of a successful implementation of the Balanced Scorecard. He says:

Consider safety, one of our scorecard perspectives. Managing with the Balanced Scorecard has provided a focus that has helped us to successfully enhance safety awareness throughout the corporation, with all staff now being competent in improving passenger safety. There is a clear line between competent staff and safety on our scorecard.

Leung adds that the scorecard has also enhanced the customer service culture within MTR. By, for example, monitoring and communicating organization-wide customer complaints the corporation has been able to raise staff awareness of what needs to be done to improve customer-facing performance.

He states:

The resources for internal processes are now better planned and implemented. And managers are encouraged to revisit their process on an ongoing basis to look for improvement opportunities based on reported measures. This has been aided by the fact that managers are, through the scorecard, clearly held accountable for performance. For example, as a result of clear accountabilities after the introduction of respective measures, preventative maintenance tends to be completed on schedule.

Leung also adds that as for efficiency, another of its perspectives, MTR's commitment to staff development is much better demonstrated as it has ensured a minimum level of staff training to meet business growth requirements.

Kwok Yiu Leung states that collectively these improvements, and others that have sprung from scorecard usage, have enabled the corporation to meet its strategy of reducing costs by 2% annually – while simultaneously improving its safety record and customer service performance.

As a powerful example of using the scorecard to improve performance, in 2002 the senior management team became worried that reliability performance was dipping, as shown on the scorecard. As a consequence, the operations manager led a work group in the identification of improvement opportunities. This led to the launching of an organization-wide program called "every minute counts" that gathered employee ideas on how to improve reliability. This became a strategic initiative to support the "reliability" objective on the Strategy Map. Importantly, people could see how the collection and implementation of improvement ideas eventually positively impacted performance on the Strategy Map.

Strategy Map

The Strategy Map for the Railway Business is shown in Exhibit 7.1. With both growth and productivity themes, the map comprises the four perspectives of financial, customer, process and efficiency (essentially learning and growth) but also a 'fifth' perspective of safety, which sits alongside both process and customer. Leung stresses that for a railway business, safety is fundamental to sustainable success and must be viewed from both internal process and customer perspectives.

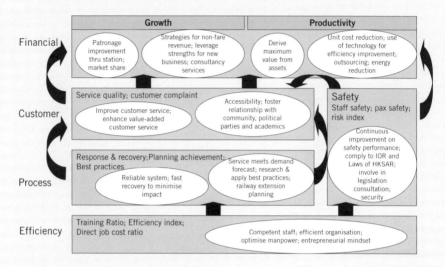

Exhibit 7.1 Railway business strategy map

Examples of strategic measures, with articulated measure purpose and formula are shown in Exhibit 7.2. These form the process and efficiency perspectives.

Strategic Goal		Measures	Purpose	Formula
Process	P1	% coverage of scheduled PM	To monitor the completion of planned PM jobs	No. of completed PM job / no. of planned PM job
	P2	Response to failure	To monitor the number of primary recovery meeting the defined targets stated in customer service standards	% of primary recovery meeting the System Performance Standards relating those train services
	P3	Capital Works Achievement against budget plan	To monitor the progress of capital works using cash flow as the approximation	Actual capital works expenses / total Capital Works budgeted for the year less contingency
Efficiency	E1	Staff efficiency index (Car-km per staff and contractor hours comparing with same month last year's)	To indicate productivity improvement of OD staff	(Revenue car km / staff & contractor hours – operations) of current month compared with (Revenue car km / staff & contractor hours – operations) of same month of **previous year**
	E2	Passenger carried per OD staff	To measure staff efficiency	No. of passengers / No. of OD staff
	E3	Training hours ratio	To measure the level of training	(Technical training hours / working hours of OD direct staff) x 100%
	E4	Direct job cost per total job cost (to be reported quarterly)	To monitor the level of direct job cost	Direct job cost per total staff cost, as defined in ABC

Exhibit 7.2 Matrix of strategies and BSC measures

An Integrated Management System

To fully comprehend the usage of the scorecard within MTR it has to be contextualized within a wider integrated management system. Kwok Yiu Leung recalls that this integration has been evident since the scorecard was first implemented. "At the time of creating the scorecard we already had in place an integrated management system and a process for strategic planning and deployment, which the scorecard slotted into."

To an extent this is not surprising, MTR has since its birth been committed to the principles of total quality management (TQM) and had fully integrated TQM approaches at each level of the corporation. As part of it's quality commitment, MTR adopted the Malcolm Baldrige framework (a US-launched quality management model comprising self-assessment and performance improvement categories such as strategic planning, customer and market focus, and process management).

For Kwok Yio Leung, "The Baldrige model helps us to identify the vital few things to monitor within the Balanced Scorecard."

Exhibit 7.3 shows how the Balanced Scorecard, which is essentially used to monitor progress against strategic goals, fits within a wider, and integrated, leadership and management framework.

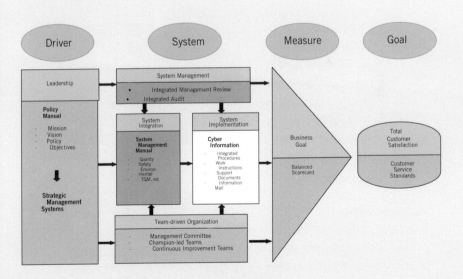

Exhibit 7.3 Leadership and management framework

Continuing with integration, Kwok Yiu Leung explains how the scorecard dovetails with the strategic and financial planning processes: *We hold a strategy planning workshop each year to facilitate senior managers and department heads in the brainstorming of strategies and initiatives for the following year. This is largely based on review of the previous year's scorecard performance. ... The strategic objectives deployed from the strategic plan will be the business line items for budgeting and eventually form part of the scorecard measures.*

On an ongoing basis MTR also used activity-based costing (ABC) to analyze cost drivers. Simply put, ABC looks at how resource costs like salaries, utilities, and rental are consumed by work activities, which are components of various processes in an organization. The activities and processes are in turn consumed by the output of the organization. ABC supports the Balanced Scorecard report in terms of cost data and performance results. It should be noted that the ABC methodology was co-created by Professor Robert Kaplan, along with Dr Robin Cooper.

As part of overall planning and implementation, MTR's scorecard helps drive the following foci and outcomes:

- clarifying and gaining consensus about MTR strategies so that managers are committed to implement vision
- linking the strings of the corporate vision to the strategic objectives and KPIs
- ensuring that key aspects of performance were visible and communicated.
- ensuring that strategies and everyday performance were linked
- evaluating business performance
- evaluating the effectiveness of action taken
- fulfilling reporting requirements
- gauging performance improvement.

Scorecard buy-in

Given that robust performance measurement systems were, thanks to the quality effort, already extant within MTR, building the original Balanced Scorecard was relatively cost-free. It was more, as Kwok Yiu Leung recalls, a case of re-mapping and reorganizing measures around different perspectives. The simplicity and minimal cost implications went some way to easing buy-in among the management population.

Securing buy-in also required a focused communication effort to sell the scorecard benefits to management teams, not least around how it built on the existing performance management systems.

That the operations director championed the scorecard at executive board level undoubtedly increased the prospect of buy-in. He is responsible for the whole railways operation, including the work of safety and quality, which is headed by Kwok Yiu Leung.

Safety and quality

The safety and quality department would support the operations director in fashioning the scorecard framework and implementation process, which would be further debated and agreed by the executive team. The safety and quality team would also take charge of the scorecard devolution process, because they best understood organization-wide processes and systems. The team has facilitated a process that has taken the high-level scorecard down through divisional and departmental levels.

Felix Kwok Wah Ng, the Standards and Performance Manager (a direct report of Kwok Yiu Leung), essentially leads the cascade process and has ongoing responsibility for the development and implementation of the Balanced Scorecard. With about 30% of his time focused squarely on the scorecard, Ng, who is supported by two assistants, meets with the department heads. Based on the divisional scorecard, he works out with them what they have to do to contribute to the divisional objectives and targets.

Ng's duties also include compiling scorecard reports for the monthly operations performance meeting, which is chaired by the operations director.

Automation

Reporting is simplified through automation, with MTR opting for a software solution from scorecard vendor SAS®. This shows objectives, measures, and targets, and provides monthly trend data. It also enables a commentary on performance to the measure. A key reason for opting for automation was the difficulties in disseminating information across the enterprise, while the data were still fresh and useful, leading to delays in responding to improvement opportunities.

The automated scorecard is now accessible over a corporate intranet by managers from their desktops, thus expediting the decision-making process. Results are also accessible by front-line staff, who also receive paper-based monthly updates. Kwok Yiu Leung stresses that for the scorecard to be effective, performance must be communicated to the deepest levels of the corporation:

It's critical to spend time communicating vision, mission, measures, and targets so that everyone understands what the leadership wants to achieve and therefore can align their performance accordingly.

Challenges

Although clearly successful, there have been challenges in the deployment of the Balanced Scorecard. Kwok Yiu Leung says that there was some resistance around a willingness to change and to agree on required leading and lagging indicators to use. But he adds that perhaps the biggest challenge is around setting stretch targets:

Within the Balanced Scorecard we have five-year strategic targets, and it can be difficult to get people to set targets that will stretch them throughout this timeframe. The most challenging part of Felix Ng's job is to convince some managers of the need to set stretch targets.

Kwok Yiu Leung stresses that the key to getting stretch targets is to get people to understand that the scorecard is about continuous performance improvement, and not a system for punishing people for poor performance.

▶▶ Conclusion

In conclusion, Kwok Yiu Leung suggests the following as critical factors for succeeding with the Balanced Scorecard:

- management commitment – from the CEO and the rest of the senior management team
- selecting the vital few strategic measures
- choosing simple measures that are easily understood and interpreted, but that are also the right measures
- making sure targets are realistic and achievable, as well as challenging
- communicating – both targets and results
- measures for improvement and motivation, and not punishment
- performance measures are balanced, or dysfunctional behaviors will result
- the scorecard is a tool for communicating, informing, and learning, not controlling.

1   Creelman, J. 2003, *Building a Strategic Balanced Scorecard*, Business Intelligence, London.

2   Norton, D.P. and Kaplan, R.S. 2004, *Strategy Maps: Converting Intangible Assets into Tangible Outcomes*, Harvard Business Press, Boston, MA.

3   Creelman, J. 2002, *Understanding The Balanced Scorecard: An HR Perspective* HR.Com, Aurora, Ontario, Canada.

4   See end note 1.

5   See end note 2.

8

Scorecard Devolution: The structural challenge

*T*he process of creating devolved and aligned Strategy Maps and Balanced Scorecards makes real the promise to "make strategy everyone's, everyday job." Ensuring alignment requires that devolved scorecards support higher level scorecards and capture local strategic and performance needs. Involving lower level employees in designing their own scorecards is crucial for securing buy-in. Functional scorecards are typically created as part of a cascade process. It is possible to create functional scorecards in the absence of an enterprise-level scorecard. But to do this, functional leaders must ensure that they understand the strategic requirements of the organization and create scorecards to deliver to those requirements. If scorecards are to be created throughout the organization, then senior management must be cognizant of the practical challenges of managing such a large-scale program. Piloting the scorecard prior to organization-wide rollout is typically an advisable step. It helps in proof of concept, and in identifying and overcoming common structural and cultural implementation challenges. The creation of scorecards for individual employees (personal scorecards) represents the final step in scorecard devolution. (However, such scorecards are relatively rare.) An example of scorecard use is provided in the case study on CSC Consultants, which concludes this chapter.

BACKGROUND

A key promise of the Balanced Scorecard Management System is that it can "make strategy everyone's everyday job" – principle three of the five principles of Kaplan and Norton's strategy-focused organization.[1] Achieving this requires the whole organization to be structurally and culturally hardwired to the enterprise-level Strategy Map and Balanced Scorecard, and this is the focus of the next two chapters. In Chapter 9 we consider the cultural challenges of scorecard devolution, which as we shall show are not inconsiderable and must not be treated lightly in a scorecard cascade. Within this chapter we will explore the more structural aspects of devolution; namely, the creation of devolved scorecards that are aligned to the highest level Strategy Map and Balanced Scorecard, how this looks schematically can be seen in Exhibit 8.1

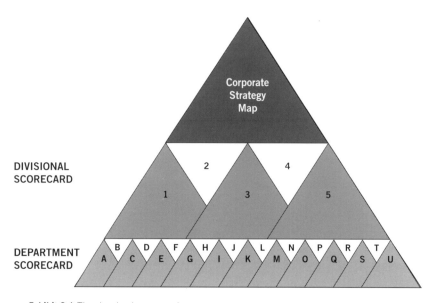

Exhibit 8.1 The devolved scorecard

CASE STUDY EXPERIENCES

The creation of devolved scorecards is common within our case study companies. For example, Saatchi & Saatchi (see Chapter 11) built scorecards for each of its 45+ business units throughout the world. Subordinate Courts, Singapore (see Chapter 3), has scorecards within each of its five divisions. In both cases the Strategy Maps are based on the enterprise-level map. However, the devolved maps are tailored to ensure that they capture the local strategic and performance requirements. And this is a critical success factor in a scorecard cascades – it is important to keep the scorecard aligned to the higher level scorecard, but appropriate and therefore meaningful at the lower level.

As Matthew Tice, Vice-President Asia-Pacific for the Balanced Scorecard Collaborative (BSCol) rightly observes:

> Successful alignment really comes down to lower level managers asking what are the things on the corporate scorecard that we really connect to, that we have a strong primary linkage to. The next question is to what extent do we not contribute to specific objectives. Obviously there needs to be an up-down review to make sure there's a solid reason for that. And [managers] need to ask what is it that's unique about the business unit that has to be articulated in their own Strategy map. It depends on the role of the group entity as to how this happens. A holding company structure, and [its] requirements, will be significantly different from a more integrated organization.

TELECOMMUNICATIONS EXAMPLE

A couple of years ago one of the authors of this book observed a simple, yet effective process for scorecard devolution and alignment within the UK-headquartered global Telecommunications organization.

The first scorecard was created at the corporate executive board level. It comprised the CEO, CFO, and divisional heads. The divisional heads then communicated the reasoning behind the objective/measure choices when working with business unit heads to create divisional scorecards.

> " Successful alignment really comes down to lower level managers asking what are the things on the corporate scorecard that we really connect to, that we have a strong primary linkage to. "

The business unit heads, in turn, then worked with their management teams to create business unit scorecards. The business unit managers communicated the scorecard objectives and measures to their own direct reports, who then communicated it to the teams and employee base.

The result – a direct connection in the process of creating and communicating scorecards throughout the organization. Everyone in the organization could see how their own outputs directly supported business unit, divisional, and corporate goals.

According to our survey of scorecard adoption in South-east Asia (see Appendix 1), 44% of scorecard users have devolved the scorecard to a functional level, 46% to a team level, and 21% to an individual employee level. A full 98% found the scorecard at least moderately effective at the functional level. There was a more mixed response at team level, where 16% found it ineffective or totally ineffective, with the rest rating performance as moderately effective or above. As for individual scorecards, although no company provided a totally ineffective score, there was an equal 25% split for ineffective, moderately effective, effective, and extremely effective.

As we can see from Exhibit 8.2, most organizations took between one and three years to devolve their Balanced Scorecard system.

Less than one year	31%
One to three years	65%
More than three years, but less than five years	4%

Exhibit 8.2 How long it took survey respondents to roll out the Balanced Scorecard System

CASE STUDY DEVOLUTION EXAMPLES

Let's look at the cascade process within some of our case study companies. Within Bank Universal (see Chapter 10) the Branch Network Scorecard was created with full participation of all managers, at both senior and branch level. The senior managers considered the wider Bank Universal vision and strategy, and decided how they could best deliver to that strategy. This scorecard was then devolved to branch level.

Mahdi Syahbuddin, who was then Bank Universal's Deputy President Director, stresses that although it is fundamentally important to involve senior management in designing the scorecard, for a successful devolution it is equally essential to involve branch management. He says that this is particularly important for the identification of branch-level metrics:

> To find the right indicators you have to involve branch managers because they are the people who really understand what makes their branches perform. If they're not involved then any performance indicators forced onto them stand a good chance of being resisted and indeed being inappropriate.

So in workshop settings, branch managers identified the key indicators that would show branch performance and how the branches were working toward corporate strategic goals.

Tata Motors Commercial Vehicle Business Unit (see Chapter 1) has created more than 300 scorecards organization-wide, covering all functions, departments, manufacturing centres of Excellence, and area offices (deepest work units within the Sales and Marketing organization).

How this works in practice is that the CVBU-level Balanced Scorecard defines the overall goals and timeframes to be achieved by the organization. These goals and targets are then cascaded into Balanced Scorecards for each division/function. Hence, each scorecard is linked to its higher level scorecard through the strategic objectives. In addition, each division/function also defines its own initiatives to help achieve its local strategic objectives.

To start the cascade process, senior executives attended a workshop delivered by Dr Norton. As a result they better understood the concept of systematic evolution of the scorecard, and the need for a strong review process to support its deployment at all levels. The cascade process also involved local Business Excellence Service Team members running strategy workshops within plants and functions. Furthermore, Business Excellence Service Team members collaborated with both the CVBU Steering Committee members and managers at lower levels to help evolve the scorecard at these levels, and set in place a review process for monitoring and analyzing performance on their local Balanced Scorecard.

Within Subordinate Courts, Singapore, the top-level scorecard serves as the focus for strategic efforts; however, the cascade process did see some tailoring in order that local objectives, measures, and targets were captured. This required the Scorecard facilitation team to work closely with unit managers to create scorecards that were operationally valuable at the local level, while maintaining the corporate focus.

At Singapore's Civil Service College (see below) the Civil Service College Consultants Business Unit created their own Strategy Map and Balanced Scorecard that reflected the corporate strategic needs and activities. Note too that the business unit created its own Strategy Map, which was not in place at the corporate level.

What we can see from these examples is a purposeful process of creating Strategy Maps and Balanced Scorecards that are hardwired to strategic objectives, but also capture local needs. And this is absolutely important, for by involving lower level managers and staff in creating their own Strategy Maps and Balanced Scorecards, it becomes significantly more likely that lower level buy-in will be achieved

A simple imposition of scorecard objectives, measures, and targets may well be resisted, or at best commitment will be limited to merely "pleasing the boss." In saying that, there may be some objectives and measures that are mandated, depending on the strategic priorities of the organization (for example, around customer satisfaction or safety).

> "...by involving lower level managers and staff in creating their own Strategy Maps and Balanced Scorecards, it becomes significantly more likely that lower level buy-in will be achieved."

FUNCTIONAL SCORECARDS

Within a conventional scorecard cascade process, it is typical for organizations to create functional scorecards, be they for Human

Resources (HR), Finance, or Information Technology (IT), as common examples.

Tata Motors is one example of an organization that has created functional scorecards (the strategy map for its Sales and Marketing function is shown in Exhibit 1.9 in Chapter 1).

BRISBANE CITY COUNCIL HR SCORECARD EXAMPLE

As a further example, the Strategy Map for the HR function within Brisbane City Council is shown in Exhibit 8.3. Note that across the top of the map are three key objectives (such as "smart, capable and innovative solutions") that describe how the work of the HR function links to the Corporate Scorecard. Importantly, delivering to these objectives becomes the vision for the HR function. The HR function, therefore, exists to deliver excellence to the organization, which in turn exists to deliver excellence to the City.

Note too that at the base the Brisbane City Council's HR scorecard is the learning and growth perspective, which describes the skills HR itself needs to deliver the vision. So, a learning and growth objective of "HR workforce trained in innovation" directly impacts, through a causal relationship, the process perspective of "[HR] processes support innovation," through the financial objective "Brisbane City Council invests in innovation" to the customer objective "Brisbane City Council fosters innovation" to the highest level objective "smart, creative and innovative solutions."

CASCADE CAUTION

Generally, the belief of practitioners and advisors alike is that functional scorecards are required if the organization is to reap full benefits from the scorecard system. After all, a well-designed functional scorecard should enable the function to demonstrate its value to the business and to move toward

" ... organizations should beware of creating functional, or any other devolved scorecard for that matter ... simply for the sake of it. "

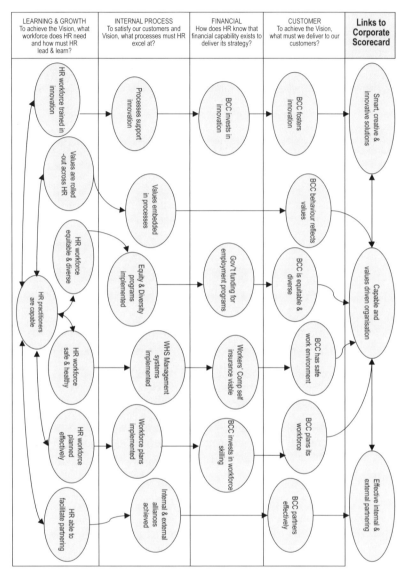

Exhibit 8.3 HR scorecard Strategy Map

the much coveted "business partner" status. However, organizations should beware of creating functional, or any other devolved scorecard for that matter (departmental and team levels, for example), simply for the sake of it.

Nigel Penny, Managing Director of the Singapore-based consultancy ClaritasAsia. comments:

I have great belief in developing scorecards down to the strategic business unit level. However, I find that functional scorecards are far less convincing in terms of benefits that are achieved. … Service and support functions clearly need aligned goals and ways to measure performance, but I have seen many examples of creating lower level scorecards and measures just for the sake of completeness rather than for any tangible benefit. Often functional scorecard creation becomes a pointless exercise in measurement for measurement sake. I believe they can add value, but often a more modified form of scorecard development is appropriate. Organizational leaders and functional heads should ask questions such as, "Are we really going to institutionalize internal customer feedback?" or "Are we going to develop service-level agreements within the organization?" For some large organizations the answer may be yes, but we must be concerned if the cost of developing and managing scorecards exceeds any potential corporate improvement in results from its usage.

As for department or team scorecards [a] similar logic applies. A scaled down form of linked measurable objectives, rather than a full-blown scorecard, is in my opinion preferable and more realistic.

The strength of Penny's argument is that it brings common sense to the scorecard cascade process. The authors have also seen many examples of organizations getting so excited by the scorecard idea that they rush out to create as may scorecards as possible, without thinking through the benefits, costs, and just as importantly whether they possess the capability to manage lots of aligned scorecards on an ongoing basis.

For example, in a fast-moving marketplace such as the computer industry, if a market shift requires significant changes to the enterprise-level Strategy Map and Balanced Scorecard, then if the

> " … we must be concerned if the cost of developing and managing scorecards exceeds any potential corporate improvement in results from its usage. "

organization had, say, 100 aligned scorecards, how quickly could these scorecards be changed? If they are not changed, then the danger is that the organization stops being strategy-focused. However, if they are changed, then there's a danger that the organization becomes focused on managing the scorecard, rather than using the scorecard with which to manage.

> " ... be clear as to the benefits of wide-scale implementation and the challenges of managing the scorecard on an ongoing basis. "

So at the outset of a cascade process, it is certainly sensible to be clear as to the benefits of widescale implementation and the challenges of managing the scorecard on an ongoing basis (see Chapter 4 for more on managing the scorecard as an ongoing competency).

STAND-ALONE FUNCTIONAL SCORECARDS

While considering functional scorecards, it is worth mentioning that it is possible to create stand-alone functional scorecards. This means that a functional scorecard is built and deployed even though an enterprise-level Strategy Map and Balanced Scorecard has not been created. Perhaps the most celebrated of all functional scorecards was the HR scorecard created within the US-headquartered telecommunications giant Verizon Communications. This has been well documented in books and also served as a best practice focus for BSCol, when it launched a research program to better align the HR organizations with the strategy of the organization.[2]

Using HR as an example, the stand-alone scorecard system creation process could follow the following six steps:

1   *Understand and internalize the strategy of the enterprise* – This is the starting point for moving forward. Without this understanding there is little point in creating the scorecard. If the functional leaders are not cognizant of, or in agreement to, the strategy of the enterprise, they must understand and internalize the strategy before proceeding.

2 *Take from the enterprise-level Strategy Map the people imperatives to deliver that strategy* – These people imperatives will serve as the steer for the subsequent scorecard creation process.

3 *HR leaders debate and agree on the HR strategic objectives that will appear on the HR Strategy Map* – The objectives will deliver to the people imperatives.

4 *The objectives are validated through conversations with business leaders and customers* – The objectives must deliver what the business needs, rather than what HR thinks the business needs, or what HR thinks it can deliver. The objective must be both business-focused, but also ensure that HR is building the internal capabilities it requires to become business-focused.

5 *HR leaders agree on the strategic measures, targets, and initiatives that will deliver to the objectives* – These too are validated with the business.

6 *The HR scorecard is communicated to the HR departments* – If required, aligned departmental scorecards are developed.

SCORECARD PILOTS

A stand-alone functional scorecard may be built and implemented as a pilot exercise, as proof of concept before rolling out organization-wide. And whether at functional, business unit, or divisional level as examples, we would certainly advise a pilot prior to full-scale implementation. It is during a pilot that a robust implementation plan can be fashioned, successes proven and communicated throughout organization, and key learnings secured, especially around cultural and structural blocks.

> **It is during a pilot that a robust implementation plan can be fashioned, successes proven and communicated throughout organization, and key learnings secured, especially around cultural and structural blocks.**

Within our survey of scorecard usage within South-east Asia (see the Appendix), about half of the scorecard users had completed a pilot prior to full roll-out and half had not.

Pilots were certainly prevalent within our case study organizations. For example, Subordinate Courts, Singapore, launched a pilot program within its Small Claims Tribunal Division in order to assess the effectiveness of the Balanced Scorecard. This division was chosen because it was self-contained and, crucially, its management team embraced change. This is a very important point. A pilot should be where successes can be easily identified and proven, and where the local management team is supportive of the concept, or at least change-embracing. Successes here will go some way to convincing skeptical managers within more resistant unit management teams. Also, pilot benefits can be extensive, as Chan Wai Yin, Director of Research and Statistics Unit at Subordinate Courts, recalls:

> The pilot program proved that the scorecard provided a clear advance over the existing performance measurement system. As the scorecard is a predictive system we were able to detect early warnings of what was going to happen and so take preventative action. The scorecard made it far easier for us to see what we were doing and how we were doing it. We also discovered that the scorecard significantly improved communications. Being a two-way system whereby employees could better report and discuss performance, we found it actually changed the whole paradigm of performance monitoring, improvement, and measurement.

As a further example, within Hong Kong's MTR Corporation (see Chapter 7) the scorecard was first successfully piloted within the engineering department before being implemented within the corporation's Railway Business.

PERSONAL SCORECARDS

A particularly challenging question in a scorecard rollout process is whether or not to create personal scorecards (that is, scorecards for each individual employee). According to Kaplan and Norton this is a crucial component of the "make strategy everyone's, everyday job" principle of the strategy-focused organization. We will look at this question in detail within the next chapter, because personal scorecards take us directly into performance appraisal and compensation systems, which are extremely cultural in nature.

For now, we will say that in an "ideal" scorecard cascade, personal scorecards serve as the final step in the process (see Exhibit 8.4) For example, we may have a series of aligned scorecards from corporate, divisional, business unit, functional, departmental, team, and individual levels – or however else the organization is structured. From our case study, companies XYZ Cellular and Summarecon (see Chapter 4) have created explicit personal scorecards, although Summarecon has so far only rolled these down to departmental managers. Even Tata Motors, which has over 300 scorecards, has not as yet created personal scorecards.

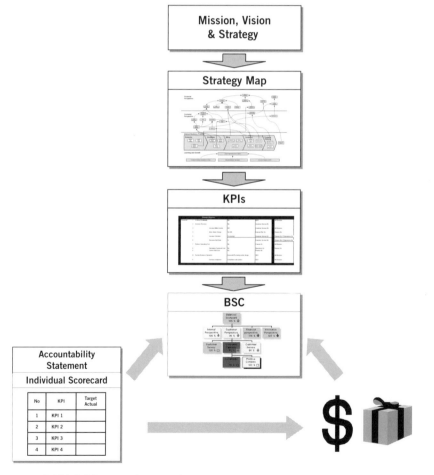

Exhibit 8.4 A personal scorecard

Personal scorecards are often avoided due to the difficulty in ensuring that they are both aligned to higher level scorecards and meaningful to the individual employee. However, there are contrary views. Chris Parsons, who was until recently Principal Consultant with the UK-based Penna Change, made this useful observation in a previous work of one of the authors of this book, a view that takes us right back to the importance of alignment in the cascade process. He said:[3]

> We have found that a key determinant of whether true alignment can be achieved is the extent to which the organization has the appropriate capability to deliver its results. It is important to put in place a system that not only helps individuals understand the targets that they need to achieve but the capability that they need to demonstrate. This we have found can be extremely rewarding for the organization and the individual.
>
> In this sense an individual is not only shown "what" they must achieve but also "how" they can achieve this. The "what" comes from the creation of an individual scorecard or the selection of key measures/targets from a team scorecard.

The "how" is provided by the identification of a set of competencies that are found to be related to the demonstration of "excellent" performance. Encouraging the individual to develop these competencies will also help to improve the organization's capability, which will over time increase their ability to achieve their strategic objectives.

> " ... in an "ideal" scorecard cascade, personal scorecards serve as the final step in the process. "

If the individual is clear on what is expected from them and what they need to achieve, they will be energized to focus on results in all quadrants of the scorecard.

The energizing process is often catalyzed by using compensation and appraisal systems to align individual performance to strategic objectives (often through a personal scorecard). The role of appraisal and compensation in the scorecard process is something we discuss in detail within the next chapter.

CASE STUDY

Civil Service College, Singapore.

Summary
When introduced at a time of dramatic change, the Balanced Scorecard has helped Civil Service College, Singapore, become a more market-oriented organization. This case study describes the development of the scorecard at the corporate level and its implementation within the Civil Service Consultants business unit.

Background
With about 165 employees, Singapore's Civil Service College (CSC) has a mission to "develop public officers for first-class Singapore public service to ensure a successful and vibrant Singapore." CSC has existed since 2001, when four previously discrete government training and development departments were brought together into a single self-financing statutory board. CSC is today organized into four strategic business units and a corporate unit. The strategic units are:
- Institute of Public Administration and Management
- Institute of Policy Development
- CSC International
- CSC Consultants.

This case study mainly traces scorecard usage within CSC Consultants, but the scorecard is being used at the corporate level. At the time of writing, CSC had not created a high-level Strategy Map. What it does have is the four quadrants of financial and strategy, customer, internal process, and people.

Adopting the Balanced Scorecard
Brigadier General (BG) Yam Ah Mee, Dean and CEO of CSC, explains how the Balanced Scorecard came to be adopted by the college.

During out transition from the departments to our present structure, we engaged an external consultant to advise on the most appropriate mechanism for articulating what CSC aims to achieve and for measuring progress toward its achievement. After a review of the options, the CSC management team agreed with the consultant's recommendation that the college should implement a Balanced Scorecard.

BG (NS) Yam was particularly keen on the scorecard as the balanced nature of the framework meant that it was possible to facilitate a mindset shift within the organization to be more outcome-, and indeed financially, driven, while still articulating a commitment to valuing and developing its people. He recalls:

We are a self-financing board so we have to be financially viable. And financial success requires our employees to be more customer-focused, especially as our customers, the public officers, are free to attend other courses or accept alternative offerings. So our employees have to deliver excellent service and be innovative in anticipating future program needs. Innovation and excellence are key focus areas for the college.

He adds that delivering excellence to the customer requires that attention be paid to delivering an equally compelling value proposition to its own employees. "Our people perspective is essentially about developing competent staff and ensuring that our three values of valuing people, integrity, and excellence are inculcated and lived organization-wide."

As well as balance, another catalyst for scorecard adoption was that the framework also served as a transparent mechanism for viewing performance at the organizational, strategic business unit, team, and individual level.

Incentive Compensation

Unusually for a public-sector organization, the scorecard is used not only to view individual performance, but also to reward it. This works though a tiered system, whereby if the college performs well against its overall scorecard targets there is a percentage multiplier for strategic business unit bonuses. These, in turn, are translated into a multiplier at the individual level. This means that an individual employee's bonus depends on his or her personal and unit's, and the college's overall performance.

According to BG (NS) Yam:

For the first time, people are seeing that they are remunerated directly to outcomes, so this is like running the organization as a commercial company with the full rigor of financial disciplines and not as a typical public-service organization, but retaining the public-sector ethos and values.

Tying remuneration to outcomes is not without its challenges, especially as employees are generally not used to such an approach, but the pay/performance link was deemed critical if a cultural shift to a more business mindset was to take root.

CSC Consultants

The incentive compensation link is now well-embedded within the 28-employee-strong CSC Consultants (CSCC), which delivers an extensive array of consulting services on people, system, and leadership development, and staff selection and assessment. It has a mission that reads: "We partner public sector organizations – in the selection, development and engagement of their people – to achieve excellence and results."

Gavin Tan, Director of CSC Consultants, and a member of CSCC's senior management team, states:

CSCC develops leaders, as well as helping them to develop their organizations. The Balanced Scorecard is one tool toward this organizational development goal. Not only do we use the Balanced Scorecard ourselves, we also partner with a reputable management consultancy to deliver a scorecard solution to our clients."

Having already gained some exposure to the scorecard concept through reading the seminal series of scorecard articles published within the Harvard Business Review,[4] Tan took his own management team and some five staff members through a three-day workshop in early 2002. It was facilitated by the boutique consultancy Balanced Scorecard Solutions. Staff members were included in the training to generate buy-in and to act as a sounding board to the eventual Strategy Map that management came up with.
Out of the workshop came a first draft of the Strategy Map. This was refined, and simplified, during subsequent in-house discussions with the group who had been through the workshop training.

CSCC Scorecard Framework

CSCC's scorecard framework comprises the conventional four perspectives of financial, customer, business process, and people and learning. For each perspective, CSCC has articulated a purpose statement.

Financial

To achieve a sustainable NEV [net economic value, see below] positive change, 10% revenue growth (for the next three years), and 60% utilization rate.

Customer

To serve as trusted advisors to public-sector organizations, offering innovative and cost-effective solutions toward people and organizational excellence.

Business processes

To leverage on IT, teamwork, agility, research, and business alliances in creating value to our clients.

People and learning

To inspire our people in high-performing teams doing meaningful work in a learning culture.

For this self-financing organization, financial is the top perspective within the Strategy Map. The top financial objective is sustainable NEV positive change. This can be traced back through supporting objectives such as revenue growth (financial), find new clients, new/improved products (customer), innovation and research (business process), and a warm and great place to work (people and learning). At the base of the Strategy Map, and as Tan says "holding up the whole scorecard framework" is servant/leadership.

Tan notes:

Leadership underpins everything we do, which is why we have it across the base of the scorecard. And leaders have to approach their role as servant/leaders to the staff and the organization. My managers and I are here to make sure this is a great place to work, that people can learn on the job, and that people are motivated. Without the right leadership support and attitudes a Strategy Map and Balanced Scorecard will not be accepted within the organization.

Communicating Strategy

Tan states that the primary reason for creating the map was as a tool for communicating strategy and to align performance. Since CSCC was a new organization, its employees required a clear sense of future direction.

At the college level we are using the scorecard to get the message across that we are self-financing and that we compete with other providers. This is even more true at the CSCC level, where we compete with other consultancies and training organizations.

Within CSCC, using the scorecard as a strategic communication tool began in 2001 when Tan shared the Strategy Map unit-wide during one of its six-monthly employee retreats. Tan provided background to the scorecard concept, described CSCC's strategy and how the Balanced Scorecard would enable everyone, in his or her own daily work, to better focus on strategy implementation.

Moreover, Tan finds the Strategy Map a powerful communication mechanism for dispelling any potential confusion that may result from seemingly opposing strategic thrusts. He says:

For example, to deliver new services demanded by our customers in their required timeframes we sometimes need to build alliances with other local providers. Yet, we ourselves need to be innovative in product and service development to provide challenges to our professionals and also not to be over-dependent on our partners.

Consequently, he says, staff may be confused as to what takes precedence – external alliances or internal innovation. But thanks to the Strategy Map, staff can see why both are important and how they fit together for the greater goal of strategy implementation.

Tan provides a compelling argument as to how using the scorecard to communicate strategy has a powerful affect on motivation.

Based on my observations, I would say that people don't mind working hard if they understand the purpose of their work. But if they feel what they are doing is pointless, then they will not likely put extra effort into their work. Without the scorecard people would not see as clearly as they should how what we ask them to do is linked to a final strategic outcome. Our staff can now see how their work is worthwhile and can also point to work that is not worthwhile and stop doing it because it does not link to a strategic objective.

On an ongoing basis, teams are expected to monitor how they are contributing to strategic goals, and monthly learning sessions are used to keep a strategic focus and to review how performance from different perspectives fits together. A CSCC-wide review of performance is held at each six-monthly retreat where the relevance of objectives and measures will be examined.

Metrics

As examples of measures used by CSCC, the people and learning perspectives have associated metrics, such as employee satisfaction and the number of people with postgraduate degrees. Internal process has measures such as new products and business alliances. From the customer perspective, measures include average value of contracts and customer satisfaction.

One particularly interesting measure is net economic value (NEV), which is found within the financial perspective. NEV is also being used at the corporate level and other strategic business units. NEV is a public-sector version of Stern-Stewart's economic value-added metric (which assesses economic profit by measuring net operating profit minus the cost of capital). NEV assesses the amount of resources exhausted in producing public-sector outputs. The purpose of NEV is to drive private-sector financial management disciplines into the management of public-sector bodies and increase performance accountability.

CSCC has set its cost of capital by benchmarking that set by similar businesses throughout the world.

Although a financially oriented, and more precisely shareholding-facing, measure such as EVA (which was designed for publicly traded organizations) would appear inappropriate to a public-sector body, Tan is certain of the worth of its public sector adaptation, NEV. He affirms, "We need to generate the value that is comparable to other training and consultancy firms, and NEV is a good way of doing this."

He adds that as Singapore aims to be an entrepreneurial and innovative society, metrics such as NEV are encouraged and mandated within the public sector by the Ministry of Finance. However, he stresses:

NEV is not just a financial measure, it's about changing the mindsets of officers and managers. The discipline forces them to think about the economic value of their projects and investments, and to understand tradeoffs, which is particularly important at the highest levels of government.

Tan adds that the Civil Service College has always taken a lead in the adoption of new and innovative public-sector management approaches.

For CSCC, and also for CSC generally, another key measure is growing the top line by 10%. Although CSCC achieved a 20% increase in revenue during the first fiscal year of scorecard usage, such a growth target has proved something of a challenge, given the economic downturn in Southeast Asia generally, and more particularly for Singapore – the economic blighting that resulted from the SARS epidemic of 2003. However, Tam points out that the strength of the scorecard is the possibility of switching priorities when required without losing sight of the longer term goals. He adds:

We were not going to drop our goal of 10% growth, but as growth slowed we spent more time on improving strategic processes and developing new products, which will put us in a good position to capitalize on opportunities when growth returns. Even with a slowdown of the economy we worked hard to ensure that we did not develop a mindset that is defeated by the external situation.

Challenges

Looking back, Tan says there have been challenges to overcome. For example, placing common measures on the scorecards of different business units or teams may be useful for cementing a unity of purpose, but there are caveats, as he explains:

A measure such as revenue per employee may be quite different in dissimilar departments, as some may be able to use external partners to grow revenue and others may not. So comparability has to be treated carefully. Also, internally I have three teams, one of which may be trying to exploit present, or mature offerings, and another developing new products, so it would not be fair to hold them accountable for the same revenue growth targets over the same timeframe.

Another ongoing challenge concerns the scorecard concept and framework itself. Tan explains:

The Balanced Scorecard has been very useful in aligning ourselves to what must be done to compete better in our business. However, the framework might not be suitable to bringing us a radically new business strategy. It tells us what to do right to deliver to our strategy, but it does not tell us what are the right things to do in a changing environment.

Future Developments

Tan says that if they were to start the scorecard journey again they would work to secure feedback from their customers, to ensure that the selected objectives were accurately capturing customer requirements. But now having this realization will help shape future scorecard developments. And Tan certainly believes that the scorecard will remain a key tool within CSCC going forward, although it will evolve. He states:

Over the next few years I don't think the approach will change, but we will refine and update it. We will also work hard to get the right data to support strategic measures and objectives. That may mean we consider an automated approach to replace our Excel-based system."

However, Tan stresses that automation is a final step as it is much more important to let the scorecard settle into the culture before adding the extra layer of a technological challenges. He adds: "If there's a large change in the external environment then there may be a change in the strategies and we will use the scorecard to support the transformation."

Conclusion

Tan states that through using the Balanced Scorecard, people are now much more conscious of how they spend their time. However, he stresses that to succeed with the scorecard it's important to dedicate the time to its creation and dissemination. In its creation he says it can be easy just to put it together quickly and then put in a drawer and never take it out. It is important to note that, "Getting your people to critique the scorecard is a good idea because ultimately you have to communicate it back to them and it will be of little value if you have something that you believe in but your people don't."

Source: Developing a Public Sector Scorecard,
James Creelman & David Harvey, Business Intelligence,
London 2004

[1] Norton, D.P. and Kaplan, R.S. 2001,The Strategy-focused Organization: How Balanced Scorecard Companies Thrive in the New Business Environment, Harvard Business Press, Boston, MA.

[2] Balanced Scorecard Collaborative HR Action Working Group, 2001.

[3] Creelman, J. 2001, Creating a Balanced Scorecard, Lafferty Publications, London.

[4] The series began with Norton, D.P. and Kaplan, R.S. 1992, "Measures that Drive Performance," Harvard Business Review, vol. 70, no 1.

9

Scorecard Devolution: The cultural challenge

*C*ultural barriers are more likely to derail a scorecard effort than any other obstacles. A properly rolled-out Balanced Scorecard system will inculcate performance transparency and accountability deep inside the organization. Some employees may be afraid of the consequences of transparency and accountability. Senior management must expect such fear to manifest itself as scorecard resistance. A cultural audit can be a powerful mechanism for highlighting potential cultural barriers. Many companies align performance appraisal and incentive-compensation systems to the Balanced Scorecard, and most companies will at some point consider the link. There is mixed opinions regarding the value of the link, especially the compensation component. If the incentive-compensation link is made, then most advisors suggest a time-lag between implementing the scorecard and aligning the compensation component. Building strategic awareness, through dedicated communication and education campaigns, is universally seen as a critical success factor for scorecard success. To highlight this point, a case study on Centrepoint Properties concludes this chapter.

BACKGROUND

More than anything else, a Balanced Scorecard program is about creating the right mindset. The "mind" of the organization must "think" Balanced Scorecard, or rather through the scorecard "think" strategically. In essence, creating a strategic mindset is not a structural challenge, or a systems or process issue. Although each of these three pillars has a key role to play, creating a Balanced Scorecard state of mind is a culture challenge.

Most Balanced Scorecard programs fail not because the Strategy Maps or accompanying Balanced Scorecards are badly designed (although, as we have explained in previous chapters, many are), but during the implementation phase. And failure during implementation is typically the result of cultural factors.

TRANSPARENCY AND ACCOUNTABILITY

In fashioning a strategic mindset, a properly rolled out Balanced Scorecard system creates two organizational performance states that for many organizations are both new and challenging; indeed, for many they are frightening – transparency and accountability. Andrew Lim, Director of the Singapore-headquartered Balanced Scorecard Solutions, rightly states: "The Balanced Scorecard cannot be very effective without there being transparency and accountability deep inside the organization. These cultural barriers must be acknowledged and overcome."

> **The Balanced Scorecard cannot be very effective without there being transparency and accountability deep inside the organization. These cultural barriers must be acknowledged and overcome.**

In planning a scorecard program these barriers must not be underestimated. Scorecard proponents would argue, and we would certainly agree, that the scorecard is a tool for continuous improvement and not for punishing poor performance. But in saying that, there can be no escaping the fact that the scorecard does unearth good, average, and poor performance. And although the goal may then be to raise the poor performance to being average, and the average to good, how well people are performing is visible at least to senior management when previously it may have been to a large extent hidden (and visibility may be organization-wide, especially if the scorecard is automated – see Chapter 10).

As few organizations will tolerate consistently poor performance, there may be good reasons for employees to shy away from the scorecard. Ning C S de Guzman, a Singapore-based scorecard and HR consultant makes this interesting observation:

> Performance against scorecard targets may be the key criteria for deciding who gets promoted. I think that top performance will welcome this as the scorecard provides an ideal framework for showcasing achievements and capabilities. However, if you are a poor performer you are not going to welcome something that threatens such transparency and accountability.

Indeed, de Guzman recalls one company that in implementing the Balanced Scorecard discovered that those managers whom had previously been seen as outstanding were in fact mediocre performers. Consequently, this group of average performance aggressively resisted the scorecard and eventually killed it.

The key point here is that some employees, at all levels, will resist the scorecard if they believe it will jeopardize their future and reputation. In planning the scorecard program senior management must expect that such resistance will take place and prepare appropriate responses. The responses fashioned by senior management and managed by the scorecard program team (see Chapter 4) will go a long way to laying the foundation for a successful scorecard effort.

The first key questions for the senior team is to decide to which level performance accountability and transparency is to be devolved. Will scorecards be cascaded down to the individual employee level, for example (see Chapter 8)? And who will have access to which scorecards? Will a supervisor in one country, for instance, be able to see team scorecards in other countries? If widespread accountability and transparency is the eventual goal, then over what time-scales will this be inculcated?

> ❝ Every one of our case companies stated that a key reason for implementing the Balanced Scorecard framework was to drive transparency and accountability deep inside the organization. ❞

TRANSPARENCY AND ACCOUNTABILITY: CASE EXAMPLES

Every one of our case companies stated that a key reason for implementing the Balanced Scorecard framework was to drive transparency and accountability deep inside the organization.

As an aside, and something we discuss in Chapter 12, the pressures for performance transparency and accountability are set to increase sharply as a result of corporate governance issues. For many organizations, in particular, those that are publicly traded, transparency and accountability may shift from "nice to have" to "must have."

Carol Yong Meng Dai, Senior Manager, Human Resources, who now acts as the scorecard champion and facilitator within Singapore's Centrepoint Properties Limited (see below), says this about its original decision to deploy the scorecard:

> This management team was looking for a way to communicate performance and quantifiable results in a format that that didn't require pages and pages of information. As the same time, they wanted to create a culture in which performance transparency and accountability was the norm.

At both the Gold Coin Group (see Chapter 5), and Civil Service College (see Chapter 9) the scorecard was perceived as being important for substantially improving transparency within the organization.

Pak Krisbiyanto, previously Vice-President, Human Capital at the Indonesia-based Bank Universal (see Chapter 10), says that the overriding benefit of scorecard usage was:

Through the Balanced Scorecard it was possible to measure the performance of our employees and of the organization more clearly. Previously, we would blame each other but through the scorecard we could see the actual causes of problems that led to targets being missed and so knew where to direct our efforts. The scorecard gave a very clear picture of accountability across the organization.

He also says that the bank became better at promotion due to there being better transparency around performance. Moreover, managers could see how they were performing against their appraisal objectives as a result of calculating their "performance points" against their scorecard's four perspectives (for more on compensation and appraisal see below).

Indonesia-based Summarecon Agung (see Chapter 4) has from the outset of its scorecard effort been cognizant of the accountability/transparency challenge, especially as a result of measurement. Director Lexy A Umiwa comments: "People can be afraid of the performance transparency that the measurement component of the Balanced Scorecard brings. Managers, for instance, may be afraid of their poor performance being visible to other managers."

He adds that overcoming this is work-in-progress:

We are working hard to get the message across to managers that prior to the scorecard they didn't always know how they were performing against strategically critical performance indicators. With the scorecard they have this information and where they find poor performance they are presented with an excellent opportunity to focus attention on improving that performance. And that improvement will be visible to all the other managers in the organization.

CULTURAL AUDITS

A useful way of assessing an organization's preparedness for an accountable and transparent culture is to conduct some kind of cultural audit. And this is certainly something that de Guzman and other advisors would recommend. There are many cultural assessment tools on the market. One tool particular liked by the authors of this book is a culture profile tool developed by the US-headquartered Senn-Delaney Leadership Consulting.[1] This tool can be quickly deployed electronically if required, and responses captured and reported. Within the tool each employee states on a scale of 1–7 which statement most accurately describes his or her view of the organization. Statements include:

"Open to change" versus "resistant to change"
(A score of 1 indicates that the employee believes the organization is always resistant to change and 7 means he or she believes the organization to be always open to change.)
   "People are highly accountable for results and actions" versus "people find excuses/blame others/feel victimized"
   "Positive/optimistic/forgiven versus insecure/fearful or negative environment."

A strength of this profile, which can show overall organization results as well as plant or department replies, is that it unambiguously points out the cultural strengths and weaknesses of the organization as perceived by the employees themselves.

Consequently, if senior teams wish to create a fully transparent and accountable organization, and such a profile tells them that their employees feel victimized and fearful, then it would almost certainly be advisable to get the culture in shape before enforcing transparency and accountability. Therefore, an organization may wish to include an objective from the learning and growth perspective around "creating a trusting culture," for example, and see significant progress here before rolling the scorecard out. Of course, the culture profile itself can be the measure of progress.

Subordinate Courts, Singapore (see Chapter 2), for example, has from their employee perspective an objective of "building a vibrant culture," which is measured through a cultural index containing components such as trust and honesty. Their belief is that the inculcation of cultural dimensions such as trust and honesty will create an organizational culture where transparency and accountability can flourish.

APPRAISAL AND COMPENSATION

Transparency and accountability are certainly important when making the link between scorecard performance and compensation and appraisal processes. According to Kaplan and Norton's five principles of the strategy-focused organization (see Chapter 1)[2], balanced pay checks and personal scorecards are sub-components of principle 3 "make strategy everyone's everyday job." Personal scorecards, which will typically serve as an individual's appraisal system, were considered in the previous chapter. In this chapter we will focus mainly on linking compensation to the scorecard, although we will often refer to appraisal systems, as compensation and appraisal typically go hand in hand, as incentive-compensation is usually based on performance to appraisal objectives.

In our survey of scorecard usage within South-east Asia (see the Appendix), 34% of users have tied compensation to the scorecard, 56% have not, and 10% plan to. Of those that have made the compensation link, most have done so at a senior management level and almost half at the general employee level, as shown in Exhibit 9.1.

Senior management	91%
Middle management	82%
Junior management	64%
General employee-base	45%

Exhibit 9.1 Scorecard usage

DIFFERING VIEWS

It is safe to say that if anything divides the scorecard community it's the link between compensation and the scorecard. Some, such as JongSup Jung, Director with the South Korea-based CalebABC, believes that it is absolutely critical to tie individual compensation to scorecard performance. Jung states, "Without this alignment, there is a significant risk that the organization will not achieve the required commitment to the scorecard."

And Matthew Tice, Vice-President, Asia-Pacific for the Balanced Scorecard Collaborative (BSCol), adds:

> Most organizations that fit into the Hall of Fame category [a status BSCol affords to organizations who achieve demonstrable performance improvement through the scorecard] would say that after the first year you should look to align compensation. I think the statistics are that between 80 and 85% of successful organizations see this as a must have.

> " ... if anything divides the scorecard community it's the link between compensation and the scorecard. "

Note that Tice states "after the first year," which is something we will talk about in a moment.

The overriding point Jung and Tice make is simply that money motivates, or as the old saying goes in Singapore, "no money, no honey." Scorecard co-creators Dr David Norton and Professor Robert Kaplan have written:

> Incentive compensation is a powerful lever to gain people's attention to company and business unit objectives. When all individuals understand how their pay is linked to achieving strategic objectives ... strategy truly becomes everyone's everyday job.

As with Tice, Norton and Kaplan recommend a time-lag between introducing the scorecard and making the compensation link, but they do not doubt the importance of compensation. Others are less certain.

Nigel Penny, founder and CEO of the Singapore-based consultancy ClaritasAsia, and previously Vice-President Asia-Pacific for BSCol, has spent a lot of time considering the compensation link and observing what does and does not motivate individual performance in the workplace. Also, he is far from convinced that the compensation lever is as significant as many believe. He says:

On the face of it, the compensation link makes good sense. For years we have bemoaned the largely inadequate process of setting annual goals at performance appraisal time. So the Balanced Scorecard offers us a new way of making this crucial linkage and focusing personal behavior on achieving wider organizational goals, through appraisal and compensation components. Yet, if we analyze this approach further, we may find some significant flaws in this logic.

He says is that although there has clearly been an increase in variable components of pay in recent years, most employees still budget on a base salary to allow them, at a minimum, to meet the key financial needs of the family (housing, food, clothing, ad so on), as well as providing for some of the desired additional lifestyle elements.

Therefore for most employees, the monetary component of "guaranteed" salary needs to be "adequate" for meet these "Base +" issues. Only a very small element of employees ("the risk-takers") would ever sign up to a package where guaranteed compensation is substantially less than that needed to meet core family needs.

For most employees, therefore, Penny says that variable components of pay will be largely based around a bonus mechanism, usually paid annually in arrears. So, it's this element that we may typically choose to link into our wider Balanced Scorecard framework. Penny qualifies:

Here's where the common wisdom of "money motivates" will often break down. Where the guaranteed salary is set at a level that allows for the employees' economic survival, market forces will inevitably dictate that the amount of money available for bonus will be a relatively small percentage of the total remuneration package.

The overall financial result of the company is likely to set the size of the pool for bonus distribution. In a bad to poor year, this inevitably means a zero bonus pool irrespective of the activities of individual employees. Even where a sizeable bonus pool may exist, it's unlikely that, across the board, this could account for more than an average of 5–10% of the total remuneration of each employee.

Given a typical distribution of performance where there may be 20% of high achievers, 10% of low achievers, and a 70% bandwidth of good, average performers, what does this mean in terms of the variable distribution of rewards? Let's assume that the poor performer gets nothing, then we may pay 15% bonus to our stars, with our average to good performers getting on average of, say, 7–8%. For an average salary of say $50,000 the annual bonus differential between our stars and our solid middle-of-the-road guys would equate to just $3,500."

As a consequence, Penny poses these questions.

1. If I were an average performer, would the once-a-year difference of $3,500 be enough to induce me to go all out to become a star performer next year? Probably not!
2. If I'm one of the poor performers, will any of this induce to me to change my ways? Again I think not. While we may encourage ways to turn around performance in this group, these are probably the employees that we will look to counsel out of the organization over time.

Penny concludes:

Given this logic, my own experiences indicate that only if the potential variable pay component represents "significant dollars" will there be a strong motivation to change behavior. Herein lies the biggest flaw in the logic of linking rewards to the Balanced Scorecard. Only where the potential for gain is substantial (in my view 25% or more of base salary), will there be a significant motivation to succeed, and hence potentially to change behavior. But the economics of this clearly means that only very few employees could benefit in such a scheme, and these are likely to be the self-motivating achievers anyway.

Penny's observations have much to commend them. Thanks to behavioral psychology we have known for some time that there are myriad influences on behavior, and the dynamics that influence one person may be diametrically opposite to that which influences another.

In an organizational setting the same rules apply (after all, we are still dealing with human behavior). Pay, especially the incentive component, may drive some people to heightened performance, but this will not be the case organization-wide. And it is certainly true that top performers are typically driven by more than the pursuit of money. The fact is they earn the most money because they are by inclination top performers.

So where does this leave us regarding the incentive-compensation debate? Although we would agree with much of Nigel Penny's reservations, we would still recommend that organizations align compensation to performance. The reason for this is simple. If the Balanced Scorecard management system is to become central to how the organization is managed, then all aspects of organizational systems, structures, policies, and so on must be aligned to the scorecard objectives. If incentive compensation becomes "the odd one out," then we jeopardize the scorecard's position as "the way we manage around here."

> " ... all aspects of organizational systems, structures, policies and so on must be aligned to the scorecard objectives. If incentive compensation becomes "the odd one out" then we jeopardize the scorecard's position as "the way we manage around here." "

Of course, organizations may decide to abandon incentive-compensation altogether, but if it remains then it has to be hardwired to the Balanced Scorecard. Everything that may have an impact on behavior (however weak) must be driving people toward the objectives on the scorecard. Organizations cannot have different systems driving different behaviors – the only outcome of this would be some degree of misalignment.

If we accept that the incentive-compensation link must be made, there are other questions to add, such as how will the compensation link be made? For example, some organizations tie the scorecard to a group incentive scheme and others to group and individual performance schemes. de Guzman states:

Personally, I would like to link a variable component of pay to the Balanced Scorecard. At the higher level it should be linked to group performance, and at the lower levels [to] more individual and key performance with about a one-third to overall performance. I don't think there's a huge disagreement here.

Our experience shows us that there are many ways to cut the incentive compensation cake. And organizations may wish to alter the balance of how compensation links to performance depending on functional requirements (that is, giving the learning and growth perspective a higher percentage weighting for HR) or depending on the organization's priorities. For example, if placing a customer-centric mindset and structure into the organization is a present performance prerequisite, then this may take precedence for a while.

Another question is when to make the incentive-compensation link? Most advisors we have spoken to would agree with Kaplan and Norton's comments that:[4] "… managers must avoid the dangers of introducing plans too quickly, before good measures have been determined and good data for the measures are available." For example, Andrew Lim states that: "The organization has to become comfortable with the scorecard before getting into performance management areas such as compensation and appraisal."

" The organization has to become comfortable with the scorecard before getting into performance management areas such as compensation and appraisal."

COMPENSATION: CASE EXAMPLES

So let's look at how our case study companies have approached the incentive-compensation.

Civil Service College, Singapore

Unusually for a public-sector organization, the scorecard is used at Civil Service College (see Chapter

8) not only to view individual performance, but also to reward it. This works though a tiered system, whereby if the college performs well against its overall scorecard targets there is a percentage multiplier for strategic business unit bonuses. These, in turn, are translated into a multiplier at the individual level. This means that an employee's bonus depends on his or her personal, unit's, and college's overall performance.

Tying remuneration to the scorecard was not without its challenges at the college, especially as employees are generally not used to such an approach, but the pay/performance link was deemed critical if a cultural shift to a more business mindset was to take root.

Further case examples

Returning to our case study companies we find just three further examples of incentive-compensation being linked to performance, although we could add Tata Motors Commercial Vehicles Business Unit (see Chapter 1), where its sales and marketing organization is beginning to explore the link.

Most employees at Centrepoint Properties have, within their appraisal system, key results areas (KRAs) in each perspective that are drawn from departmental or divisional Strategy Maps. Success against the KRAs impacts both incentive and annual compensation awards.

At Summarecon the performance management/scorecard link is through individual scorecards, which has been rolled-out down to departmental managers. On these individual scorecards, managers have accountability statements and have objectives and measures set against the perspectives they most impact, thus enabling line-of-sight from individual performance up to unit and corporate scorecard performance.

Over the next couple of years bonuses will also be introduced to support individual scorecard performance and more widely to reward employees for success against the scorecard. Although an important element of moving toward becoming a "performance-based" organization, there is some caution around paying for performance, largely for local, cultural reasons. President Commissioner Liliawati Rahardjo explains:

When it comes to performance, in Indonesia we do not have the same approach to reward and punishment as the United States and some other countries. It's not a question of a big bonus if you do well and you're fired if you don't. Culturally, we still have more of an emotional connection with employees and tend to put as much emphasis on personal relationships as we do on individual performance. However, competition is becoming increasingly global, so individual performance is becoming more of an issue."

At The Gold Coin Group a substantial percentage of the pay of management was tied to scorecard results (well in excess of the 25% which Nigel Penny stated earlier in the chapter that would make a difference to motivating an individual's performance).

Throughout the Group the split between fixed and variable pay is standard according to management level. So group directors received 50% fixed pay and 50% variable, and sales managers received 60% fixed and 40% variable. However, the variable percentage will alter, depending on local needs. As an example, in one country, customer retention may be a pressing priority, while in another it may be customer acquisitions. Therefore the variable compensation may be configured according to local needs, as will the measures weighting on the local scorecard.

Although there are examples of Asia-based organizations making the link between compensation and performance to scorecard results, for most regional companies the link is still some way down the road. This is a result of two reasons. First, scorecards are typically, but not exclusively, well embedded in the organization prior to the compensation link being explored. Second, even in North American and European organizations, where the scorecard is a mature management tool, there is not a wealth of best practice incentive-compensation stories. It is proving the least popular, and certainly the most challenging of all the sub-components of Kaplan and Norton's principles of the strategy-focused organization.

STRATEGIC AWARENESS

Unlike compensation, a sub-component of "make strategy everyone's everyday job" that is universally viewed as popular is "strategic awareness." And this brings us to the final piece in overcoming the cultural barriers to scorecard implementation.

Strategic awareness is about education and communication. It is about making employees fully cognizant about why the scorecard is being deployed, how it functions, and keeping employees up to date on progress toward strategic objectives. Education and communication is also about inculcating in the employee-base an understanding of how his or her own day-to-day actions impacts scorecard results.

Communicate, Communicate, Communicate

Just about every practitioner and advisor alike concurs that strategic awareness is a critical success factor in a scorecard program. Or put another way "communicate, communicate, communicate."

A successful communication campaign should be waged through as many communication channels as possible: electronic, print, and, most importantly, face-to-face. Email, intranet (see Chapter 10 for more on this), posters, newsletters, town-hall meetings, and regular unit/team briefings should all play their part. Communications should be regular, structured. and tell the same story.

Within our survey of scorecard usage within South-east Asia we can see various communications being used, as shown in Exhibit 9.2.

Senior management briefings	58%
Cascaded briefings	49%
Training sessions	37%
Email	35%
Intranet	33%
Internal newsletters	14%
Town-hall meetings	21%
Automated scorecard on desktop of all employees	7%

Exhibit 9.2 Communication mechanisms used by survey respondents

> " A successful communication campaign should be waged through as many communication channels as possible: electronic, print, and, most importantly, face-to-face. "

COMMUNICATION AND EDUCATION: CASE EXAMPLES

Let's consider some case study examples of communication and education approaches. At Subordinate Courts, Singapore, the scorecard steering committee made concerted efforts to communicate progress and learnings to the other units during the time that the scorecard was being piloted in one its divisions. This was a purposeful strategy in order to build awareness and to pre-emptively tackle cultural difficulties that may emerge, such as around a fear of measurement, for example. The thinking was that when it came to full rollout, the scorecard would be "nothing new." A focused communication campaign would give people enough time to get used to the scorecard idea.

Within Civil Service College Consultants (CSCC), the scorecard is seen as a powerful strategic communication tool. This began in

2001, when Director Gavin Tan shared the Strategy Map unit-wide during one of its six-monthly employee retreats. During this retreat he provided background to the scorecard concept, described CSCC's strategy, and how the Balanced Scorecard would enable everyone, in his or her own daily work, to better focus on strategy implementation.

Tan finds the Strategy Map a powerful communication mechanism for dispelling any potential confusion that may result from seemingly opposing strategic thrusts. He says:

> For example, to deliver new services demanded by our customers in their required timeframes we sometimes need to build alliances with other local providers. Yet, we ourselves need to be innovative in product and service development to provide challenges to our professionals and also not to be over-dependent on our partners.

Within Tata Motors Commercial Vehicles Business Unit (CVBU), every year the Executive Director initiates the strategic awareness process by sharing the company's vision, mission, future directions, and strategies at a town hall meeting with all employees. He repeats this communication session personally at all locations of the company, to ensure that all employees have a strong, consistent understanding of the business unit's future.

To ingrain the understanding further, the Balanced Scorecard core team conducts score-carding cascading workshops at each division/function, to communicate the CVBU Strategy Map, Balanced Scorecard, and initiatives. Communication systems include internal publications, intranet websites, and presentations made by senior leaders. According to KC Girotra, Head of Business Excellence Services Department:

> This has created a tremendous amount of awareness among employees of all categories from front-line and shop-floor staff to supervisors and middle management. The monthly scorecard review meetings and the quarterly scorecard audits conducted across the organization to ensure alignment of all divisions/departments/functions/plants to the overall CVBU objectives further reinforce the deployment of the Balanced Scorecard system."

At times there is also a requirement for external training support to buttress the scorecard message. Nigel Penny, for example, recently led a two-day workshop for 80 employees to sharpen their understanding of how more effectively to cascade scorecards.

Another very popular way to communicate the scorecard organization-wide is through an automated software solution. Automation is the subject of the next chapter.

CASE STUDY

Centrepoint Properties

Summary

Centrepoint Properties Limited has created separate Balanced Scorecards for its four divisions. This case study explains how the design and usage of the scorecard has evolved since being introduced into one division only and the critical role of CEO leadership, keeping the scorecard simple and focused, and of concerted communication.

Background

Headquartered in Singapore and with about 800 employees worldwide, Centrepoint Properties Ltd (CPL) is a property investment, development, and management company with a portfolio of premier retail, commercial, and residential properties worth over S$1 billion. It is a subsidiary of the diversified Fraser and Neave Group, which has business operations in the fields of soft drinks, breweries, dairies, properties, publishing, and printing.

CPL has a mission that reads:

CPL aims to be a major developer of quality homes and a leading manager of shopping centres, serviced residences and property fund/asset management business.

CPL will be a leading Singapore based property company with broad international footprint of oversees operations.'

To achieve its mission, CPL has identified four strategic thrusts going forward:
- increase focus on property development;
- de-emphasize ownership in investment properties;
- expand internationally
- increase fee-based and service content business.

Structurally, CPL comprises three divisions: Investment Properties (Malls of Centrepoint), Development & Property (Centrepoint Homes), and Hospitality (Fraser Serviced Residences). There is also a Corporate Division encompassing the Chief Executive Officer's Office, Business Development,

Finance and Human Resources. This division provides leadership and support to the other three divisions. As shall be explained, all four divisions have their own Balanced Scorecard.

The First Balanced Scorecard

The Balanced Scorecard was introduced first into the Hospitality Division in 1998. Hospitality was then a new division within CPL and the division's management team arrived with experience of performance measurement systems and a desire to more widely embrace performance management principles.

Carol Yong Meng Dai, Senior Manager, Human Resources, who now acts as the scorecard champion and facilitator within CPL, recalls:

This management team was looking for a way to communicate performance and quantifiable results in a format that that didn't require pages and pages of information. At the same time, they wanted to create a culture in which performance transparency and accountability was the norm."

An environmental scan of extant frameworks led to the identification of the Balanced Scorecard as the team's preferred performance model. Yong adds, "The scorecard framework was perceived as a logical framework for capturing and reporting results simply yet quantifiably."

As a result, and facilitated by a local consulting group, the Hospitality Division created its Balanced Scorecard. Although the Division certainly found value from their scorecard, not least in learning to see through "balanced" perspectives, the effort was somewhat constrained by the lack of a Strategy Map to show the causality between objectives.

Full Scorecard Rollout

This "missing link" was addressed in 2000 when the remaining CPL divisions embraced the scorecard concept. Strategy Maps were created for each division, including Hospitality. It should be noted that there isn't an aggregated map at CPL level. According to Yong: "We were originally looking for one overarching map, but quickly found that this didn't work as we are three quite different business units."

The challenge therefore was to ensure coherence and alignment, while allowing different emphases, depending on the industries served. Yong says that although this is a challenge the process actually highlights a key strength of the scorecard:

With the scorecard you can cut it any way you want. You can say the financial perspective is the most important and the other three support it, or see the customer as the most important and everything supports that, as would be the case for the Hospitality Division.

It is therefore the responsibility of the respective divisional senior managers to align their scorecards to the dynamics of their own environments, but the four maps are linked through the financial perspective. The corporate division holds the umbrella as it also encompassed the CEO's targets for CPL.

Creating the Scorecards

Creating the divisional scorecards began with pre-consulting where consultants from the Singapore-based Balanced Scorecard Solutions met up with divisional general managers to elicit an understanding of how they saw the strategy and to draw preliminary maps. The senior management team then collectively went on a retreat, facilitated by the consultant, to create maps, which were fine-tuned on their return.

According to Carol, a strength of the divisional scorecards is their relative simplicity, each scorecard typically housing only about 15 objectives, focused through the conventional scorecard perspective hierarchy of financial, customer, internal growth, and learning and growth (which CPL calls human capital). Yong reflects: "From the scorecard beginnings within Hospitality we've been focused on keeping performance reporting and communication simple. That would have been compromised if we'd built complex Strategy Maps."

However, creating simple Strategy Maps that really drive performance did present challenges. This required divisional leaders to be very disciplined and focused on identifying, and agreeing upon the right critical success factors (CPL's term for strategic objectives). Carol states that successful Strategy Map creation is dependent upon senior management being sharp on vision and direction.

If they are clear about vision and direction, then the map is not difficult to create. If they lack this clarity, they will not be sure whether the critical success factors are right. ... This year we revisited the maps and redrew. The redrawing of the maps demonstrated the higher confidence managers had in using the scorecard and in confirming the right critical success factors."

CEO Commitment

Yong also firmly believes that the successful creation of the Strategy Map and Balanced Scorecard, and rollout, was dependent on the fact that the CEO, Mr Jeffrey Heng, was totally committed to the score-carding process, which he demonstrated within the original workshops.

We had a few senior managers who weren't sure whether the scorecard would work for them, or that it offered anything new. The CEO's determination to "give it a shot" went some way to ensuring the scorecard was implemented.

Deputies Committee

Overcoming potential resistance, both at managerial and staff levels, was also addressed by the formation of a Balanced Scorecard Deputies Committee. It comprised senior managers working together to gain clarity and iron out problems. According to Yong, who facilitates the committee, this group has become a driving force for change within CPL.

Communication

To overcome potential resistance at staff levels, CPL uses a highly interactive workshop-based communication process, here described by Carol:

The crux of the Balanced Scorecard is about getting people to see the business from an owner's point of view. So in a workshop setting, we begin with a session where we get staff to act as entrepreneurs, making a proposal for a retail space in our shopping mall. They go through an actual proposal submission process. At this stage, we deliberately did not discuss the Balanced Scorecard, as we wanted staff to be themselves, to think through how best to set up their own business. So they created the business concept, with figures, projections etc.

After they had completed the exercise, we then introduced the four perspectives of the Balanced Scorecard, and it made sense to them because they could see how they needed all four perspectives to successfully manage a business.

Yong adds that this business experiential exercise helps overcome the typical problem of staff being segmented in their vocational fields and thus unable to appreciate business operations from a macro level. For example, engineers will typically only look at operational plans and won't necessarily see how it all links up to financials, or the importance of human capital development. Yong continues:

After the exercise, we explain the divisional maps and get them to brainstorm across the four perspectives and understand how they can contribute within their own departments. At the end of workshop, people are much clearer about the company's direction and how they can individually contribute towards achieving this direction.

Appraisal and Compensation

Linking Balanced Scorecard results to performance appraisal and compensation (incentive and annual) also catalyzes individual contribution. In the appraisal process most employees have key result areas in each perspective that is drawn from the overall departmental (CPL has developed the scorecard to departmental levels – such as HR within the corporate division) or divisional map.

CEO Review

Appraising the divisional scorecards themselves is through a quarterly CEO review. Yong says that he will challenge managers if he thinks that targets are too low, or alternatively if he thinks the targets represent too much of a stretch. Such a review process highlights the fact that through the Balanced Scorecard, performance becomes more transparent than had been the case previously. Therefore it is much more evident which division is not performing financially. But of course the power of the balanced Scorecard is that it enables a view of performance that is wider than narrowly financial. According to Yong:

Through the Balanced Scorecard we are getting people to think strategically and to understand that it's acceptable to put in place long-term plans that may not reap immediate financial returns but are building value for tomorrow. This ties in with how we see ourselves – as a company that will be here for the longer term.

Yong also makes this valuable observation:

Mr Heng values divisions that may not be delivering as well financially, but possess intrinsic value in terms of reputation and branding, and certainly building the foundations for tomorrow's success. The balancing view of the CEO is important in how he looks at numbers and synergies across divisions, and how they complement each other without just looking at the financial numbers.

This stance was important – rather than transparency being a problem, it is has led to greater peer support as people realized they could do a lot more together, share frustrations, and get better synergies.

Budgeting

Such insights have also proved invaluable in ensuring that financial planning and resource allocation takes into account the wider value proposition of each division. Within CPL, there is a direct tie-up between the Balanced Scorecard and budgeting cycle, as Yong explains:

Each year the second quarterly review is when we formally assess the scorecard and do our Strategy Mapping for the following year. This is then used to shape the thinking that goes into the budgeting process. So we get the revised Strategy Map in May and complete the budget during June and July."

Scorecard benefits

Carol Yong believes that CPL's experience of deploying the Balanced Scorecard has led to many benefits: at organizational, departmental, and individual levels. She emphasizes:

The Balanced Scorecard creates a more team-based, performance-oriented culture. The transition the company is experiencing is the move from an operational to strategic mode. That is a major paradigm shift and people across the business are getting better and better at thinking strategically, and through the scorecard are sharing a common strategic language.

She describes departmental level benefits by highlighting the value of the scorecard to her function – human resources.

If it wasn't for the scorecard and the way it shows the cause and effect relationship from human capital performance through to financial, we would not be seen as a business partner. We'd be seen as the people who take charge of hiring, firing, and handling training. Through the scorecard we can show how what we do drives the numbers.

At the individual level the scorecard shows how each person contributes to overall strategic goals, but also: "Through the platform of the Balanced Scorecard we have previews of how the Board thinks. And it helps us all learn much more about the business and how it works."

Critical Success Factors

As for critical factors for succeeding with the Balanced Scorecard, Yong stresses CEO and senior management commitment. She also points to learning. She says that CPL is still learning about how best to capture the most meaningful non-financial metrics, as they find that the best metrics are often difficult to measure, while easy-to-find metrics are not necessarily good measures. They are also striving to get a better balance between leading and lagging performance indicators, with the latter more prevalent at the moment. Yong concludes, "The Strategy Map has to be a dynamic tool offering ongoing learning opportunities. It should not be a piece of art to put in a drawer and then to be taken out to look at now and again."

[1]   See ww.sdlcg.com

[2]   Norton, D.P. and Kaplan, R.S. 2001, The Strategy-focused Organization: How Balanced Scorecard Companies Thrive in the New Business Environment, Harvard Business Press, Boston, MA.

[3]   See and note 2.

[4]   See end note 2.

[5]   See end note 2.

10
Scorecard
Automation

*I*mplementing the Balanced Scorecard Management System is not an IT project. There are a growing number of vendors of scorecard automation solutions. Balanced Scorecard Collaborative has a process for certifying scorecard products that meet specified functional standards. For most organizations, the favored software support tools are still Excel-type spreadsheets and PowerPoint, but there are clear limitations to such conventional tools. The greatest benefit of automation is that it enables effective strategy communication. There are many other benefits, such as ease of access of mission-critical information and data. A key consideration is when to automate the scorecard. It is also important to ensure adequate training is provided in using the automated system. Guidance is provided on vendor/product selection. To highlight this, a case study on Bank Universal concludes this chapter.

BACKGROUND

With regards to scorecard automation we will make the most important point at the outset. Implementing the Balanced Scorecard system is not an IT project: you cannot buy a scorecard software solution and simply "plug and play." Automation cannot replicate the critical scorecarding process of the senior executive team debating and agreeing on the critical few objectives and measures that will deliver strategic success. Put another way, no matter how clever a piece of software may be, it cannot create an organization's Strategy Map or Balanced Scorecard. Neither can it overcome the myriad cultural barriers that, and as we explained in Chapter 9, are much more likely to derail a scorecard effort than technical issues.

> *... we have seen too many examples of organizations waste time, effort, and not inconsiderable amounts of money buying software with the mistaken belief that the simple purchase will somehow turn them into a strategy-focused organization.*

The reason why we counsel caution regarding software is not because we are opposed to scorecard automation; on the contrary, and as we shall explain, we firmly believe it to be an absolute must for securing the full benefits from a scorecard program. Rather, this counsel is proffered because we have seen too many examples of organizations waste time, effort, and not inconsiderable amounts of money buying software with the mistaken belief that the simple purchase will somehow turn them into a strategy-focused organization.

A European-based scorecard practitioner (whose organization is known for effectively automating its scorecard) recently said this to us: "I regularly receive telephone calls from managers from other organizations who ask me, 'I've just bought this scorecard software, what do I do now?' Quite simply, a golden rule is to know what you want to achieve with the Balanced Scorecard Management System itself before you consider software support."

VENDORS

If the decision is made to opt for an automated solution, there are a large number of offerings in the market to choose from. Given that the scorecard has proven such a popular and enduring management approach, it is not surprising that such a large software support industry has evolved, as can be said about consultancy support.

A comprehensive list of scorecard providers is found within the Balanced Scorecard Software Report, which is compiled annually by Professor Andy Neely and Bernard Marr of the UK Cranfield School of Management.[1] This report evaluates the product offerings of more than 30 vendors (see Exhibit 10.1) and is a valuable in-depth aid for any organization considering a software solution.

Company name	Product name	Internet address
Accrue Software	Pilot Balanced scorecard	http://www.accrue.com/
Active Strategy	Active Strategy Enterprise	http://www.activestrategy.com/
Cash Focus Pty	20–20 BALANCED SCORECARD Software	http://www.cashfocus.com/
Cognos	Cognos KPI Business Pack	http://www.cognos.com/
Comshare	Comshare MPC	http://www.comshare.com/
Corporater	Corporater Balanced scorecard	www.corporater.com
CorVu	RapidScorecard/ CoreManage	http://www.corvu.com/
Crystal Decision	Balanced scorecard Analytic App.	http://www.crystaldecisions.com/
Dialog Strategy	Dialog Strategy	http://www.dialogstrategy.com/
EFM Software BV	Bizzscore	http://www.efmsoftware.com/
Fiber	FlexBI Te	http://www.fiber.com/
Hyperion	Hyperion Performance Scorecard	http://www.hyperion.com/
IC Visions	Dolphin Navigator System	http://www.icvisions.com/

Source: Marr, B. and Neely, A. (2003) Automating your Scorecard: The Balanced Scorecard Software Report, Gartner and Cranfield School of Management, InfoEdge, Stamford, CT.

Exhibit 10.1 Software vendors with solutions to support a Balanced Scorecard implementation

Company name	Product name	Internet address
IFUA Horvarth & Partner	Score IT!	http://www.horvarth-partner.com/
InPhase Software	Performance Plus	http://www.inphase.com/
Lawson	Lawson Scorecard	http://www.lawson.com/
Online Development	PM-Express	www.pm-express.com
Open Ratings	Gentia Balanced scorecard	www.openratings.com
Oracle	Oracle Balanced scorecard	http://www.oracle.com/
Panorama Business Views	PB Views	http://www.pbviews.com/
Peoplesoft	Balanced scorecard	www.peoplesoft.com
Procos AG	Strat&Go Balanced scorecard	http://www.procos.com/
ProDacapo	Balanced scorecard Manager	www.prodacapo.com
QPR Software	QPR ScoreCard	http://www.qprsoftware.com/
SAP	SEM Balanced scorecard	http://www.sap.com/
SAS Institute	Strategic Performance Management	http://www.sas.com/
Show Business Software	Action Driven BALANCED SCORECARD	http://www.showbusiness.com/
Simpel	SIMPEL scorecard	http://www.simpel.com/
Smart 4	Strategic Management Tool	http://www.smart4.com/
Solvision	Scorecard.nl	http://www.scorecard.nl/
SQL Power	Power*Scorecard	http://www.sqlpower.com/
Stratsys AB	Runyourcompany	http://www.runyourcompany.com/
Vision Grupo Consultorues	Strategos	http://www.visiongc.com/
4GHI Solutions	Cockpit Communicator	http://www.4ghi.com/

Source: Marr, B. and Neely, A. (2003) Automating your Scorecard: The Balanced Scorecard Software Report, Gartner and Cranfield School of Management, InfoEdge, Stamford, CT.

Exhibit 10.1 Software vendors with solutions to support a Balanced Scorecard implementation (continued)

To narrow the choice down, readers may wish to consider one of the 19 software vendors (such as Panorama Business Views, SAS, CorVu, and Hyperion) whose product has been certified by the Balanced Scorecard Collaborative (BSCol) as conforming to Kaplan and Norton's view of the scorecard.[2] Hence, if you want to build a Balanced Scorecard system according to Kaplan and Norton's principles then this can be enabled through the products of BSCol-certified vendors.

As part of the scorecard certification process, vendor products must be able to demonstrate, as a minimum, the following four capabilities, as laid down by a set of functional standards published by BSCol.[3]

1. Balanced Scorecard Design

The functional standards state: "The application should be able to flexibly accommodate the basic elements of a proper Balanced Scorecard design. The application must be able to 1) view the strategy from four perspectives (financial, customer, internal and learning and growth), 2) identify strategic objectives from each perspective, 3) associate measures with strategic objectives, 4) link strategic objectives in cause and effect relationships, 5) assign targets to measures, and 6) list strategic initiatives."

2. Strategic Education and Communication

The functional standards state: "One of the key reasons for implementing a Balanced Scorecard software solution is the facilitation of strategic education and communication. Therefore, a certified application will enable users to document and communicate descriptions of objectives, measures, targets and initiatives aligned with the strategy."

3. Business Execution

The functional standards state: "Initiatives (discretionary investment programmes) are the testing grounds for the strategy expressed in the Balanced Scorecard. Therefore, a certified application must make explicit the relationship between initiatives required and the associated strategic objective."

4. Feedback and Learning

The functional standards state: "Through proper system design, the feedback cycle time for management information can be significantly reduced. Analysis of the measure results against targets will allow managers to understand which areas of the organization require further attention. However, the system should not override the judgment of a senior executive – the balanced scorecard should rely on objective and subjective judgments, as well as graphical indicators, to report on progress of a particular measure against target functionality."

CASE STUDY USAGE

So let's consider the extent of software usage within our case study companies, which is shown in Exhibit 10.2.

Case company	Software used to support Balanced Scorecard
Bank Universal	Pbviews
Centrepoint Properties	Non-exclusive tools such as Excel and PowerPoint
Civil Service College, Singapore	Non-exclusive tools such as Excel and PowerPoint
Gold Coin Group	Pbviews
MTR Corporation	SAS
Saatchi & Saatchi Worldwide	Began with Excel and PowerPoint and Hyperion for financials. Has since built its own system, which incorporates an OLAP product.
Singapore Prison Service	Non-exclusive tools such as Excel and PowerPoint, although there may soon be a need for automation
Subordinate Courts, Singapore	Non-exclusive tools such as Excel and PowerPoint
Summarecon	Pbviews
Tata Motors Commercial Business Unit	Non-exclusive tools such as Excel and PowerPoint
XYZ Enterprises	Non-exclusive tools such as Excel and PowerPoint

Exhibit 10.2 Case study companies' use of software

What is striking from the case study companies is that just four of the 11 profiled organizations have as yet purchased a recognized scorecard automation system (we've excluded Saatchi & Saatchi, which has built its own). Three of these four companies have opted for Pbviews, and we will be honest and say that this reflects the fact that both of the authors of this book have relationships with Panorama Business Views (the owners of Pbviews), and therefore should not be viewed as in any way representative of market share in Asia. It can also be noted that what was probably the first scorecard automation project in Asia was a Pbviews solution implemented in Indonesia in 1995 by one of this book's co-authors, Naresh Makhijani.

BARRIERS TO AUTOMATION

Our observations are that globally most scorecard users still prefer simple tools such as Excel and PowerPoint for scorecard reporting and communication. This is often because organizationally they have ready access to such tools, or may reflect the maturity of the scorecard project, or they may not be ready for the disruption of yet another large-scale IT project.

A further barrier is the sheer cost of automation. According to Neely and Marr, software package prices vary enormously from a few thousand US dollars to far over a million dollars, with typical spend in the region of US$200,000 for reasonably sized organizations.[4]

> " ... software package prices vary enormously from a few thousand US dollars to far over a million dollars, with typical spend in the region of US$200,000 for reasonably sized organizations. "

EXCEL DOWNSIDES

There are certainly downsides to using conventional tools. Neely and Marr state the following as the major disadvantages of standard spreadsheet documents:[5]

1. No scalability – scorecards quickly reach the capacity that desktop spreadsheets can handle.
2. Time-consuming to update – usually they are manually fed and updated, which is slow and leaves immense room for errors.
3. No collaboration and communication support – data is stored in individual spreadsheets, often scattered around on different machines, and it requires enormous discipline to work on the same spreadsheet.
4. Difficult analysis – because data is stored in individual spreadsheets, it is difficult and time-consuming to bring them together for analysis.

Nigel Penny, the Managing Director of the Singapore-based consultancy ClaritasAsia, expands on this theme, "Automation is a must for any organization with more than five scorecards. We see many Balanced Scorecards falling into disuse purely because of the overhead of trying to produce Excel-based reporting month after month."

Matthew Tice, BSCol Vice-President Asia-Pacific, adds: "Ultimately, if you're going to have your organization connected, or at least a reasonably sized organization of say 1000+ employees, then you have to automate."

We would certainly agree that automation is a must. If the Balanced Scorecard is to be the steer for everything that happens within the organization, there must be the capacity for employees to quickly and easily access the information and data contained within the scorecard. And if the scorecard is to be real value, employees must be able to enter a dialogue with colleagues, often in dispersed locations, based on what the scorecard tells them. Simply put, automating the scorecard enables rich strategic conversations based on current, consistent, and "balanced" information.

> " … automating the scorecard enables rich strategic conversations based on current, consistent and "balanced" information. "

SURVEY

Our survey of scorecard usage in South-east Asia (see the Appendix) found that 70% of present scorecard users had automated their scorecard. The effectiveness of automation is shown in Exhibit 10.3. As we can see, the all but 10% of those that had automated the scorecard found software support to be at least "moderately effective."

Totally ineffective	10%
Ineffective	0%
Moderately effective	20%
Effective	30%
Totally effective	40%

Exhibit 10.3 Balanced Scorecard automation effectiveness

CASE STUDY BENEFITS

Our case study companies that have opted for an automated solution are certainly reaping the benefits. For example, MTR Corporation (see Chapter 7) used an SAS product that, as with most other products, shows objectives, measures, and targets, and provides monthly trend data and enables a commentary on performance to the measures.

Kwok Yiu Lueng, MTR's Safety and Quality Manager, says that a key reason for opting for automation was that MTR had identified difficulties in disseminating information across the enterprise, while the data was still fresh and useful, leading to delays in responding to improvement opportunities.

The automated scorecard is now accessible over a corporate intranet by managers from their desktops, thus expediting the decision-making process. Results are also accessible by front-line staff, who also receive paper-based monthly updates. Kwok Yiu Leung stresses that for the scorecard to be effective, performance must be communicated to the deepest levels of the corporation.

And consider too the words of Pak Krisbiyanto, formerly Vice-President, Human Capital at Bank Universal (a Pbviews user, see below). He also speaks of the power of automation for communications purposes: "We wanted to automate the scorecard, as we saw it, as a way to significantly improve communications and enhance performance transparency.

Mahdi Syahbuddin, formerly the bank's Deputy President Director, adds that through automation it became clear how individual branches were performing against indicators within all four perspectives. Importantly, where excellence was identified, say in customer service scores, then the branch best practices that caused these scores could be shared throughout the network, thus serving as a powerful knowledge-sharing tool.

STRATEGIC COMMUNICATION

These case comments highlight what is by some distance the biggest benefit of an automated system. It transforms the scorecard into a powerful, near real-time strategic communication system, rather than something management looks at once a month. Such communication triggers huge potential for strategic learning. Indeed, Dr David Norton has said that strategic learning is probably the most important part of scorecard usage. It is through this learning that an organization tests the hypotheses of the Strategy Map and Balanced Scorecard and makes any requisite fine-tuning or wholesale changes.

Through automation the strategy can be disseminated to the desktops of all managers (and if required all employees) in an instant – or at a click of a button. Everyone will receive the same messages as to what the strategy is, and what will drive its success (strategic objectives, measures, and initiatives).

> "Through automation the strategy can be disseminated to the desktops of all managers (and if required all employees) in an instant – or at a click of a button."

KNOWLEDGE-SHARING

Rapid performance dissemination also makes possible powerful knowledge-sharing organization wide. Not only can organizations see performance in terms of measures, but also where good, or excellent performance is found, the reason behind the success can be captured through commentaries within the automated system and shared enterprise-wide. Hence, a database of internal benchmarks can be collated with clear explications of how the best performing units/teams achieve these results. This knowledge can be used to drive up performance in poorer performing units.

A software solution also shows performance to objectives, typically reported through green (above target), amber (on target), and red (below target) traffic-light indicators. This has powerful benefits, as it is by monitoring progress according to set indicators that the organization can ensure performance is on track and identify where improvements can be made, and make them in an appropriate time-scale. And given the recent vertiginous rise in interest of corporate governance issues, an unanticipated benefit is that such performance-tracking can go some way to providing the higher level of transparency required as part of an organization's governance responsibilities.

However, a potential downside of such performance visibility is that people may be afraid of the consequences of their "poor" performance becoming widespread corporate knowledge. For this reason, the cultural barriers to scorecard rollout must be understood before such transparency is sanctioned (see Chapter 9).

CEO BENEFITS

Overcoming cultural barriers may be particularly important because through an automated scorecard the CEO can have instantaneous access to the performance of all of his or her units, functions, or teams, whereas previously they may have been safely outside the CEO's radar screen.

Andrew Lim, Director of the Singapore-based Balanced Scorecard Solutions (which vends Pbviews), provides this summary of how the CEO benefits from scorecard automation:

The CEO can get a quick high-level and aggregated performance overview, and is also able to drill down to problem areas and learn of corrective action plans under way. Really, an automated solution saves a lot of time as all strategically relevant information, text, and data are in one place, and the CEO can use that information for rich and informed strategic dialogues with their management team.

WHEN TO BEGIN

A key consideration is when to begin the automation process – at the very beginning of the scorecard journey, after about a year or following a longer time-scale for embedding the "idea" of the scorecard, testing the scorecard, and dealing with change management issues.

There is not a set answer to this. We have spoken to many practitioners who report that it was a success perquisite that they automated their scorecard from very early in the scorecard journey – particularly evident when the primary reason for scorecard implementation is as a mechanism to effectively communicate strategy widely in an organization where this had previously been weak. Other organizations state that it required several years to "bed the scorecard in" before automation became a sensible option.

Our survey of scorecard usage in South-east Asia asked when organizations automated their scorecard. The replies are shown in Exhibit 10.4.

At the same time as we built the scorecard	45%
Immediately after we built the scorecard	40%
Less than one year after we built the scorecard	5%
Between one and three years after we built the scorecard	10%
More than three years after we built the scorecard	0%

Exhibit 10.4 Scorecard automation

We would typically recommend that the scorecard had been at least piloted prior to considering software. If the pilot is successful and a wider rollout is planned, we can then expect that there is a good chance that the scorecard will be in situ over the longer term.

We would also suggest that toward the end of the pilot, once the scorecard concept and methodology has taken hold, it might be appropriate to introduce software. Consequently, from the pilot it will be able to show the rest of the organization that the Balanced Scorecard works as a strategy implementation framework and that strategy implementation can be greatly enabled through dedicated software support. Bank Universal, for example, piloted both the scorecard approach and the Pbviews software solution before they created (and subsequently automated) the corporate scorecard.

TRAINING

Another question to ponder is who will be trained in using the automated system. As with any IT solution there's always the danger that it's under-utilized or not used all by some key people, simply due to their inability to use the system fully or at all.

The first people to be trained should be the employees who will manage or facilitate the scorecard program (see Chapter 4). As these will be the people responsible for collecting data and for ensuring the accuracy and timeliness of information and reports, they will need to be the in-house system experts. End-users such as managers and other employee groups will also need to be shown how to use the system, whether it's just reading and making sense of the information required, or inputting information/metric updates.

There will also be a need for people from the IT function to be clear as to how the system interfaces with other systems, and for finance staff and planners and so on to understand how an automated scorecard works alongside other tools for budgeting, scenario planning, and forecasting. We would suggest that representatives from IT, finance, and planning should be involved during the application "scoping" period to ensure the scorecard software is right for the organization's own needs.

VENDOR/PRODUCT SELECTION

A critical part of the automation process is vendor/product selection. Little benefit will be secured (and much time and money wasted) if you can't work with the vendor or the product doesn't meet your requirements for example. Identifying your requirements can prove challenging. Matthew Tice states:

> The question comes down to what is it that you are automating. Also, what are you trying to achieve. If you are looking to reengineer your whole data infrastructure then that speaks to one kind of solution. If you already have that done and you just need a report, that speaks to another set.

> **If you are looking to reengineer your whole data infrastructure then that speaks to one kind of solution. If you already have that done and you just need a report, that speaks to another set.**

Sandy Richardson, Managing Consultant with the US-based Strategy Focused Business Solutions Inc., provided this simple but useful five-step systems selection formula within an article she wrote for Panorama Business View's Perform magazine.[6]

1. Develop your Balanced Scorecard/Performance Management Principles First

This is a very important activity that should be completed early on in the development phase of your performance management journey … consider the following questions:

- How do we want to build our performance measurement measures? (e.g., top down? Via two-way communication?

- Who will use the results information? (senior management only? All employees?)
- How will they use it? (e.g., to manage business performance? to evaluate employee performance? To distribute incentive compensation?)
- How will employees access the results? (e.g., via paper reports? Via a systems application available on their desktop?)
- How will data get into the performance management system? (e.g., via manual data entry? Via automated data feeds?)
- How will we ensure data quality (e.g., through data audits? Automated data feeds?)
- How will results be communicated within the organization (via the systems application? Team meetings? Town hall meetings?...

2. Define your system application requirements?

Using your performance management principles as your guide ... brainstorm on your system functionality requirements. Use the following categories to define your requirements:

- Data-entry processes (e.g., manual or automated data entry? Will the system complete calculations? Will the system automatically assign results icons?)
- Data display (e.g., graphs? Tables? Results icons/color coding? Commentary?)
- Accessibility (e.g., who has write access? Who has read-only access?)
- Security needs or requirements (e.g., what corporate security standards must be adhered to? Do we need variable levels of security?)
- Other (e.g., budget limits, resource considerations, flexibility for enhancements, system scalability)

... Creating this list is the first step in ensuring that you select the right system application for your organization. ...

3. Detail and prioritize your system application requirements

The next step in the process is to take your system requirements and assign priority to each item on your list. That is, review your list and determine what should be defined "have to have" versus what should be defied as "nice to have."...

4.   Complete an objective review of system/software options using your prioritized system application requirements

Once you have prioritized your system requirements, create a marking template that can be used in your review of system application options. List your "have to have" and "nice to have" system features and apply these evaluation standards to every system application reviewed. ...

5.   Select a system application that delivers the majority of your required/must have system application requirements

[To] select the performance management system that is right for your organization ... take each of the completed marking templates and compare your evaluation and notes ... Needless to say, you should seriously consider selecting the application that satisfies the majority of your "have to have" systems requirements.

For the Balanced Scorecard Software Report, Neely and Marr created a two-directional matrix in which organizations put weightings against each of 10 criteria (which are summarized below). This matrix can then be used to compare available software products against the organizational requirements (see Exhibit 10.3).[7]

Selection Criteria 1: Company and Product

At the outset it is critical to check the vendor background as well as basic product information and pricing options. Also, do not be too impressed by the size of the vendor as a boutique firm may have more people focused on a scorecard product.

Selection Criteria 2: Scalability

Scalability is a key consideration. The application must be able to easily incorporate new scorecards and cope with quickly amassing data. The communication approach should be scalable so that it is easy to disseminate the information through mediums such as the Web.

Selection Criteria 3: Flexibility and Customization

The authors suggest that organizations look at how the offerings interface with other reporting and performance management tools that the organization uses. Also, ensure that the software has the flexibility which allows users to add their own perspectives, create personal views, or add personal scorecards.

Selection Criteria 4: Features and Functions

This is where the organization ensures that its needs are reflected in the application's features and functions. Discussions with the vendor will focus on areas such as administrative tasks and access control, exception alerting, collaboration, and reporting.

Selection Criteria 5: Communication

This is where organizations consider their required levels of communication functionality within the application. For example, do they want software to be Web-enabled, or even WAP-enabled? Furthermore, will users be able to communicate on all aspects of the scorecard from strategy down to individual activities, or will the ability to comment be restricted to any group; for example, managers responsible for certain aspects in the balanced scorecard?

Selection Criteria 6: Technical Specifications

It is critical that through the scorecard application one can extract data from existing data sources, so any new piece of software should support the existing desktop or network operating system. A lack of support can be a major obstacle to any implementation.

Selection Criteria 7: User Interface/ Data Presentation

Here organizations have to decide how they want the data to be presented, and applications vary between very graphical to more text- and tables-based formats.

Selection Criteria 8: Analysis Functionality

The authors state that tools offer different levels of analysis capabilities, stretching from simple drill-down capabilities to multidimensional analysis, complex statistical functionality, forecasting, and even scenario-planning. Companies that require more complex analysis functionality often have tools for this in place and have to decide whether to integrate or replace these.

Selection Criteria 9: Service

Organizations must be clear as to the amount of service support available during implementation and ongoing usage stage. Vendors offer differing levels of service, with some offering no implementation support. Other vendors offer a comprehensive service, including their own implementation service and an international service hotline. So organizations need to ensure that their service requirements match the vendor's service offering.

Selection Criteria 10: Future

According to the authors this criteria includes future developments and release frequency of the product, which might indicate the vendors' attention and commitment to the product. It is also important to understand the future vision of the software vendor, which will influence the future product development direction. Organizations want to share the future vision with the software vendor in order to ensure future compatibility.

Exhibit 10.5 provides a selection matrix, which Neely and Marr suggest is useful for assessing vendor offerings against organizational requirements. Through this tool, organizations are able to weight their requirements against Neely and Marr's 10 criteria and use that as a basis for vendor selection.

Criteria	Required	Weight	Product A	Product B	Product ...
Company / Product Sub-criteria I Sub-criteria II ...	Yes/No Yes/No	1–10 1–10			
Scalability Needs Sub-criteria I Sub-criteria II ...	Yes/No Yes/No	1–10 1–10			
Flexibility Needs Sub-criteria I Sub-criteria II ...	Yes/No Yes/No	1–10 1–10			
Features & Functions Sub-criteria I Sub-criteria II ...	Yes/No Yes/No	1–10 1–10			
Communication Needs Sub-criteria I Sub-criteria II ...	Yes/No Yes/No	1–10 1–10			
Technical Needs Sub-criteria I Sub-criteria II ...	Yes/No Yes/No	1–10 1–10			
User Interface Sub-criteria I Sub-criteria II ...	Yes/No Yes/No	1–10 1–10			
Analysis Needs Sub-criteria I Sub-criteria II ...	Yes/No Yes/No	1–10 1–10			
Service Requirements Sub-criteria I Sub-criteria II ...	Yes/No Yes/No	1–10 1–10			
Future Developments Sub-criteria I Sub-criteria II ...	Yes/No Yes/No	1–10 1–10			
Score:					

Source: Marr, B. and Neely, A. (2003) Automating your Scorecard: The Balanced Scorecard Software Report, Gartner and Cranfield School of Management, InfoEdge, Stamford, CT.

Exhibit 10.5 Selection matrix for Balanced Scorecard software

▶▶ CONCLUSION

According to Kaplan and Norton's five principles of the strategy-focused organization (see Chapter 1), strategic learning along with analytics and information systems (which will include automated scorecards) are two of the three sub-components of principle four – Make Strategy a Continual Process. Organizations that wish to fully leverage the power of the Balanced Scorecard, and that want to make strategic learning a real-time capability, should invest in an automated scorecard solution. However, organizations should also keep firmly in mind that software enables, but doesn't drive scorecard success. The third sub-component of the Make Strategy a Continual Process strategy-focused organization principle is to "link budgets and strategy," which we consider in the next chapter.

Bank Universal, Indonesia.

Summary

This case study describes the Balanced Scorecard experiences at Bank Universal prior to its merger into Bank Permata. It illustrates the importance of a successful scorecard pilot prior to full rollout, involving lower level managers in identifying their own performance metrics and of building the internal capability to manage the scorecard program.

Introduction

Headquartered in Jakarta, Indonesia, Bank Permata was formed through the 2002 merger of Bank Universal, Bank Bali, and several other banks. With about 8,000 employees, Bank Permata is one of Indonesia's largest financial services organizations. At the time of the merger, Bank Universal boasted about 2,200 employees and assets of about US$1.2 billion.

Asian Currency Crisis

The banking industry within Indonesia has been in a state of change since the Asia Currency Crisis of 1997, which precipitated the closure/merger of almost 40% of the country's 240+ banks. Those that survived (including Bank Universal) were placed under Government supervision through the Indonesian Banking Restructuring Agency (IBRA). Hence, the banking industry became essentially state-controlled while it was being reshaped. However, Bank Universal's shares were still publicly traded.

Three Strategic Themes

This is important when considering Bank Universal's Balanced Scorecard. Mahdi Syahbuddin, who was Bank Universal's Deputy President Director and is now Bank Permata's Managing Director, explains:

When we created our Balanced Scorecard we started with our corporate vision, which was "to be the best Indonesia regional bank." And in designing the scorecard it forced us into an executive discussion around what we meant by "best," given our own set of circumstances.

The senior management team concurred that being the best required delivering according to three strategic themes (which would be articulated on the Balanced Scorecard). These are outlined by Mahdi Syahbuddin:

The first theme was around handling past problems caused by the non-performing loans from the previous years. The goal here was to minimize loss for the shareholders. The second theme was focused on becoming "a good bank." Here we were setting out to build a new business model and launch a new market strategy post-crisis, and therefore were keen to ensure this new model and strategy would be profitable. So here we were looking to create future value for our shareholders. The third theme was really around communication and building confidence in the eyes of our stakeholders – government, shareholders, and customers – that we were on the way to becoming a "good bank," one that would be profitable and trustworthy.

The Balanced Scorecard captured the three strategic themes in cause and effect relationships through the perspectives of people, process, customer satisfaction, and finance. For example, the "good bank" strategic theme 1 focused on becoming profitable. As we can see in Exhibit 10.6, strategic objectives for the financial perspective included profit and fees income. Customer objectives included effective selling, whereas an internal perspective objective was cross-selling. And an example objective from the employee perspective was core competencies professional growth.

Mahdi Syahbuddin explains that the scorecard represents a commonsense approach to managing a business and that this starts with "people."

As leaders it's of the utmost importance that we appreciate the people who serve the customers, the people who improve the processes, and the people who train others. Quite simply, if we don't have the best people in each area, it is impossible to have efficient processes. And if we don't have efficient processes then it is impossible to serve the customer well and thus, as a consequence, it is impossible to have a good and sustainable return on investment.

The First Pilot

Though commonsense should prevail, it is not to say that scorecard implementation is devoid of complex practical challenges. A first attempt at implementing the Balanced Scorecard within Bank Universal began in 1997. This was triggered when Mahdi Syahbuddin became aware of the scorecard through his readings. As a result, he sent a few of his senior team

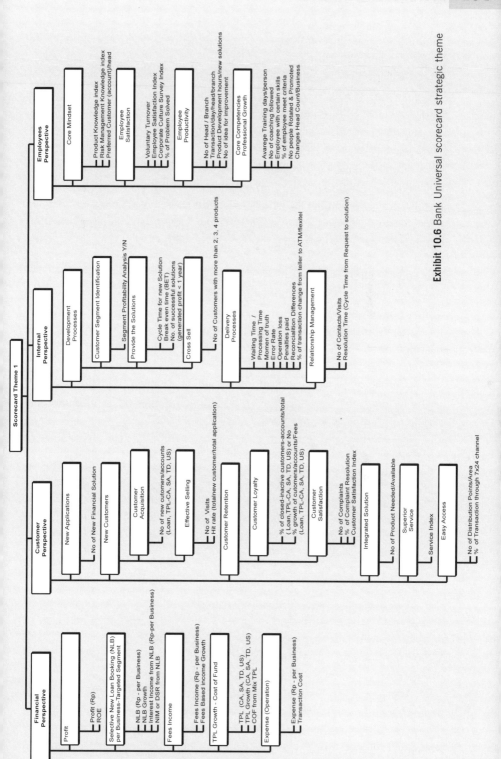

Exhibit 10.6 Bank Universal scorecard strategic theme

to attend scorecard awareness-raising sessions in several locations, including Singapore and Jakarta.

Believing the scorecard could be a valuable tool within the bank, the decision was made to launch a pilot scorecard pilot within the Branch Banking Network (the largest Bank division with 900 employees).

However, Mahdi Syahbuddin admits this effort was less than successful. This, he recalls, was largely due to the fact they had not developed the capability internally for successfully building and implementing a scorecard into an organization with its unique set of challenges, and partly due to a lack of robust measures, particularly around people. And launching a major change exercise when the fallout from the Asian currency crisis was still raining down on the bank might not, in hindsight, have been appropriate.

The Second Pilot

Pak Krisbiyanto, who was Bank Universal's Vice-President – Human Capital, and is now Vice-President, Human Resources for Bank Permata, recalls that despite the pilot challenges there was still a feeling within the senior management team, especially Mahdi Syahbuddin, that the Balanced Scorecard was the most promising tool with which to successfully manage strategy implementation within Bank Universal. This led to the involvement of the Indonesian consultancy, Organizational Transformation International (OTI), in a new scorecard effort.

Pak Krisbiyanto, who acted as a project manager for the scorecard program, recalls:

In 2000 Naresh Makhijani [a senior OTI consultant] came and gave a presentation to the top 14 managers on how the scorecard could help drive the organization forward. Following this he ran a workshop for the top 28 senior managers and it was decided that we should recommence the scorecard effort, again starting with a pilot within the Branch Banking Network.

It was also agreed that this time round a consultancy would be asked to assist in the scorecard effort (they were not used first time round because due to the Asian currency crisis, the budget was not available). According to Pak Krisbiyanto, "We are experts in financial services, not in building Balanced Scorecards, so it seemed sensible to bring in consultancy support."

After being appointed in 2001, OTI's involvement came to an end, as agreed, about eight months after the their involvement began. In this period, the pilot was completed and the pilot scorecard automated, a corporate scorecard created, and, importantly, knowledge transfer took place between

OTI and bank employees.

With OTI facilitation, the Branch Network Balanced Scorecard was created with full participation of all managers, at both senior and branch level. The senior managers considered the wider Bank Universal vision and strategy and decided how they could best deliver to that strategy. This scorecard was then devolved to branch level.

Mahdi Syahbuddin stresses that although it is fundamentally important to involve senior management in designing the scorecard, for a successful devolution it is equally essential to involve branch management. He says that this is particularly important for the identification of branch-level metrics.

To find the right indicators you have to involve branch managers because they are the people who really understand what makes their branches perform. If they're not involved, then any performance indicators forced onto them stand a good chance of being resisted and indeed being inappropriate.

So in workshop settings, branch managers identified the key indicators that would show branch performance and how the branches were working toward corporate strategic goals.

Pilot Indicators

As examples of indicators chosen (there were between 15 and 20 measures for each branch) financial metrics are, as expected, around "revenue" and "expenses." Customer satisfaction metrics include "how long customers wait for tellers or service delivery," and there was an annual customer satisfaction survey that measured the branch network performance collectively, and branches individually.

From a process perspective, measures included how long it took to process a check, to submit a deposit, or to open an account. And finally, on the people side, measures included succession planning at branch level and the product knowledge of branch employees. However, Mahdi Syahbuddin stresses: "The branch managers defined all these measures, not the head office."

The managers must have done something right, for in 2001 an independent survey conducted by a leading business magazine rated Bank Universal as the number one bank in Indonesia, based on its customer service, operational efficiency, and human resource practices (1, Ref). Hence, it covered key parts of each of the three "non-financial" Balanced Scorecard performance perspectives.

Within Branch Banking the scorecard was monitored on a weekly basis at a senior level. This led to the need for a powerful communication process within the network.

Scorecard Automation

This communication process has been greatly enabled through the automation of the Branch Network's Balanced Scorecard, as Pak Krisbiyanto explains:

We wanted to automate the scorecard as we saw it as a way to significantly improve communications and enhance performance transparency. On OTI's advice we opted for Pbviews [a solution provided by the vendor Panorama Business Views], which was both easy to use and to update.

Mahdi Syahbuddin says that through automation it became clear how individual branches were performing against indicators within all four perspectives. Importantly, where excellence was identified, say in customer service scores, then the branch best practices that caused these scores could be shared throughout the network, thus serving as a powerful knowledge-sharing tool.

The Corporate Scorecard

While the pilot was progressing, the process began in February 2001 to create the corporate-level scorecard (a new post-crisis strategy had been shaped in November/December 2000).

The creation of this corporate scorecard (which was subsequently automated) was achieved through a series of senior management workshops. Within these, the senior team benefited from the learnings that came out of the Branch Banking pilot and were greatly encouraged by the pilot success. The Board management group reviewed the corporate scorecard on a monthly basis.

Knowledge Transfer

As OTI provided consultancy support for a specified period, it was critical to the long-term success of the scorecard program that knowledge transfer take place between the consultancy and bank personnel. Pak Krisbiyanto explains how he sees a consultancy role in a scorecard program:

The role of the consultancy is hugely important in the early stages. They can explain what the scorecard is, provide best practice information based on other corporate implementations, and they have the expertise to facilitate the scorecard design and pilot process. But their skills must be transferred to the company itself. For it is the organization that must own this and manage the scorecard on an ongoing basis.

This was certainly true within Bank Universal, where responsibility for the scorecard program resided in the human capital group, where each of the three strategic themes had a designated program manager from within the group. Trained by OTI, each theme "manager" was charged with securing data from an identified scorecard contact in finance and for putting that data into reporting formats. Pak Krisbiyanto states:

Placing responsibility in the human capital group made sense because this was essentially about change management, leadership, and communications. And as part of their work in the bank, human capital has primary responsibility for ensuring those performance aspects are well managed as a process.

Scorecard Benefits

Given that the original scorecard effort was not a success, it is notable that both Pak Krisbiyanto and Mahdi Syahbuddin state that second-time-around successes were secured and rapidly so. Pak Krisbiyanto says that the overriding benefit was around transparency and accountability.

Through the Balanced Scorecard it was possible to measure the performance of our employees and of the organization more clearly. Previously we would blame each other but through the scorecard we could see the actual causes of problems that led to targets being missed and so knew where to direct our efforts. The scorecard gave a very clear picture of accountability across the organization.

He also says that the bank became better at given promotion due to there being better transparency around performance. Moreover, managers could see how they are performing against their appraisal objectives as a result of calculating their "performance points" against the four perspectives of the scorecards.

Mahdi Syahbuddin adds that the transparency afforded by the scorecard also led to better cross-functional teamwork and understanding. "The marketing people could appreciate the service people and the service people could appreciate the operational and process people, who in turn could appreciate the human resource people." Accordingly, another benefit is resource allocation.

Previously, it was difficult to allocate both people and the budget for our investments because each group of directors wanted their area to be a priority. With the scorecard we knew what was important and it became easier to decide where we should prioritize.

Syahbuddin adds that the scorecard also helped the bank's external relations (a key theme in the scorecard). "We could tell the shareholders how we're handling the aftermath of the problems caused by the crisis. And we could communicate our strategy to all of our stakeholders and show them the areas we could control and the areas we could not."

Conclusion

In conclusion Mahdi Syahbuddin stresses that by far the most important critical success factor in using the scorecard is that the senior management team believes in the value of the scorecard. Pak Krisbiyanto agrees with this, and both concur that management support should be gained at each level, which was why the bank placed a significant focus on involving the branch managers.

At the time of writing, Mahdi Syahbuddin was planning to launch the Balanced Scorecard within Bank Permata. This in itself is a powerful testament to the value the senior team of Bank Universal derived from using the scorecard.

Source: Building a Strategic Balanced Scorecard,
James Creelman, Business Intelligence, 2003

1   Marr, B. and Neely, A. 2003, Automating your Scorecard: The Balanced Scorecard Software Report, Gartner and Cranfield School of Management, InfoEdge, Stamford, CT.

2   See <http://www.bscol.com/>

3   See end note 2.

4   See end note 1.

5   See end note 1.

6   Richardson, S. 2003, "Build In-house or Buy Off the Shelf?" PERFORM, vol. 2, issue 1, pp. 20–4.

7   See end note 1.

11

Advanced Usage: An integrated financial and strategic management system

*T*he Balanced Scorecard has to become "the way we manage around here" and not a discrete project. For most companies it is proving difficult to hardwire the budgeting process to the Balanced Scorecard. The budget represents an annual performance cycle, whereas the Balanced Scorecard does not conceptually, or practically, conform to financial year cycles. The budget was created for the industrial era, the Balanced Scorecard Management System for the knowledge era. Rolling forecasts are emerging as alternatives to the budget. They are more attuned to the needs of the knowledge era and so more compatible with the Balanced Scorecard. Management meetings within the organization must be focused around the Balanced Scorecard. The senior team should hold quarterly reviews of performance to the scorecard. These meetings should focus only on the scorecard and strategy. Monthly management meetings should be used to track how successful the organization is proving to be in translating strategic objectives into operational actions. As an example, a case study on Saatchi & Saatchi Worldwide concludes this chapter.

BACKGROUND

Throughout this book we have stressed that the Balanced Scorecard Management System has to become "the way we manage around here." Put another way, it must be the overarching performance management system to which everything in the organization responds to and feeds into. We are uncompromising in our belief that the Balanced Scorecard should not be a discrete project happening on the edges of management's horizon and vying for funding with a host of other programs. The Balanced Scorecard provides the process for deciding which projects are funded.

> " Placing the emphasis to initiatives rather than measurement ensures that the Balanced Scorecard becomes an "action-oriented" system, rather than merely an assessment tool. "

In Chapter 8 we explained the role of strategic initiatives as an integral component of a Balanced Scorecard Management System. We will not repeat those learnings here, but will restate our view that it is through strategic initiatives that the real work of the Balanced Scorecard (or more accurately strategy implementation) takes place. The actions that are completed as a result of scorecard creation are, we argue, much more important than the measures that are chosen to monitor performance. Placing the emphasis to initiatives rather than measurement ensures that the Balanced Scorecard becomes an "action-oriented" system, rather than merely an assessment tool.

It was interesting that on a number of occasions within their book Strategy Maps, scorecard co-creators Dr David Norton and Professor Robert Kaplan, illustrate the Balanced Scorecard Framework as comprising three parts:[1]

1. A Strategy Map of strategic themes and objectives.
2. A Balanced Scorecard of measurements and targets.
3. An action plan of initiatives and budget.

This decomposition of the Balanced Scorecard Framework serves as a powerful illustration of the importance of initiatives and the critical role of allocating scarce financial resources to these strategic initiatives.

BUDGETING

This brings us to the role of budgeting within the Balanced Scorecard system and the linking of budgets to the strategy. Anybody who has observed the Balanced Scorecard since its inception in the early 1990s, as we have, will have become all too aware of the difficulties many organizations get into in trying to hardwire the budgeting process (and also other planning processes such as forecasting) to the Balanced Scorecard.

Robert Kaplan recognized these problems when he said that: "One aspect of the Strategy-Focused Organization that has lagged is the integration with the budgeting system. It's less developed than the objective setting or the links to incentive systems, human resource systems, or communications systems." But he adds: "I think, however, if we don't establish the link with budgeting, then the scorecard initiatives may wither"

According to our survey of scorecard adoption in South-east Asia (see Appendix 1) almost half of scorecard users claimed their budgeting process was partially integrated with the Balanced Scorecard, as shown in Exhibit 11.1. Further analysis will be required to probe the level of integration because a figure of 74% partially or fully integrated seems extraordinarily high and contrary to our experience and observations.

Fully integrated	28%
Partially integrated	46%
Not integrated	26%

Exhibit 11.1 The scorecard and budgeting

THE DIFFICULTIES IN ALIGNING BUDGETS

On one level the reason for the difficulty in establishing the link is simple to understand. The budget represents an annual performance cycle, fixed to the organization's financial year. Financial targets are set and financial, and other resources are allocated to meet these targets.

At the end of the year the performance to the budget is reported, and for public organizations the investment community receives updates of financial performance each quarter. Success or failure of the organization, and by association the senior management team, is based squarely on performance to the budget.

> **" The very essence of cause and effect cannot be shoehorned into a financial year. "**

Conceptually, or practically, the Balanced Scorecard Framework is not tied to an annual performance cycle. A Strategy Map describes those objectives that if delivered will mean the successful implementation of a strategy – which typically has a horizon much in excess of one year. The very essence of cause and- effect cannot be shoehorned into a financial year. For example, resourcing programs within the learning and growth perspectives may well in turn lead to desired changes in the process and customer perspectives, and ultimately financial success. However, this chain of causal relationships may, for example, start in Q2 of the financial year 2004 and not translate into the hoped for financial outcome into Q1 of financial year 2005.

As a learning and growth initiative such as skills training, for example, will be expensed as opposed to capitalized, the cost of the program will hit the bottom line in 2004 where the revenue will not hit until 2005. So if there were severe pressure to hit the 2004 targets, it would be expedient to "kill" the training program or not start it all. This clearly will be to the detriment to the longer term strategy.

Matthew Tice, the Balanced Scorecard Collaborative's (BSCol) Vice-President Asia-Pacific, puts it nicely when he says: "The solar cycle should not be the basis on which you allocate resources."

INFLEXIBILITY

Tice adds that for most organizations it is proving a difficult task to align the budget to the scorecard simply because of the inflexibility of their budgeting process. One of the most useful ways we find to define a strategy-focused organization is to describe it as the opposite of a budget-focused organization.

Dr David Norton provides this overview of why in the knowledge-era we need to create a new management approach that moves away from the inherent principles that dictate a budget-focused organization; precepts that were laid down to galvanize success in the industrial age.

If the world is stable [as the industrial age essentially was] you want a management system that works incrementally and we developed the perfect system for incremental change – it was called the budget. The budget essentially uses the past as a point of reference and gives you a way to manage change incrementally. The whole concept of the budget was based on the idea of control. That the threat to the organization did not come from outside but within. However, if we have systems today that manage incrementally, they're a liability, they get in the way of our ability to change. So management systems have to adapt from incrementalism to permitting a dynamic, far-reaching transformation and change.

And continuing with the downsides of the budget, most budgeting systems prohibit dynamic management simply due to the length of the process. Empirical research by the US-headquartered Hackett Group found than an average company required 80 business days to complete a budget, with many requiring more than a 100.[2] It is hard to be dynamic if takes a third of a year to complete a budget.

However, the fact is that most organizations still put themselves through the rigors of the annual budgeting process. So let's look at how some of our case study companies approach the challenge of linking budgets to strategy through the Balanced Scorecard.

> " ... one of the most useful ways we find to define a strategy-focused organization is to describe it as the opposite of a budget-focused organization. "

CASE STUDY EXAMPLES

Perhaps the most advanced example of integration within our case study organizations is found within Saatchi & Saatchi Worldwide (see below), where the Balanced Scorecard (or CompaSS as they brand it) plays a significant role in the financial planning process. Paul Melter, the organization's Worldwide Director, CompaSS, explains:

> We now have CompaSS and 100-day plans, which are action plans linked and aligned to CompaSS objectives. So what we are saying to units is manage strategy, not costs. Although judicious financial management is critical, what we are saying is, 'Put the budget in a CompaSS format and show how you are ensuring that resources are supporting important strategic initiatives.'
>
> To secure investment, managers have to show how the predicted financial results are achieved through cause and effect relationships between CompaSS objectives and measures. People know the information required in order to fund their investments. So now they show up at meetings with the right data and get straight to what the challenge and action plan is.

At Centrepoint Properties (see Chapter 9) there is also a direct link between the scorecard and the budget, as Carol Yong Meng Dai, Senior Manager, Human Resources, explains:

> Each year the second quarterly review is when we formally assess the scorecard and do our Strategy Mapping for the following year. This is then used to shape the thinking that goes into the budgeting process. So we get the revised Strategy Map in May and complete the budget during June and July."

Safety & Quality Manager Kwok Yiu Leung, explains how the scorecard dovetails with the strategic and financial planning processes within Hong Kong's MTR Corporation (see Chapter 7):

> We hold a strategy planning workshop each year to facilitate senior managers and department heads in the brainstorming of strategies and initiatives for the following year. This is largely based on review of the previous year's scorecard performance. The strategic objectives deployed from the strategic plan will be the business line items for budgeting and eventually form part of the scorecard measures."

So what we are seeing from our case study companies is typically the collocation of the budgeting process with the Balanced Scorecard system. Typically, once an annual scorecard review (and therefore requisite changes or reprioritization) has taken place, this information is used to inform the budgeting process. By such a process it becomes more likely that annual targets do not compromise the progress of longer term strategic initiatives.

In their book The Strategy-Focused Organization: How Balanced Scorecard Companies Thrive in the new Business Environment, Norton and Kaplan make this valuable observation:

> Companies have discovered that they need two kinds of budgets: a strategy budget and an operational budget. This distinction is essential. Just as the Balanced Scorecard attempts to protect long-term initiatives from short-term suboptimization, the budgeting process must also protect the long-term initiatives from the pressures to deliver short-term financial performance.[3]

Kaplan and Norton suggest this process for making the transition from high-level strategy to budgeting for local operations, which includes both strategy and operational budget elements.

1. Translate the strategy into a Balanced Scorecard, defining the strategic objectives and measures.
2. Set stretch targets for specific future times for each measure. Identify planning gaps to motivate and stimulate creativity.
3. Identify strategic initiatives and resource requirements to close the planning gaps, thereby enabling the stretch targets to be achieved.
4. Authorize financial and human resources for the strategic initiatives. Embed these requirements into the annual budget. The annual budget comprises two components: a strategy budget to manage discretionary programs and an operational budget to manage the efficiency of departments, functions, and line items[4].

ROLLING FORECASTS

This process accepts that a conventional budgeting process remains in place, and for most companies this will certainly be true. However,

> " ... a number of pioneering organizations ... are dispensing with conventional budgets altogether. "

there are a number of pioneering organizations that are dispensing with conventional budgets altogether – such as the Scandinavia-headquartered organizations Ikea Systems (supplier of hone furnishing and products), Svenska Handelsbanken (which actually hasn't had a budget since 1972, but has consistently been Europe's most profitable bank), and Borealis (at the leading edge of polymer research and development). All three of these organizations are users of the Balanced Scorecard, with Borealis being a member of BSCol's prestigious Hall of Fame.

What these organizations essentially do is replace the budget with an ongoing series of strategic reviews leading to resource prioritization and re-prioritization, which is much more aligned with the business environment. The most popular way to do this is by deploying what is called a rolling forecast.

Simply put, a rolling forecast can be defined as a forecast with a time horizon not limited to the current business year. A rolling forecast with four quarters covers this time period, regardless of the business year. But forecasts can be spread over five, six, seven, or more forecasts.

In his paper "The Perils of the Budget," UK-based consultant Jonathan Chocqueel-Mangan, provides this explanation of how Borelais used a rolling forecast alongside the Balanced Scorecard.[5] Borealis is probably the leading example of an organization that used a rolling forecast alongside a Balanced Scorecard.

The problem [Borealis] faced was that the budgeting process provided the illusion of control when, in reality, its core assumptions were based on volatile oil prices and a highly unpredictable business cycle. So it replaced the target setting, planning, measurement and control functions of the budgeting process by integrating them within a Balanced Scorecard that directed their attention away from short-term budget contracts and toward a number of strategic themes (such as reducing fixed costs) that underpin medium-term goals (such as reducing fixed costs by 30 percent over five years).

He went on to say that targets are now set by reference to industry benchmarks (cost targets are an example) and the annual review process takes only a few weeks, compared with four to five months spent previously on the budget. Rolling forecasts support quarterly performance reviews, and costs are managed through medium-term targets and trend analysis.

Performance is now reviewed quarterly and Scorecard measures are a feature of web pages and bulletin boards that are eagerly followed by all staff. Project leaders reckon they have saved 95 percent of the time that used to be spent on budgeting and forecasting.

Chocqueel-Mangan quotes Borealis project leader Bjarte Bogsnes as saying "We now achieve what the planning and budgeting did in a simpler, more direct way. In fact I would go further. The new system is not just simpler – it gives us far more information and far more control than the traditional budget ever did."

MANAGEMENT MEETINGS

At the start of this chapter we highlighted our assertion that the Balanced Scorecard System must become "the way we manage around here." Naturally, as well as being the way organizations identify strategic initiatives and allocate scarce financial and human resources, the scorecard has to be the central focus of management meetings.

Nigel Penny, founder of the Singapore-based consultancy ClaritasAsia, observes:

I favor using the scorecard at two levels. First, there should be a formal quarterly review of progress against the objectives housed on the Strategy Map. In this review organizations can check our progress (good and bad) and use it as a feedback mechanism to revisit whether the assumptions behind the strategy map, and the strategy itself are still valid. I find this quarterly formal review very helpful in managing "course corrections."

On a monthly basis I prefer an approach whereby we just target "volatile measures," progress of key initiatives, and any action item agendas for the quarterly formal review.

What Penny is recommending, and we would certainly agree with this, is that two complementary scorecard-focused management meetings take place. The first is a strategic review where leaders focus squarely on performance to the scorecard, and indeed do nothing within this meeting apart from focusing on, and discussing, the Balanced Scorecard.

Within the monthly management meeting, we can track scorecard progress as part of the day-to-day cauldron of managing a business in the knowledge era. But in this case, the meeting still revolves round the scorecard insomuch as it is a forum for ensuring that operational performance is progressing according to the dictates of the strategic objectives. It is where we instill the managerial disciplines required to turn strategic aspirations into operational actions.

CASE STUDY EXAMPLES

We'll now consider how our case study organizations place the scorecard at the heart of their management meetings. Within Tata Motors Commercial Vehicles Business Unit (CVBU, see Chapter 1), performance to strategic initiatives is monitored during monthly scorecard review meetings that are held at each organizational level. Moreover, quarterly scorecard audits are conducted across the organization. The meetings and the audits ensure alignment of all divisions/departments/functions/plants to the overall CVBU objectives.

At Singapore Prison Service (see Chapter 2) monthly meetings are held at the department level (the highest prison level) and are chaired by the Director (the most senior officer). Performance to key performance indicators are discussed. In this session the superintendents report and they are held accountable for the performance of their branches.

Wee Yik Keong, Staff Officer, Research and Planning, states: "This monthly exercise ensures that the scorecard remains high on people's agenda. Without this discipline we would probably find that the scorecard would wither."

Both Bank Universal (see Chapter 10) and the Gold Coin Group (see Chapter 5) discussed scorecard performance at the top management level on a monthly basis. Paul Melter says that the Balanced Scorecard focuses the discussions of every management meeting at Saatchi &

Saatchi. At Centrepoint Properties, appraising the divisional scorecards (it has Strategy Maps and Balanced Scorecards at the divisional and not corporate level) is done through a quarterly CEO review. At the India-based XYZ Cellular (see Chapter 6), the CEOs conducts a review of performance to scorecard measures with his direct reports on a weekly

> " The Balanced Scorecard is becoming "the way we manage around here" and strategy is what we manage. "

basis. Furthermore, there's a periodical (typically quarterly) review by the senior team of the objectives, measures, weights, and targets on the scorecard to ensure the scorecard remains aligned with changes in the business environment or strategy. This helps ensure that the Balanced Scorecard continues to remain relevant.

What we are seeing in each of these case examples is the Balanced Scorecard directing the content of both quarterly and monthly performance review meetings. The Balanced Scorecard is becoming "the way we manage around here" and strategy is what we manage.

Although there is no doubt that the Balanced Scorecard Management System has proven its continued relevance to organizations since its inception in 1992, the next questions is how likely it is to remain relevant in the future? We ponder this question in Chapter 12, which concludes this book.

CASE STUDY

Saatchi & Saatchi Worldwide

Summary

In the mid-1990s Saatchi & Saatchi Worldwide was on the brink of bankruptcy. In 2000 the Publicis Groupe acquired it for about US$2.5 billion. This occurred after the Balanced Scorecard had been deployed as Saatchi & Saatchi's strategic tool to manage an ambitious turnaround strategy. This case study describes what Saatchi & Saatchi has learnt to be the critical factors in working with the Balanced Scorecard – not least the importance of senior management commitment, global consistency, and keeping the Strategy Map uncluttered and laser-focused.

Background

Headquartered in New York City, and with annual billings topping US$7 billion, Saatchi & Saatchi is one of the world's leading creative organizations. The corporation has more than 7,000 employees within 138 offices in 82 countries. Services range from communication and marketing strategy, advertising scripts and production (for all media channels), consumer research and forecasting, among others. The organization positions itself not as an advertising agency, but as an "ideas' company."

Within Asia, Saatchi & Saatchi is headquartered in Hong Kong and comprises two regions: South-east Asia (with operations in, as examples, Singapore, Malaysia, Thailand, Vietnam, and India) and Greater China (Hong Kong, Taiwan, and China). It has three offices in China (Beijing, Shanghai, and Guangzhou), a country where Saatchi & Saatchi claims market leadership and where it represents organizations such as the P&G, Danone, and Mead Johnson.

Indisputable success

That Saatchi & Saatchi is successful is indisputable. With the vision "To be revered as the hothouse for world-changing creative ideas that transform our clients' businesses, brands and reputations," the corporation represents over 50 of the world's most valuable global brands. The impressive client list includes household names such as Toyota/Lexus, Procter & Gamble, General Mills/Pillsbury, Visa International, Mead Johnson, and Danone.

As one measure of its success, in September 2000, the Paris, France, headquartered Publicis Groupe SA (the world's fourth-largest communications group) purchased Saatchi & Saatchi for close on $2.5 billion. Equating to about 4.5 times Saatchi & Saatchi's then net worth, this purchase price is remarkable in that just three years earlier the corporation was teetering on the brink of bankruptcy. This brings us to a story of transformation and one of the truly great Balanced Scorecard implementations.

Experiencing a classic burning platform due to over-extension through acquisitions throughout the 1980s, coupled with severe financial pressures in the recession of the early 1990s, turnaround started with the appointment of a new senior management team in the mid-1990s. Bob Seelert became Chairman and he appointed Kevin Roberts as CEO Worldwide, and Bill Cochrane as CFO Worldwide. They still hold these positions and were, as a team, catalytic for the scorecard implementation that was to follow.

Turnaround strategies
First though was the requirement for significant organizational restructuring and redirection. A key trigger for this was the December 1997 de-merger of Saatchi & Saatchi from Cordiant Communications. With Saatchi & Saatchi now out on its own, the senior team presented to its Stakeholders a detailed strategic blueprint for recovery, which included the following three very ambitious targets within a timeframe of three years.

- growing the revenue base better than market;
- converting 30% of that incremental revenue to operating profit;
- doubling its earnings per share.

These goals were to support the new vision, articulated at this time and explicated earlier in this case study. The corporation had an ambitious vision and even more ambitious financial targets. But the trick would be to deliver on its goals, which would clearly require a rapid implementation of the new strategy. And giving the high failure rates of strategy implementation, coupled with the corporation's precarious financial position, this would not be without a significant risk of failure. As Paul Melter, Worldwide Director, CompaSS (how the company brands its Balanced Scorecard), explains: "We didn't have the luxury of getting it wrong, we had one shot and the clock was ticking."

After spending about three months during late 1997 on the road visiting the majority of the organization's 45+ globally dispersed agencies, Kevin

Roberts realized that although great work was being done, each location was essentially working to its own agenda. Simply put, there was no commonality of purpose or cohesion of identity – not surprising, given the organization had grown through acquisition. Roberts therefore realized that he required a management tool that would help communicate and make operational the new vision in a commonly understood process and language.

Arriving at the scorecard

A few months later that tool presented itself when CFO, Bill Cochrane, attended an executive seminar at the seminal Harvard Business School. One of the guest lecturers was Professor Robert Kaplan, who introduced the assembled delegates to the Balanced Scorecard. Melter recalls:

> On hearing Dr Kaplan speak, Bill Cochrane knew immediately that the scorecard was the ideal tool for our strategy implementation efforts. It was simple, intuitively sensible, and if it was designed and aligned correctly it would lead to immediate and lasting results."

Scorecard steering committee

With the top team collectively championing the scorecard effort, a first important decision was to appoint Renaissance Worldwide (the president of which was Dr David Norton) as consultants to the program.

The next step saw the creation of a Balanced Scorecard Steering Committee to lead the scorecard program. The committee comprised three representatives from Renaissance and three from Saatchi & Saatchi – Paul Melter and colleagues from client services and strategic planning. The committee had to report to the executive management team on a weekly basis.

Melter, who was then a finance director for a Saatchi & Saatchi division clearly recalls the day he first came across the Balanced Scorecard.

Bill Cochrane invited me onto the steering committee on September 1, 1998. He called me up and said, "Come into my office, I've got something very interesting to show you." He had a stack of papers on his desk about the scorecard. He then told me that the consultancy firm Renaissance was coming in the next day to begin the scorecard design and implementation process. I read the papers, joined the committee, and I've been hooked ever since.

Melter also recalls how the corporation came to brand the scorecard CompaSS:

During late 1998 we architected our first Balanced Scorecard and tested the concept within several of our business units, one of which was Saatchi & Saatchi Canada. This unit's CEO, Dick Olsen, is a keen sailor and he observed that the Balanced Scorecard was really a compass, navigating us in the direction we wanted to sail. The senior team loved this image, especially as the SS represented the company's initials, and so we branded the scorecard CompaSS.

Interestingly, Melter states that whereas everybody within Saatchi & Saatchi today knows about CompaSS, they will not necessarily recognize the term Balanced Scorecard.

The Corporate Strategy Map

The corporate-level Saatchi & Saatchi CompaSS was built in a three-month period from September to November 1998. The corporate Strategy Map, which was used until 2003, is shown in Exhibit 11.2. Note that despite the pressure the organization was under at the time it first created the scorecard, and the complexities of managing a global organization, the Strategy Map is remarkably simple, comprising just 12 strategic objectives. Note there is just one objective from the "people and culture" perspective (One team: One dream: create a rewarding, stimulating environment where nothing is impossible) and from the client perspective (create permanently infatuated clients). This simplicity was purposeful, says Melter.

A Strategy Map should show the critical few objectives that will make the difference in delivering to the strategy. And these should be strategic objectives, not operational. Too many Balanced Scorecards and Strategy Maps include both.

The Map

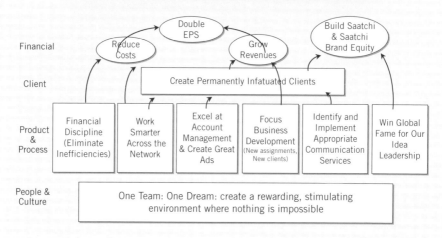

Exhibit 11.2 The map

RASCIs

From the steering committee evolved a process of setting out RASCIs – an acronym for Responsible, Approval, Support, Consult and Inform. According to Melter:

The "A" was Kevin Roberts, as he would be the one who would give the final approval to our work. As for the "Rs" – we first identified a theme owner for each perspective (therefore responsible for that perspective). For Finance it was Bill Cochrane, from North America. For Client it was a Senior Executive/Regional Director from Asia. For Product and Process it was another Senior Executive/Regional Director from Australia, and for People and Growth it was another Senior Executive/Regional Director, from China.

Melter goes on to say that that these "Rs" then worked with the steering committee to choose objectives that would eventually be essential links in the Strategy Map, which was then presented to Roberts for approval. He adds that having one "A" and just one "R" for each perspective was vital for taking out any bottlenecks and ensuring the process moved rapidly.

From here, further "Rs," typically CEOs from agencies around the global network, were assigned responsibility for detailing how specific objectives would be achieved, such as identifying the key measures. These "Rs" also worked closely with the steering committee in delivering to his task.

The RASCI of designing and aligning CompaSS was taking shape:

R – local CEOs

A – Kevin Roberts

S – support (those who worked with the CEOs doing the "real work" providing analysis/data)

C - steering committee

I - people who needed to know about decisions but did not necessarily need to be involved in the decision-making process and could therefore be informed after the fact.

Global Rollout

With the corporate level CompaSS in place, the next process step was global rollout to all 45+ business units. Keeping with the goal of commonality of purpose and the desire to keep scorecards simple and focused, devolved Strategy Maps are essentially the same as at the corporate level. Melter states:

So, for example, the Strategy Map for Asia-Pacific would be almost an exact replica of the corporate map. There will be some tweaking to capture important local objectives and measures (that is, Global – To be in the top 3 at Cannes; Local – Dominate Creative Effectiveness, Media, and Cyber Awards), but we can take the regional map and overlay it onto the corporate map.

Importantly, the corporate map defines the performance conversations with the regions, as Melter explains:

We will say to regional CEOs, "Here's the corporate scorecard. As you can see, our customer focus is to build permanently infatuated clients. We expect you to do the same, so what are you doing to make this happen? What initiatives are in place? How are you measuring this?" So by using the scorecard as a strategic communication tool nobody can be in any doubt as to what we want to achieve as an organization and the contributions we expect from our people.

Senior Management Commitment

Responsibility for CompaSS performance within each unit ultimately lies with the local CEO, just as at the corporate level the performance "buck" stops with Kevin Roberts. And the unwavering commitment of Roberts and the other members of the executive team largely ensure getting local CEO buy-in, as Melter explains:

Without having the unconditional, unequivocal backing of the senior executive group this will fail. All of the 45+ unit-based CEOs have mentors among the senior executive group and if there's a feeling that the CompaSS doesn't have to be done this month, or if they believe there's something more important then it will fade. But our three executive leaders make it clear to all the local unit CEOs that this is a great tool and this is the way we manage the business.

Roberts, for example, uses the CompaSS as the framework for his performance discussions with Saatchi & Saatchi's parent company Publicis. According to Melter:

With the CompaSS, Kevin Roberts can talk to Publicis about the whole Saatchi & Saatchi performance in one or two documents – financial, client, processes, and products, and what's going on in every unit. Once senior managers at the units see this commitment and the usefulness of the CompaSS they will want to use it.

Scorecard Support

In saying that, the management of each unit does receive proper training and ongoing support in how to work with the scorecard. Paul Melter is the full-time CompaSS director and two full-time staff support him. One is involved in managing and developing the scorecard software system. The other person is involved in quality control. Melter also has the support of over 40 part-time scorecard champions in the units who are responsible for collecting and collating their own CompaSS and forwarding these to the center. Melter elaborates:

By the time I look at an individual CompaSS, it is to see whether it makes sense and if there are any disconnects from strategy. Almost always, I give feedback and discuss the scorecard with the individual unit's CEO.

As an important learning, Melter is convinced that in a global organization, responsibility for the scorecard has to be a full-time vocation:

I find it difficult to imagine how any large organization can manage the scorecard as a part-time effort. When we set up the steering committee it was essentially a part-time responsibility, but once CompaSS was being rolled out it had to be full-time. To do the CompaSS on a quarterly basis there's a great deal of education, training, and logistics that go into the process.

But the job isn't over when CompaSS is up and running. Then you get into managing the scorecard as an ongoing program. We are using the scorecard with the aim of building a strategy-focused organization. The scorecard therefore impacts planning, communication, people and culture, budgeting, and feedback as examples. It focuses the discussions of every management meeting. In short, the scorecard is an essential tool in the way we manage our global organization. It's the means for setting priorities and allocating resources.

Where the scorecard is managed part-time I'd be interested to know how effective the scorecard is, whether the company is truly setting out to become a strategy-focused organization and how deeply ingrained it is in their cultures.

100-day plans
Being on a trajectory to become a strategy-focused organization means that the CompaSS plays a significant role in the financial planning process. Melter explains:

We now have CompaSS and 100-day plans, which are action plans linked and aligned to CompaSS objectives. So what we are saying to units is manage strategy, not costs. Although judicious financial management is critical, what we are saying is put the budget in a CompaSS format and show how you are ensuring that resources are supporting important strategic initiatives. To secure investment, managers have to show how the predicted financial results are achieved through cause and effect relationships between CompaSS objectives and measures. People know the information required in order to fund their investments. So now they show up at meetings with the right data and get straight to what the challenge and action plan is.

Despite the undoubted success Saatchi & Saatchi had in implementing its strategy through the CompaSS (for example, it delivered to its three-year stretch targets six months ahead of schedule), there have been some challenges along the way. One has been the complexity of reporting the scorecard results from all 45 business units back up to the corporate level in a meaningful fashion. Melter states:

We consolidated the non-financial measures based on assumptions and modeling. You can always aggregate financial data but the way you aggregate non-financial data is through weighted averages on some measures and straight averages on others based on relevant assumptions and criteria.

He admits that some of the definition is subjective, especially around client satisfaction, but they do try and get all non-financial metrics calibrated at least annually. In addition, where there are subjective measures, they try and include at least one substantive measure to support it (that is, Client Satisfaction rating, supported along with a Brand Sales Growth measure).

The 45 units roll up to 11 regions, which then get consolidated to make the Worldwide (enterprise) CompaSS. Performance is typically discussed from a regional perspective.

Scorecard results, are delivered quarterly, and expressed through the "traffic-light" reporting system of green (ahead of target), yellow (meeting target), or red (off target). When green, executives are expected to share best practices for use elsewhere in the organization (thus strengthening the "one team, one dream" people and growth objective).

Melter recalls that the "traffic-light" system did cause some early concerns. "Nobody wanted to be red because they knew Kevin Roberts would see this. We called it "red status phobia" and it had to be overcome.

He says they did this by predefining the financial measures based on conditional formatting. Therefore, making them either red or green, there was rarely ever a "yellow" status. So the manager was either beating target or not. Fudging therefore is not an option.

We also said that excellent leaders do not see "red" as a failing, but as a signal to identify, and deliver solutions. It was an opportunity to earn your feathers, which exemplified what becoming a "chief" was all about.

Melter adds that where managers were reporting "green" for people, process, and customer, but "red" for financial, it highlighted a strategic disconnect that needed to be addressed. Identifying such disconnects is, says Melter, one of the strengths of the scorecard system. Keeping focus to avoid such disconnects is assured by the scorecard being central to every management meeting.

Once you're over this important hurdle, the brilliance is:

- stating the true issue(s) and challenge(s) in a clear and simple way;
- then figuring out what action(s) and initiative(s) are needed to drive performance;
- applying RASCI to ensure it gets done.

But Melter stresses that the initial greatest challenge is getting the strategy right. "Go back to the Balanced Scorecard mantra – 'You can't manage what you can't measure, you can't measure what you can't describe.' It's real simple, you need a clear strategy."

Once this is clear, he says that the next challenge is changing people's roles to make sure that everybody is focused on the strategy and they do not get side-tracked.

About 80% of our revenues come from 20% of our clients, so we must all focus on making sure these clients are permanently infatuated. So even in countries where the top 20% of clients represent only a small part of that country's revenue the message is still "these clients are very important."

A new strategy: Lovemarks

It is now more that five years since Saatchi & Saatchi began its scorecard journey. The CompaSS is now part of the corporate lexicon, but the language is evolving to deliver to a new strategy. Melter emphasizes that:

Strategies don't last forever. Our new strategic focus is taking us beyond doing the best creative work in our clients markets to creating and perpetuating Lovemarks. This is a phenomenal strategy that we believe will set us apart from our competition."

Within a speech given at The Tuck Academy of Management Symposium in Seattle in August 2003, Kevin Roberts provides this definition of Lovemarks[6].

Lovemarks [are] powerful emotional connections between a company, its people, its brand and its customers …Lovemarks are not owned by companies, managers or marketers. They are owned by the people who love them …Lovemarks take loyalty beyond reason through three heat signatures:Mystery to draw together past–present–future, great stories, dreams, myths and icons, and the inspiration that gives a relationship its texture.Sensuality to enthrall the emotions. Vision, sound, smell, touch, taste. This is how we experience the world.The warm breath of Intimacy. Empathy, commitment and passion. The intimate connections that today no one takes for granted. The job of every smart executive is to turn their organization into a Lovemark.

Big transformative ideas

To help achieve Lovemarks, Saatchi & Saatchi now has scorecard objectives around creating "big transformative ideas (BTIs)." Melter states:

These BTIs are not so much about quantity but quality. We set the target (number of BTI's) low; that is, three per quarter, even for big agencies like New York, London, and Beijing. But the focus on the status/color they give is high. We come up with tens or hundreds of ideas every day, but we only want to capture the true, few BTIs you've come up with and we want to celebrate those. A BTI should transform a brand and yield big business impact for our clients.

He explains how the new strategy has led to a reshaping of the Strategy Map:

We took our Strategy Map and made it a little different. We've taken the top rung and instead of focusing on financial/shareholders, as we don't really have a direct line to shareholders per se, we decided to replace it with something our people can relate to. We've called our top perspective "sharing the dream," and one measure is BTIs. Once you state it, and it's indeed deserving of a "green" status (best in class), we then want to share it around the world and celebrate it. Sharing the dream is supported by customer (which we call our focus) and people and culture (which we now call our spirit) perspectives.

The new CompaSS was rolled out as this case study was prepared. It shows how continued success in using the Balanced Scorecard concept has provided Saatchi & Saatchi with the confidence, and capabilities to adapt the scorecard to their own performance requirements. This is a mighty accomplishment for an organization using intangible assets (intellectual capital) to produce an intangible product (ideas).

This is certainly a CompaSS that is hardwired to Saatchi & Saatchi's vision: "To be revered as the hothouse for world-changing creative ideas that transform our clients' businesses, brands and reputations."

[1]   Norton, D.P. and Kaplan, R.S. 2004, *Strategy Maps: Converting Intangible Assets into Tangible Outcomes*, Harvard Business Press, Boston, MA.

[2]   Calabro, L. 2001, "On Balance," CFO Magazine.

[3]   *Quo Vadis, Budgeting? A nswerthink/The Hackett Group Study of Budgeting Practices and Trends in Europe*, 2003, Hackett Group, London.

[4]   Norton, D.P. and Kaplan, R.S. 2001,*The Strategy-focused Organization: How Balanced Scorecard Companies Thrive in the New Business Environment*, Harvard Business Press, Boston, MA.

[5]   See end note 4.

[6]   Chocqueel-Mangan, J. 2003, *The Perils of The Budget*, Tyler Mangan Ltd, Reigate, UK.

[7]   Speech by Roberts, K. CEO, Saatchi & Saatchi, 2003,The Tuck Academy of Management Symposium, Seattle, WA.

12

Conclusion: The Balanced Scorecard – The Future and Action Template

T *In the first part of this chapter we prognosticate on how the Balanced Scorecard Management System may evolve over the next few years. This evolution will continue an already remarkable evolutionary process that the scorecard has gone through. The scorecard will certainly be around for the long term; it has already proven that is not a management fad. With corporate governance becoming a key organizational concern, as a result of recent accounting scandals, the Balanced Scorecard is well placed to play a crucial role in the governance movement. We believe the scorecard will take hold and flourish within Asia. Given management disciplines and approaches within Asia, the scorecard may prove more enduring in this region than in other parts of the world. In the second part of the chapter we provide 20 action-oriented questions that draw together the key learnings of this book.*

BACKGROUND

This book serves as a guide for designing and implementing a Balanced Scorecard Management System. We have provided case examples of organizations that are among the pioneers of scorecard adoption in Asia, be they private sector (such as Centrepoint Properties (see Chapter 9) or public sector (such as Singapore Prison Service (see Chapter 2). Or be they locally focused, such as Indonesia's Summarecon (see Chapter 4) or truly global, such as the US-headquartered Saatchi & Saatchi, which has an extensive presence in Asia (see Chapter 11).

In the second half of this concluding chapter we will draw together the key learnings from this book that organizations will find valuable as they scope and start on their scorecard journey. Although the learnings, which we articulate as 20 action-oriented questions, are primarily aimed as Asia-based companies, they would be of equal value to other organizations in the geographic regions embarking on, or already progressing along a Balanced Scorecard program.

THE FUTURE OF THE SCORECARD

First we will prognosticate on how the Balanced Scorecard concept may evolve over the next few years. Although our views are founded in observation, anything that has a large predictive component should be viewed as informed opinion rather than fact. In saying that, we can be fairly confident that the Balanced Scorecard System will be here over the long term. The mere fact that it has been used in organizations since 1992 proves that it is not a "management fad." The simple truth is that it has endured so long because it works and organizations have found great, and myriad, benefits as a result of their scorecard implementations.

It must also be stressed that the scorecard's survival is the consequence of its careful observation of a basic rule of continued existence – it has evolved! From being a simple four-box "balanced" measurement system that set out to solve a narrow problem of organizational reliance on financial metrics, it has grown to embody the principles of a strategy-focused organization.

And given the speed of change these days it is noteworthy that this evolution took place in just a 10-year period. Given that the knowledge-era organizations are best able to reap substantial financial benefits by taking "first-mover" advantage, or developing products or capabilities that are "just ahead of market requirements,"[1] it is interesting that the most successful management model thus far in the knowledge-era adheres to the same rules. The Balanced Scorecard Management System has always managed to position itself at the next level that organizations would want to go – from measurement, to the strategy implementation framework, to the all-embracing principles of being strategy-focused. Naturally, the successful evolution of the Balanced Scorecard concept is essentially the result of the excellence of the scorecard research, education, and application by Kaplan and Norton, and the Balanced Scorecard Collaborative (BSCol). So in looking into the future, we should consider some of the present work of BSCol for guidance.

> " The Balanced Scorecard Management System has always managed to position itself at the next level that organizations would want to go ... "

CORPORATE GOVERNANCE

What is particularly interesting is that BSCol has been doing much work to position the Balanced Scorecard as the natural tool to help organizations deal with much of the challenges thrown up as a result of the recent, and quite catastrophic, corporate governance failings of some Western organizations – most notably, Enron and WorldCom.

Much of the governance challenges fall on ensuring greater transparency in, and accountability for, corporate performance, which is something the scorecard is well able

> " Much of the governance challenges fall on ensuring greater transparency in, and accountability for, corporate performance, which is something the scorecard is well able to provide. "

to provide. Although CEOs and their most senior executives have responsibility for inculcating such transparency and accountability within the organization (best achieved through deploying a Balanced Scorecard), the concerns for improving both governance and transparency have also focused increased attention on the role of boards of directors in monitoring and evaluating the performance of the CEO and other senior corporate managers.

As a consequence, bodies such as CMA (Certified Management Accountants) Canada have recommended that boards of directors use the Balanced Scorecard to:

- improve both the evaluation and management of performance of boards of directors and individual board members;
- improve the evaluation and governance of both corporate performance and CEO performance;
- use performance measurement and strategic management systems for communicating the performance of boards of directors, the corporation, and the CEO to external stakeholders.[2]

Exhibit 12.1 shows the Balanced Scorecard Framework to evaluate board performance.

> If, as we predict, over the next few years the Balanced Scorecard becomes the tool for overseeing corporate governance, the scorecard concept will move to being an "absolutely must-have" for organizations.

CMA's seminal report "Measuring and Improving the Performance of Corporate Boards"[3], recommends that a Balanced Scorecard for the Boards of Directors can be used alongside a CEO Scorecard. A CEO Scorecard will typically house objectives and measures around areas such as ethical behavior, legal compliance, and relationships with the board.

So in the future we will find organizations with a cascading series of scorecards from Corporate Board level, thought CEO and corporate levels all the way down to the departmental/team level, and even individual employee level. This will

Exhibit 12.1 Board strategy map – how the board will contribute

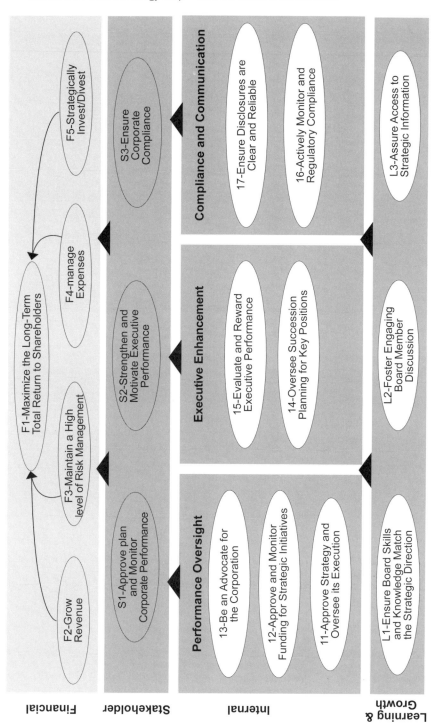

Exhibit 12.2 Board Scorecard Framework

Executive Enhancement Theme	Objective	Measure(s)	Target(s)	Owners
Financial	• Maximize the Long-Term Total Return to Shareholders	• ROE Relative to Peers	• 2003 75th percentile	• Executive Management
Stakeholder	• Strengthen and Motivate Executive Performance	▪ Are executive and affiliate CEOs on track with development plans?	• Yes	• Compensation Committee
Internal	• Oversee Succession Planning for Key Positions	• Share of executives with a current succession plan in place	• 75% Year 1 • 100% Year 2	• Governance Committee
Learning & Growth	• Assure Access to Strategic Information	• Board member survey on relevance of information presented	• Above Avg. Year 1 • Excellent Year 2	• Full Board

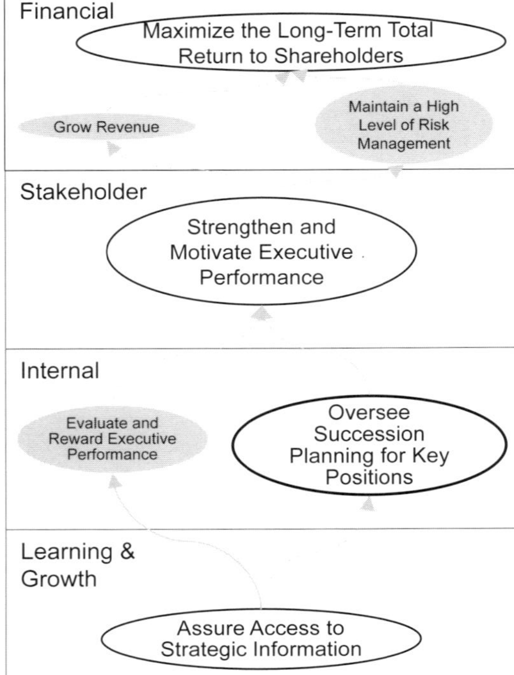

Strategy map (Executive Enhancement Theme):

Financial: Maximize the Long-Term Total Return to Shareholders; Maintain a High Level of Risk Management; Grow Revenue

Stakeholder: Strengthen and Motivate Executive Performance

Internal: Oversee Succession Planning for Key Positions; Evaluate and Reward Executive Performance

Learning & Growth: Assure Access to Strategic Information

create high levels of organizational transparency and accountability, providing the right conditions for exemplary corporate governance.

If, as we predict, over the next few years the Balanced Scorecard becomes the tool for overseeing corporate governance, the scorecard concept will move to being an "absolutely must-have" for organizations.

DEVELOPMENTS IN ASIA

So how do we see the Balanced Scorecard concept developing is Asia? We believe the scorecard will take hold in Asia and that it will spread in popularity from its early strongholds of Singapore and Hong Kong to other countries.

It was notable that in 2004, BSCol's prestigious Hall of Fame welcomed into its esteemed membership an organization from Korea (Korea Telecom) and India (Tata Motors Commercial Vehicles Business Unit, which we profiled in Chapter 1). This points to rising interest in those countries and we are seeing countries such as Thailand and Malaysia following suit.

One reason for this is that as Asia emerges from the economic downturn that has negatively impacted the region, organizations will be looking for new tools with which to grow. The scorecard is a proven approach for doing this (the Balanced Scorecard is not effective when cost-cutting is a primary objective as the focus is then overly financial and short term).

Nigel Penny, Managing Director of Singapore-based ClaritasAsia, adds that the scorecard will grow in popularity as a consequence of a heightened requirement for robust strategic planning processes:

Generally, companies in Asia are still in their infancy in terms of strategic planning. Many organizations have no formal strategic planning group, and often only a limited annual strategic planning process. However, as this area matures these organizations will need tools and approaches and the Balanced Scorecard is the market leader.

Asian organizations have a wealth of successful case examples from the West to draw from and to distil key learnings. Another benefit is that Asia-based companies new to the scorecard will be building and deploying scorecards after Kaplan and Norton have evolved their thinking through their three books. Peter Ryan, Strategy and Performance Planner at City of Brisbane (another 2003 inductee into BSCol's Hall of Fame), states that a problem his organization had as an early adopter was the need to change the mindsets of people each time the scorecard evolved:

Our biggest challenge occurred four years ago when we moved from the old KPI [key performance indicator] view of the Balanced Scorecard to one driven by strategy. Worldwide the thinking and the literature moved in 1999, but many people didn't. Once people see the Balanced Scorecard as KPIs in four boxes, moving them to strategy and mapping strategy is incredibly difficult. So there's a real danger of finding yourself in the odd position of having the biggest resistors to contemporary scorecard thinking being those who believe themselves to be scorecard enthusiasts. It took a lot of work to undo that.

> **In Asian organizations, and in sharp contrast to Western companies, once something becomes a process it tends to stick.**

This is an important observation. Most Asian scorecard adopters will come to the scorecard system with the concept of Strategy Maps, Balanced Scorecards, and the principles of the strategy-focused organization already established. This may lead to a common agreement in Asia as to what constitutes a Balanced Scorecard Management Framework – concurrence that is sadly lacking in other regions of the world.

Intriguingly, Matthew Tice, BSCol's Vice-President, Asia-Pacific, believes that the Balanced Scorecards will prove even more enduring in Asia that it has in the West:

In Asian organizations, and in sharp contrast to Western companies, once something becomes a process it tends to stick. It might take a bit longer to get embedded into the fabric of Asian management, but the psyche is much more process-driven. And many of the cultures in Asia are more willing to take a longer term view."

TWENTY ACTION-ORIENTED QUESTIONS

We will now provide 20 action-oriented questions that essentially pull together the key learnings from this book. Each question (except number 20) has a number of supporting questions. All in all, these questions will help the reader take their scorecard to the next stage and ensure that the scorecard does remain in situ over the longer term.

1. Why do you wish to build and deploy a Balanced Scorecard Management System?

At the very beginning of the scorecard effort it is important to be clear as to exactly what you want to achieve through the Balanced Scorecard. In Chapter 2 we explained that the scorecard can be deployed purely as a measurement system, for control purposes, to communicate strategy or to become a strategy-focused organization, as examples. Being clear of how the scorecard will be used early on will help secure commonality of purpose and buy-in organization-wide. Also, it will then be possible to plan the evolution of your scorecard usage toward strategy-focused status. Moreover, be very clear about what changes you expect to see within the organization as a result o scorecard usage. As examples:

- How will decision-making processes be improved?
- How will communication (internal and external) improve?
- How will the culture change for the better?
- How will employees understanding of, and commitment to, strategic goals improve?
- How will financial results improve?

2. What will the role of the most senior leaders be in the scorecard program?

In chapter 3 we stated that the single most important condition for success with the Balanced Scorecard is the ownership and active involvement of the executive team, most particularly the CEO. So at the start of the scorecard journey, it is important to assess the commitment of the senior team (not just the lip service paid) and the

> " ... it is important to assess the commitment of the senior team ... and the likelihood that they will dedicate the time and effort to building the scorecard system and ensuring its implementation. "

likelihood that they will dedicate the time and effort to building the scorecard system and ensuring its implementation. Consider how much time is required to build scorecard understanding within the top-team and ensure that concerns or doubts of individual leaders are unearthed and addressed. Remember that a senior manager has every right to question the appropriateness, or effectiveness, of the Balanced Scorecard, so make sure you can answer their questions. Case studies can be useful in demonstrating what can be achieved with the scorecard.

Other key questions to ask:

- What is the CEO's view of the scorecard? If he or she is not totally convinced what does this mean for the likelihood of scorecard success?
- If the CEO is supportive, what will happen to the scorecard program if the CEO were to suddenly leave the organization?
- Which senior manager is championing the scorecard effort and what influence has he or she on the other members of the top team?
- Will senior support still be evident if financial performance dips one quarter?

3. How will we inculcate into the organization the requisite skills for working with the Balanced Scorecard?

Too many Balanced Scorecard programs eventually fail because the capabilities to manage with the scorecard over the long term have not been inculcated. It can be argued that if the scorecard is to be "the way we manage around here," the competencies in using the scorecard should be as crucial as any other organizational capabilities – IT, HR, and so on.

There are many required competencies in working with the scorecard: understanding the principles of causality, cognizance with the science of measurement, knowing what strategy is and how it can be put into operation and communicated, and understanding how to make use of strategic feedback. Key questions could include:

- How will people at each level of the organization be trained in using the Balanced Scorecard?
- Will we appoint a full-time scorecard manager? If so, what will be their merit and qualifications?
- Will we create a dedicated scorecard unit?
- Will we have a core scorecard team supported by part-time scorecard facilitators in the business?
- How will the scorecard unit be viewed in comparison with other functions – as an equal or as something inferior?

4. Will you use management consultants? If so, how?

In Chapter 5 we opined that management consultants can play a vital role in a Balanced Scorecard program, as long as there are clear parameters around the consultants' responsibilities and that the organization's expectations of the consultants are well defined. Importantly, we stressed that the consultants cannot own your Balanced Scorecard – ownership must remain within the organization and particularly within the executive team. Key questions include:

- Will we use management consultants or do it ourselves? If we do it ourselves, do we really possess the internal skills and can we spare the resource?
- How will we choose our consultants: what skills must they have, such as facilitation, and do we expect deep industry knowledge?
- Over what time-period will we use consultants and what do we expect by the end of that time-scale; for example, number of scorecards, the inculcation of in-house knowledge, and so on?

5. How will you integrate the Balanced Scorecard with other performance management/measurement frameworks?

Few organizations will introduce the Balanced Scorecard into an organization devoid of existing performance management frameworks/systems. Total quality models (such as the Singapore Business Excellence Framework), activity-based costing approaches, or economic value-added, as examples, may well be in use. So think through how the scorecard will work alongside such approaches. Key questions include:

- Will the scorecard be the overarching performance management framework that all others support?
- How will you ensure that all the frameworks work together without causing organizational confusion or "frameworkitis"?
- How will you overcome sensitivities such as other framework champions believing that their favored approach should take precedence?
- What role will people such as quality managers have with the scorecard? Will they become the in-house facilitators, for example?

6. How will you view the Strategy Map?

Throughout the book we have repeatedly stressed that the Strategy Map is the most important component of the Balanced Scorecard Management System. The Strategy Map is a visual representation of the cause-and-effect relationships among the components of an organization's strategy, and therefore as part of a strategy implementation framework it must take precedence over other components such as metrics. We also stated that there should be a limited number of objectives on the Strategy Map – only those objectives that keep the CEO awake at night! The key questions in this section are:

- Is the senior team aware of the importance of the Strategy Map?
- How will we gain consensus within the senior team as to what we mean by strategy and the key drivers of strategic success?
- How will we decide on the strategic themes of the map and the critical few objectives?

7. How will you view the role of measurement?

We have made it clear within this book that the Balanced Scorecard Management System is not a measurement system. We have continually reiterated this fact because it is proving the hardest message to get across to new and current scorecard users. Measures, along with targets and initiatives, play a supporting role to the Strategy Map. In saying that, metrics are still an important component of the system. Measures, as with objectives, should be kept to the vital few – perhaps two measures for each objective.

> " ... the Balanced Scorecard Management System is not a measurement system. ... it is proving the hardest message to get across to new and current scorecard users. "

The key questions are:

- How will we ensure that the scorecard is not seen as a metrics project while still getting across the important role of measurement?
- How will we ensure that a balance of leading and lagging metrics appear on the scorecard?
- Will individual measure owners be identified, or will there be a more collective ownership?
- How will we make the trade-off between the value of the measure and the cost of creating the measure?

8. How will we set performance targets?

The targets within the Balanced Scorecard should be both stretching and achievable. Within any organization, targets are set for financial measures, since scorecard adopters' targets are equally important for non-financial measures. Causality within the scorecard framework means that it is by hitting non-financial targets that financial targets are achieved. The key questions in this section are:

- What criteria will be used for target-setting; for example, comparative external benchmarks?

- How will we overcome the challenges of people negotiating "easier" targets, especially when performance is related to incentive compensation?
- Conversely, how will you ensure that managers don't commit to overly stretching targets as a result of their scorecard enthusiasm?

9. How will we select strategic initiatives?

Simply put, it is the successful implementation of strategic initiatives that enable targets to be hit and objectives to be met. As we stressed in Chapter 7, it is through initiatives that the real work of the Balanced Scorecard takes place. It is where theory is translated into action. The key questions are:

- How will we use the Strategy Map to prioritize the allocation of resources to action programs?
- How will we ensure that we fund a balance of strategic initiative so that we are improving performance within each perspective?
- How will we monitor the progress of initiatives?
- How will we know whether the funded initiative is really having the desired impact on performance?

10. Will we create devolved and aligned scorecards?

As we explained in Chapter 8, the process of creating aligned Strategy Maps and Balanced Scorecards makes real the promise to "make strategy everyone's, everyday job." We also stated that ensuring alignment requires that devolved scorecards both support higher level scorecards, but also captures local strategic and performance needs. But key questions may be:

- How deep in the organization do we intend to devolve the scorecard system? And what do we see as the benefits of such devolution?
- How will we ensure that lower level employees are involved in designing their own scorecards?
- What are the structural challenges in devolving the scorecard and how will these be overcome?

- What are the logistical challenges in devolving the scorecard and how will these be overcome?
- How do we ensure that the performance on lower level scorecards is reported up to the higher levels?
- If we change strategies at the top of the organization how quickly will we be able to make required changes on lower level scorecards?

11. Will we pilot the scorecard methodology?

In Chapter 8 we also stated that piloting the scorecard prior to organization-wide rollout is typically an advisable step. It helps in proof of concept and in identifying and overcoming common structural and cultural implementation challenges. The key questions are:
- What do we believe will be the key benefits, or deliverables, of a scorecard pilot?
- How will we choose the location for the scorecard pilot? What criteria will we use?
- How will we communicate pilot results organization-wide?

12. What are the cultural barriers to scorecard rollout?

Within the book we have stressed that cultural barriers are more likely to derail a scorecard effort than any other obstacles – much more so than structural, logistical, or technological barriers. A Balanced Scorecard program is a major change effort, and any change program has a substantial cultural component. The cultural challenges of building and implementing a Balanced Scorecard can be particularly irksome due the performance transparency and accountability that a scorecard infuses.

> The cultural challenges of building and implementing a Balanced Scorecard can be particularly irksome due the performance transparency and accountability that a scorecard infuses.

The key questions are:

- Do we know how accommodating our corporate culture will be to the precepts of the Balanced Scorecard? Do we, for example, have a culture well used to using measurement for continuous improvement, or has it been used to identify and punish poor performance?
- How transparent is present performance within the organization?
- If performance is not presently transparent how will we overcome the fear of transparency?
- Similarly, how much accountability is there for performance, and how will we overcome any fear of accountability?

13. Will we align compensation to scorecard results?

Most organizations will eventually ponder the questions of whether to align compensation, especially incentive-compensation to scorecard results. In Chapter 9 we detailed the pros, cons, and challenges of making this link. The key questions are:

- What do we see as the key benefit (if any) of aligning incentive-compensation with the scorecard; for example, galvanizing behavioral change?
- Will compensation be aligned at all organizational levels, or just for managerial levels?
- How will the compensation be calculated?
- How will we ensure that employees are rewarded for performance to balanced objectives and not just financial outcomes?
- Will we weight compensation according to function (for example, provide a higher weighting for learning and growth performance to HR managers).

14. How will we link performance-appraisal systems to the Balanced Scorecard?

Most scorecard adopters also eventually consider linking performance-appraisal systems to the Balanced Scorecard to ensure congruence of individual performance objectives with corporate strategic objectives. The key questions are:

- How will we ensure that employees are appraised against performance they can positively influence, rather than a strategic objective that they have only a limited impact on?
- Will the appraisal system be in the form of a Balanced Scorecard?
- If personal scorecards are created will employees have objectives, measures, targets, and initiatives within all four perspectives, or just some of the perspectives?

15. How will we use communication to support the scorecard?

Building strategic awareness, through dedicated communication and education campaigns, is a critical part of scorecard rollout. It is something we also discussed in Chapter 9. Employees must know why the scorecard is being used, understand how they can contribute to strategic success, and be kept up to date with progress against the scorecard. The key questions are:

- Who will be responsible for scorecard communication?
- Which communication mechanisms will we use: paper, electronic, face-to-face, town-hall meetings, or a mix of all?
- How do we ensure that the communications are regular, meaningful, and honest?
- How do we use the communication process to deliver messages and capture feedback?

16. Will we automate the Balanced Scorecard

As we explained in Chapter 10, automating the Balanced Scorecard, especially through a dedicated scorecard software package, can deliver large benefits. However, we also made clear that implementing the Balanced Scorecard Management System is not an IT project. The key questions are:

- What do we perceive to be the main benefits, or deliverables, of scorecard automation?
- How can we be sure that the benefits outweigh the cost and time-requirement of automation?
- When will we automate – at the start of the scorecard effort or once the scorecard framework itself is embedded, and has been accepted, within the organization?
- What criteria will we use to choose software?
- Who will have access to the scorecard via software and will there be levels of access?

17. Will we align the budgeting process with the Balanced Scorecard?

In Chapter 11 we explained that for most companies it is proving difficult to hardwire the budgeting process to the Balanced Scorecard. This is largely because a budget is an annual target-setting process, whereas the Balanced Scorecard is about strategy implementation, which cannot be confined to a lunar cycle. The key questions are:

- How will we ensure that the budget supports, rather than defines, the strategic goals on the Balanced Scorecard?
- How can we make sure that the pressure of meeting the budget does not compromise longer term strategic objectives by, for example, canceling strategically critical investments in training?
- Would we consider new alternative approaches to the budget, such as rolling forecasts, which are more attuned to the Balanced Scorecard?

18. How will the scorecard be used in management meetings?

If the Balanced Scorecard system is to be "the way we manage around here," then management meetings within the organization must be focused around the Balanced Scorecard. The key questions are:

- Will the senior team hold strategic reviews of scorecard performance? If so, how often will these reviews take place and what will be agenda for such reviews?

- How do we ensure that strategic performance, as reported through the scorecard, receive adequate airtime within monthly management meetings?

19. How do we capture strategic feedback?

A critical role of the Balanced Scorecard system is to capture feedback on how well the strategy is being implemented and to help build an understanding of whether the right strategy is being prosecuted, or whether the strategy is supported by the right mix of objectives. The key questions are:

- How will be institutionalize a process so that strategically critical findings at the front-line can be fed back into the organization and filtered up to the highest organizational level?
- How will we ensure that strategically critical knowledge is captured and shared organization-wide?

20. Will we do it?

Organizations will only secure the benefits of the Balanced Scorecard Management System if they actually do it. So if you are considering launching a scorecard program take the learnings from this book, and also from other materials, and start the task. For over 10 years, many companies have gained substantial financial and other benefits from using the Balanced Scorecard. They all had one thing in common – they decided to do it and made it happen!

> " For over 10 years many companies have gained substantial financial and other benefits from using the Balanced Scorecard. They all had one thing in common – they decided to do it and made it happen! "

[1]   See Saint-Onge, H. and Armstrong, C. 2004, *The Conductive Organization, Elsevier Butterworth Heinemann*, Burlington, MA.

[2]   Epstein, M.J. and Marie-Josée, R. 2002, *Measuring and Improving the Performance of Corporate Boards*, CMA Canada, Mississauga, Ontario.

[3]   See end note 2.

Appendix

SURVEY

To support this book the following survey was distributed to organizations primarily within South-east Asia to determine the extent of scorecard usage. At the beginning of 2005 the survey will form the basis for an annual pan-Asian survey.

SECTION 1: PERSONAL DETAILS

1.
- Name
- Job title
- Company name
- Number of employees
- Industry/Sector
- Revenue
- Telephone number
- Email

SECTION 2: SCORECARD BACKGROUND

2. Do you use the balanced scorecard within your organization?

Yes	Planning to	No

If yes or planning to go to Question 4.

3. If no, is this because:

We evaluated the Balanced Scorecard but decided not to implement the framework	
We have never considered using the Balanced Scorecard	
The scorecard failed to deliver expected results	
Management interest faded	
Management couldn't reach agreement on the composition of the scorecard	
It proved too difficult to implement	
Cultural resistance	
The champion left the organization	
Change of CEO	
The scorecard was removed following a merger or acquisition	
Other reasons (please specify)	

4. How important were the following reasons for implementing a Balanced Scorecard?

	Totally unimportant	Unimportant	Moderately important	Important	Extremely Important
	1	2	3	4	5
To rectify poor financial performance					
To contend with increasing competition					
To better understand the drivers of strategic success					
As a tool to increase accountability for performance					
As a tool to increase performance transparency					
To communicate the strategy to the employee base					
To align the performance of all employees to strategic objectives					
As a framework for aligning bonuses with performance					
To better prioritize initiatives and allocate resources					

SECTION 3: SCORECARD EFFECTIVENESS

5.   To which level has the scorecard been deployed (tick all that apply) and how long has it been used at this level?

	Planning stage	Less than 1 year	1–3 years	3–5 years	Over five years
Corporate					
Division					
Business unit					
Function					
Team					
Individual employee					

6.   On a scale of 1–5, with 1 being totally ineffective and 5 being totally effective, how effective has the Balanced Scorecard proven to be at improving performance at each level?

		Totally ineffective	Ineffective	Moderately effective	Effective	Extremely effective
	Too early to say	1	2	3	4	5
Corporate						
Division						
Business unit						
Function						
Team						
Individual employee						

SECTION 4: ENTERPRISE-LEVEL SCORECARD

The following questions concern the process for building the enterprise-level scorecard. If you have only built a scorecard at the functional level and below, go to Section 5.

7. How long did it take to build the enterprise Balanced Scorecard System?

We are presently building the scorecard	
Less than 1 month	
Over 1 month, but less than 3 months	
Over three months, but less than 6 months	
Over 6 months, but less than 9 months	
Over 9 months, but less than 1 year	
Over 1 year	

8. How many perspectives does the Balanced Scorecard contain?

Too early to say	3	4	5	6	Other (please specify)

9. How many strategic objectives are housed within the Balanced Scorecard?

10. How many key performance indicators are housed within the Balanced Scorecard?

11. Who championed the Balanced Scorecard effort?

CEO or equivalent	
Other executive board member	
Non-executive board member	
Other (please specify)	

12. How often does the executive team formally assess performance to the Balanced Scorecard?

As an agenda item within each monthly management meeting	
The scorecard sets the agenda for the monthly management meeting	
As an agenda item once a quarter	
Within a specially convened quarterly meeting	
Once a year	
As an occasional requirement	
Other (please specify)	

13. How closely is the budgeting process integrated with the Balanced Scorecard?

Fully integrated	
Partially integrated	
Not at all integrated	

14.   Is the Balanced Scorecard used alongside other management tools, and how successful has the integration been in improving performance?

Tool		Totally ineffective	Ineffective	Moderately effective	Effective	Extremely effective
	Too early to say	1	2	3	4	5
EVA or equivalent						
Six Sigma						
Quality framework (such as Malcolm Baldrige)						
ABC						
Other (please specify)						

15.   Who now has primarily responsibility for facilitating the scorecard process on a day-to-day basis within the organization?

A dedicated full-time in-house Balanced Scorecard team of 5 or more people	
A dedicated full-time in-house Balanced Scorecard team of less than 5 people	
The finance function	
The HR function	
The IT function	
Other (please specify)	

SECTION 5: DEVOLVED SCORECARD

16. If you have rolled the scorecard out deeper than enterprise-level, how long has it taken you to complete the process?

Less than 1 year	
More than 1 year, but less than 3 years	
More than 3 years, but less than 5 years	
More than 5 years	

17. Did you complete a local scorecard pilot prior to wider scorecard rollout?

Yes	Presently in a pilot stage	No

18. If yes, where was the pilot undertaken?

Business unit	
Country	
Function (specify which function)	
Team (specify which team)	
Other (please specify)	

SECTION 6: USE OF CONSULTANTS

19. Did you employ an external consultant to facilitate the scorecard creation and implementation process?

Yes	No

If no go to section 6

20. If yes, was this consultant:

A large general management consultancy	
A specialist balanced scorecard consultancy	
An academic	
A functional specialist consultancy	
Other (please specify)	

21. How effective was this consultancy in supporting the scorecard effort?

	Totally ineffective	Ineffective	Moderately effective	Effective	Extremely effective
Too early to say	1	2	3	4	5

SECTION 7: AUTOMATION

22. Have you automated the Balanced Scorecard?

Yes	No

23. If no, how do you capture and report scorecard results? For example, Excel or PowerPoint.

Now go to Section 8.

24. If yes, which software provider did you use?
25. When did you automate the scorecard?

At the same time as we built the scorecard	
Immediately after we built the scorecard	
Less than 1 year after building the scorecard	
Between 1 and 3 years after building the scorecard	
Between 3 and 5 years after building the scorecard	
More than 5 years after building the scorecard	

26. How effective has the automated solution been in supporting the scorecard program?

	Totally ineffective	Ineffective	Moderately effective	Effective	Extremely effective
Too early to say	1	2	3	4	5

SECTION 8: COMPENSATION

27. Have you tied incentive compensation to scorecard results?

Yes	Plan to	No

28. If yes, at which levels is the compensation link applied? Tick all that apply.

Executive Board	
Senior management	
Middle management	
Junior management	
General employee base	

29. How effective has the compensation link proven to be in improving performance to scorecard objectives, measures, and so on?

		Totally ineffective	Ineffective	Moderately effective	Effective	Extremely effective
	Too early to say	1	2	3	4	5
Executive Board						
Senior management						
Middle management						
Junior management						
General employee-base						

SECTION 9: COMMUNICATIONS

30. Which of these mechanisms have you used to communicate the Balanced Scorecard within the organization? Tick all that apply.

Intranet	
Internal newsletters	
Town-hall meetings	
Posters and other visual displays	
Email	
Senior management briefings	
Cascaded briefings	
Training sessions	
An automated scorecard on the desktop of all employees	
Other (please specify)	

SECTION 10: CONCLUSION

31. What has been the greatest benefit in using the Balanced Scorecard?

32. What has been the single greatest challenge in you scorecard implementation efforts?

33. What is the most important success factor in succeeding with the Balanced Scorecard?

Index